Virginia Woolf
against Empire

Virginia Woolf against Empire

Kathy J. Phillips

The University of Tennessee Press / Knoxville

Copyright © 1994 by The University of Tennessee Press / Knoxville.
All Rights Reserved. Manufactured in the United States of America.

First Edition.

The following excerpts are reprinted by permission of the publisher, Harcourt Brace & Company: from *The Waves* by Virginia Woolf, copyright © 1931 by Harcourt Brace & Company and renewed 1959 by Leonard Woolf; from *The Voyage Out* by Virginia Woolf, copyright © 1920 by Harcourt Brace & Company and renewed 1948 by Leonard Woolf; from *The Years* by Virginia Woolf, copyright © 1937 by Harcourt Brace & Company and renewed 1965 by Leonard Woolf; from *Growing: An Autobiography of the Years, 1904–1911,* copyright © 1961 by Leonard Woolf and renewed by Marjorie T. Parsons; from *Night and Day* by Virginia Woolf, copyright © 1920 by George H. Doran & Company and renewed 1948 by Leonard Woolf; from *The Diary of Virginia Woolf: Volume III, 1925–1930,* copyright © 1980 by Quentin Bell and Angelica Garnett; from *Jacob's Room* by Virginia Woolf, copyright © 1922 by Harcourt Brace & Company and renewed 1950 by Leonard Woolf; from *Mrs. Dalloway* by Virginia Woolf, copyright © 1925 by Harcourt Brace & Company and renewed 1953 by Leonard Woolf; from *Between the Acts* by Virginia Woolf, copyright © 1941 by Harcourt Brace & Company and renewed 1969 by Leonard Woolf; from *A Room of One's Own* by Virginia Woolf, copyright © 1929 by Harcourt Brace & Company and renewed 1957 by Leonard Woolf; and from *To the Lighthouse* by Virginia Woolf, copyright © 1927 by Harcourt Brace & Company and renewed 1954 by Leonard Woolf.

Short excerpts from *Collected Essays* and *Complete Shorter Fiction, Diaries, Letters* by Virginia Woolf and from *After the Deluge: A Study of Communal Psychology, Diaries in Ceylon, 1908–1911,* and *Stories from the East: Three Short Stories on Ceylon* by Leonard Woolf courtesy of Hogarth Publishers.

The paper in this book meets the minimum requirements of the American National Standard for Permanence of Paper for Printed Library Materials. ∞ The binding materials have been chosen for strength and durability.

Library of Congress Cataloging in Publication Data

Phillips, Kathy J., 1950–
    Virginia Woolf against empire / Kathy J. Phillips. —1st ed.
        p.   cm.
    Includes bibliographical references (p.   ) and index.
    ISBN 0–87049–833–9 (cl.: alk. paper)
    1. Woolf, Virginia, 1882–1941—Political and social views.
2. Literature and society—England—History—20th century. 3. Women and literature—England—History—20th century. 4. Imperialism in literature.   I. Title.
PR6045.072Z859   1994   93-43714
823'.912—dc20   CIP

Contents

Illustrations

Introduction

From her first book to her last, Virginia Woolf consistently satirizes social institutions. She accomplishes this criticism in her novels chiefly by means of incongruous juxtapositions and suggestive, concrete detail, which can be interpreted as metaphor. One of her most interesting juxtapositions associates Empire making, war making, and gender relations in a typical constellation. Although these three elements might seem to cluster together as a random sign of the times, Woolf links the items in a complicated and shrewd critique. A representative passage in *Jacob's Room*, for example, jumps abruptly back and forth among these international topics, while the surface action acknowledges only a young English woman serving tea in the drawing room or walking her dog, "Troy":

> "Wait till we cross the road," she said to the dog, bending down. . . .
>
> "What's all this about England?"—a question poor Clara could not have answered, since, as Mrs. Durrant discussed with Sir Edgar the policy of Sir Edward Grey, Clara only wondered why the cabinet looked dusty, and Jacob had never come . . .
>
> And Clara would hand the pretty china teacups, and smile at the compliment—that no one in London made tea so well as she did.
>
> "We get it at Brocklebank's," she said, "in Cursitor Street."
>
> Ought she not to be grateful? Ought she not to be happy? Especially since her mother looked so well and enjoyed so much talking to Sir Edgar about Morocco, Venezuela, or some such place. . . .
>
> "But you'll get run over if I let you go," she said to the dog.
>
> "England seems all right," said Mr. Bowley.
>
> The loop of the railing beneath the statue of Achilles was full of parasols and waistcoats . . . [as] a horse galloped past without a rider. (166–67)

Colonies such as Morocco, coveted territories such as Venezuela, and apologists for Empire such as Sir Edward Grey form an insistent bass note in Woolf's novels. She had a detailed knowledge of colonialism, derived particularly from her husband Leonard Woolf's writings on imperialism and international government. When his *Empire and Commerce in Africa* was published in January 1920, she reported, "I'm reading it for the second time—to me it seems superb" (*Letters* 2: 413). In fact, in summer 1917 she had helped with the research for this book, before Leonard had narrowed the focus to Africa (*Diary* 1: 229n). Woolf was well aware, therefore, that Morocco was a prize "given" by England to France in 1904; in exchange, France had allowed Britain to seek dominance in Egypt (*Empire and Commerce* 59; Lloyd 275). Control of Morocco was part of a much larger imperialism; by 1914, France and Britain alone had appropriated more than seven million square miles, through a system whose effects in Africa Leonard Woolf called "almost wholly evil" (*Empire and Commerce* 24, 352).

Although the characters in the passage quoted from *Jacob's Room* do not go on to discuss Morocco, Woolf continues to comment on imperialism through juxtaposition. "Morocco" abuts "Troy," a dog, and "Achilles," a monument. The location of a colony next to names that conjure up the *Iliad* and war implies that when the European powers try to amass territory and monopolize trade at all costs, then force necessarily follows. By further juxtaposing Mr. Bowley's offhand comment that "England seems all right" with Clara's fear that the dog might get run over, Woolf casts doubt on Bowley's opinion. She insinuates instead that, because England participated in the European "policy of grab" (*Empire and Commerce* 55), the country also risked getting "run over." The passage warns, in fact, that England was courting World War I, the disaster announced throughout *Jacob's Room*.

Various historians have argued, like the Woolfs, that the European rivalry for colonies contributed significantly to the war: "The participation of Britain in the World War, viewed in its longest perspective, was the inevitable consequence of her world-wide supremacy, both economic and naval, during the mid-Victorian era: for that supremacy was something she was losing, but which she would not be likely to bring herself to accept as lost without a struggle to retain it" (Thomson 219). Woolf makes her similar point not through discursive language but through informed juxtapositions. "Troy" and "Achilles," when placed next to a reference to a territory in Africa, recall that in the years before the First World War, public schools were likely to alternate "reports of the English campaign against the Ashanti with accounts of heroic deeds beside the walls of Ilium" (Eby 99). Popular culture in England was actively invoking the *Iliad* to glorify militarism: "The Epic of England, George Jones said in his 1897 history for young people, was waiting for England's Homer or Virgil. Perhaps Rudyard Kipling, that 'strong, sweet Singer of the Seven Seas,' would take on this 'most splendid of all possible tasks'" (MacDonald 25). Virginia Woolf, however, displays no such reverence for soldiering or for Kipling, whose "orgy" about "Men" and the "Flag" she calls "immature" (*Room of One's Own* 106). In the passage quoted above from *Jacob's Room*, she undercuts the freedom and power presupposed in the warrior by showing that a lowly dog, with a name evoking heroes, really runs at someone else's command. Achilles, now a statue, remains rigidified, as in death. Moreover, Clara's discreet injunction to Troy, "Wait till we cross the road," announces bluntly enough that the military ideal is, to put it politely, excrement.

As Woolf enjoys her rude joke, she also pursues a serious analysis of the connections among imperialism, war, and gender relations. Her novels suggest that these three topics interrelate through economics, school training, professions, life-styles, sexual mores, religions, and so on: institutions that a recent theorist, Louis Althusser, would call "Ideological State Apparatuses" (143). Terry Eagleton defines ideologies as "the ideas, values and feelings" by which people "experience their societies at various times" (viii). Woolf, without using the word "ideology," profited from the concept. The narrator-biographer in *Orlando*, for example, dissects London society and concludes, "Nothing exists. The whole thing is a miasma—a mirage," i.e., a social construct (192). Eagleton further pinpoints ideology as "false consciousness," implying that a few privileged observers might arrive at an underlying true consciousness without any ideology (17). Woolf, on the other hand, expressing what might be termed a post-structuralist view, doubts that people can live without cultural constructs altogether. Thus Orlando muses during her centuries-long lifetime, "I am losing some illusions . . . perhaps to acquire others" (174).

Nevertheless, if no one can achieve a completely disinterested, illusion-free "truth," some ideologies, as times change, begin to seem more distorting than others. Woolf caustically suggests, for example, the fantastic "constructedness" of Victorian gender expectations: "If you say to the public with sufficient conviction: 'All women have tails, and all men humps,' it will actually learn to see women with tails and men with humps, and will think it very revolutionary and probably improper if you say, 'Nonsense'" (*Collected Essays* 1: 332). Despite the "naturalness" that ideologies may seem to possess for people enmeshed in them, Woolf frequently exposes assumptions *as* ideologies, by insisting on their artificiality and transitoriness. In *Orlando,* a carnival that plays out typical Renaissance life looks permanent during the Great Frost. Nevertheless, the carnival and the ice—along with Renaissance presuppositions about life—will be swept away (62). Similarly, a monument of Victorian England, advertising solidity, will melt by the Edwardian age: "top hats, widows' weeds, trumpets, telescopes, wreaths, all had vanished and left not a stain, not a puddle even" (*Orlando* 296).

Althusser maintains that "the ideology by which [state apparatuses] function is always in fact unified, despite its diversity and its contradictions" (146). Woolf, too, as I hope to show in this study, sees that the seemingly diverse institutions which she examines remarkably reinforce each other. Chapter 1, "Devouring the Lamb," illustrates how unacknowledged economic relations and gender relations, in *Mrs. Dalloway* and *The Years,* contribute to imperialism and war. Chapter 2, "Staking a Territory," discusses the institution of Victorian marriage as a product of imperial needs, as shown in *The Voyage Out, Night and Day, To the Lighthouse,* and *Freshwater.* Chapter 3, "Securing the Circle," argues that Woolf systematically investigates how elementary schools, universities, the Christian church, professional life, international finance, and gender expectations together function to train warriors (like Jacob in *Jacob's Room*) and totalitarian Empire-builders (like Percival and Louis, in *The Waves*). Chapter 4, "Playing Out History," looks at a broad overview, in *Orlando* and *Be-*

tween the Acts, of England's march since the Renaissance toward colonialism and war. The conclusion summarizes the complicated ways in which Woolf sees the British Empire, militarism, and gender relations interacting.

It is only in the past fifteen years or so that Woolf has been recognized as a social thinker, let alone as someone with a sophisticated grasp of complex ideologies. Critics such as Naomi Black, Berenice Carroll, Jane Marcus, and Alex Zwerdling have taught readers that Woolf did look at society in cultural terms. In light of this research, statements about her supposed divorce from social issues now seem shortsighted. In the 1967 volume of his autobiography, Leonard Woolf assesses his wife as "the least political animal that has lived since Aristotle invented the definition" (quoted in Gottlieb 242). Quentin Bell believes that "she belonged, inescapably, to the Victorian world of Empire, Class and Privilege. Her gift was for the pursuit of shadows, for the ghostly whispers of the mind and for Pythian incomprehensibility, when what was needed was the swift and lucid phrase that could reach the ears of unemployed working men or Trades Union officials" (Bell 2: 186). Marcus, however, effectively counters this judgment of Woolf's naiveté with the evidence that she taught at a working men's college, led meetings of the Women's Co-operative Guild, and served as secretary of the Rodmell Labour Party, "scarcely a shadowy voice of Empire and Privilege" (*Art and Anger* 107–8). Woolf's novels might be "Pythian," but the Pythian oracle told Oedipus as plain as day that he would kill his father and marry his mother; if the Pythia was incomprehensible, she became so only because her listeners were unprepared to hear her. Similarly, Woolf's complaints against such institutions as the British Empire, capitalism, the military, and marriage were literally unthinkable to many in her audience. For the rest of this study I will be using "Empire" as an inclusive term, encompassing economics, gender relations, and war making, as these forces operate both at home and abroad.

Perhaps Leonard Woolf and Quentin Bell misjudged Woolf as apolitical because she disliked meetings—"mudcoloured moonshine"—and scorned politicians (*Letters* 2: 582; Nicolson 20; Schlack 69). Nevertheless, for all her impatience, she did attend meetings. Naomi Black has documented that, at one time or another, Woolf took an active role in suffrage groups, the Women's Co-operative Guild, the Fabian Society, the Labour Party, and the London and National Society for Women's Service (183). Marcus further explains Woolf's skepticism about individual politicians' motives within the larger need for change: "Her criticism of reformers . . . derives not from snobbery but from an intimate knowledge of her own reforming heart's desire to dominate. She was an insider to labor and left politics, not a 'lady' who looked on them with disdain. She called the Labour Party 'that timid old sheep' because its politics were not radical enough for her" (*Art and Anger* 163).

Such attendance at meetings, albeit grudging, attests to Woolf's social awareness, but did these interests carry over into her fiction? The prevailing aesthetic of her time, from Ezra Pound's Imagism to Ernest Hemingway's "iceberg method," avoided discursive commentary and didactic messages, substituting concrete "showing" for authorial "telling." She subscribed to this aesthetic to the extent of preferring "subterranean" satire, as Zwerdling emphasizes (42). Reading D. H. Lawrence's letters, Woolf complained, "It's the preaching that rasps me. . . . The moral is, if you want to help, never systematize—not till you're 70: and have been supple and sympathetic and creative and tried out all your nerves and scopes" (*Diary* 4: 126). Yet this absence of overt moralizing does not mean that Woolf muted her criticism. Elaine Showalter, for instance, impatiently chides her for tactics to "choke and repress her anger," until "self-deception becomes habitual" (*Literature of Their Own* 264, 291). Even Zwerdling—who recognizes that Woolf's directly satiric portraits, such as that of the doctor in *Mrs. Dalloway,* do "not support the theory of her unconscious repression of anger"—still speculates that Woolf's usually indirect manner derives from "the familial and societal training that encouraged women to suppress their own feelings to please men" (251, 55). However, to assume either repression or suppression seems to confuse Woolf with a character like Orlando, who fears that her writing might offend the spirit of the late nineteenth century, which she eventually inhabits. Orlando, despite the "contraband" in her mind, gives up composing as a "satirist, cynic, or psychologist—any one of which goods would have been discovered at once" (265–66). Although Woolf entertains similarly "contraband" opinions, she is not nearly so accommodating as Orlando. Just a few months after rejecting Lawrence's didacticism, she indicates that aesthetic "nerves and scopes" do not, after all, preclude the social criticism of "satirist, cynic, or psychologist": "And there are to be millions of ideas [in *The Years*] but no preaching—history, politics, feminism, art, literature—in short a summing up of all I know, feel, laugh at, despise, like, admire, hate and so on" (*Diary* 4: 152).

Far from muting her criticism in her novels, Woolf expresses it through juxtaposition and imagery. If indirect, these methods, once recognized, demolish her targets perhaps more powerfully and economically than essayistic prose. Typical of Woolf's devastating use of imagery is a scene in *The Years* in which North Pargiter, who has raised sheep in an African colony, watches blood from underdone mutton drip into the well of a dish. Because North's cousin refers to the "switch in your hand" by which he exacted labor, the unpleasant mutton becomes a Dantesque punishment (321). The visual imagery of the blood dripping into the well vividly sums up North's career, based on the blood not just of sheep but of Africans. Once the reader is alerted to her methods, Woolf's condemnation of Empire could not be more apt or brazen.

Until about fifteen years ago, Woolf criticism generally did not focus on her satiric bluntness because we were trained to define a modernist as someone who composes in a random, meandering style and prefers aesthetic, not referential, problems. We were prepared to see Woolf in particular as someone who adhered to a "Bloomsbury" ethic, which supposedly prized personal relations over social action. Once assigned this program, Woolf was thought to emphasize individualized characters, from a psychological point of view, and to highlight mundane detail as a way of praising the domestic over the public sphere. However, as a result of post-structuralist contributions to literary theory, and in the wake of post-colonial studies, more recent readers are likely to reverse these judgments, as the following paragraphs will indicate. Nowadays, the "random" fragments point to a consistent social criticism. Her works can be seen to de-emphasize the failings of characters in their personal relations and instead to investigate personalities as products of dangerous ideologies. Small details are now read to expose the tedium, not the glory, of domesticity. In addition, domestic details seem to comment indirectly, through implied metaphor, on issues of worldwide scope.

Supposedly, modernists juxtapose fragments at random. The Marxist critic Georg Lukács, for example, regrets that modernists jumble together "naturalistic" details of immediate experience, without situating them in a historical context (21, 34). In fact, Woolf has been thought to scatter sensory impressions onto the page just this haphazardly, and, as critical fashion has changed, readers alternately have blamed or praised her for a desultory style. A past contributor to *The Pelican Guide to English Literature* reprimands her condescendingly, "Such all-inclusiveness has its dangers, and in trying to record everything, in refusing to select and discriminate between the significance and value of different experiences, the novelist may merely end by reproducing the chaos from which it is the function of intelligence to save us" (Bradbrook 259).

More recent critics may convert this supposed lack of selectivity from a liability into an asset—still assuming Woolf's random gaze, however. Toril Moi, while rightly defending Woolf against Showalter's implication that only personal experience and realism can be "feminist," suggests that critics usefully might follow Julia Kristeva to read Woolf's "sportive, sensual" language as the "rhythms of the body and the unconscious" (Moi 4, 11). Although Moi criticizes Kristeva for assuming that a "revolution within the subject somehow prefigures a later social revolution," she still interprets as a basically unconscious product any occurrence in Woolf's books of the "abrupt shifts, ellipses, breaks and apparent lack of logical construction" that Kristeva prefers (15, 11). Moi thus approves Woolf for creating a "free play of signifiers [which] will never yield a final, unified meaning" (9).

However, in the passage quoted from *Jacob's Room* at the beginning of this chapter, Woolf's abrupt shifts from Sir Edward Grey to Achilles to parasols do not testify merely to sportive "free play." Instead, such breaks and ellipses yield a coherent pattern of satire. Although no meaning can be viewed as "final," some reflections may be traced provisionally. Sir Edward Grey, touting England's right to rule the entire length of Africa "from Cairo to the Cape," had in 1895 warned France out of North Africa, ensuring the continued rivalry of the European countries (Lewis 57). As we have seen, such rivalry made the mobilization of a modern Achilles more likely. The riderless horse which frightens Clara near the statue thus suggests a funeral cortege, prefiguring Jacob's death in the war. "'Tut-tut!' said Mr. Bowley in his dressing-room an hour later. 'Tut-tut!'—a comment that was profound enough, though inarticulately expressed, since his valet was handing his shirt studs" (*Jacob's Room* 167). It is Bowley and the valet, one might say, who remain in an unspeakable "semiotic" (Moi 161). Far from liberating, the preverbal "tuts" only demonstrate the repressions of the master-servant relationship. The master hides his fears for the country, while the servant in turn reserves his opinions. As Woolf insists throughout her books, English society can be stifling; the inequalities of class divisions are one of the reasons that people become "cramped and squashed into featureless masses by hedges" (*Collected Essays* 2: 179). Deadening at home, England is also actively soliciting the deadliness of war.

A frequently quoted line from Woolf's "Modern Fiction" (1919) might seem to support Lukács's characterization of modernism as fragmentary, unanalyzed chaos: "Let us record the atoms as they fall upon the mind in the order in which they fall, let us trace the pattern, however disconnected and incoherent its appearance, which each sight or incident scores upon the consciousness" (*Collected Essays* 2: 106–7). In fact, she is here describing James Joyce's method in *Ulysses*. Her own method places side by side only those "atoms" which illuminate each other as "homologies": "resemblances, in seemingly very different specific practices, which may be shown by analysis to be . . . a general social process" (Williams 104–5). In *Jacob's Room*, Clara with her teacups does belong next to Morocco, because she and the Moroccans suffer corresponding oppressions. Gender expectations in the decades before World War I kept middle-class women out of the public arenas of business and intellect and confined them to the private drawing room, "chained to a rock . . . eternally pouring out tea" (*Jacob's Room* 123). Chapter 3 will show that Jacob's training to see all men as excelling all women prepares him for the simplifications that enable wars: Britons universally must be superior to Germans; the French unquestionably must be superior to Moroccans. Jacob's grounding in gender prejudice makes it easier for him to reduce other whole groups to a subhuman "enemy."

To explain how the "atoms" of teacup and Morocco do trace a coherent pattern, Woolf might have borrowed an argument from another modernist with a social purpose, Bertolt Brecht (cf. Marcus, *Art and Anger* 78). When Lukács advises artists to present a "total" social picture and charges that modernists only heap up fragments, Brecht objects that, in a complex society, artists only gradually can build up a comprehensive view of the interweaving effects of corporations, bureaucracies, the military, and so on, by means of a "montage" of "nonlinear images" (Lunn 87). Such a montage is, in fact, just what Woolf typically creates. Clara's trip to Brocklebank's in Cursitor Street does not lead to Troy linearly. However, when Woolf tosses out the reminder of a London tea shop, she starts ripples that include, first, the colony in which the tea must have been grown and, then, the soldier, the modern Achilles, who has to secure that colony. In the decade before World War I, "popular art on imperial, royal, and military subjects" appeared everywhere in advertisements, on packaging tins, and in marketing gimmicks: "Lipton's . . . illustrated their advertisements with elephants bearing tea chests from Ceylon to the home retailer. Horniman's, Mazawattee, the C.W.S., and other tea companies used similar images and sentiments in their advertising. Camp coffee associated itself with the army in India" (MacKenzie 26). The jumps in *Jacob's Room* from tea to colony to Achilles might not be linear, but they do follow a logic. Woolf insistently exposes the logic that imperial rivalry over commerce would lead to military skirmishes, which in turn would lead to full-scale war.

It might seem odd at first to compare Woolf and Brecht. In some ways, of course, the two are poles apart. She wrote mostly prose fiction, while he staged plays. She did not share his "pro-industrial attitudes" (Lunn 122). Nevertheless, they held many goals and methods in common, even in areas where they seemed to differ. Brecht, for instance, derides what he takes to be a modernist "eternalizing of the presently immediate" (Lunn 122). Woolf, on the other hand, favors "moments of being" (*Moments* 73). Her appreciation of privileged moments, however, does not preclude an urgent interest, like Brecht's, in their historical development. In *Jacob's Room* she builds up to the moment when the riderless horse near the statue of Achilles brings tears to Clara's eyes, not to let the reader savor the intensity of an isolated experience, but to discover its political sources and effects. When she adds that the "loop of the railing beneath the statue of Achilles was full of parasols and waistcoats," she implicates the attitudes of the people carrying the parasols and wearing the waistcoats—send me my tea cheaply, keep ladies delicate—in a dangerous enterprise that eventually kills Jacob (167).

The most important technique shared by Woolf and Brecht is juxtaposition, designed to shock the audience. Thus Brecht sets up disorienting overlaps in a "cubistic" project of revealing a "multifaceted and contradictory outer reality, estranging his audiences from habituated mental assumptions so that they may be able to truly master the social world" (Lunn 122). Woolf, too, wants to jar, not soothe, the reader. In March 1921, she decides that, in writing, "you must be able to screw up into a ball and pelt straight in people's faces" (*Diary* 2: 97). Like Brecht, she jumps from fragment to fragment so that the reader will think and judge. It might be bizarre to put Clara's crockery next to Venezuela, but it is also silly, she implies, to say that women can do nothing but pour out tea. It is, moreover, incongruous and untenable for England to claim disinterest in Venezuela. In the 1890s, England used its colony British Guiana as a base to maneuver for territory in Venezuela. After a fall in coffee prices halted the Venezuelan repayment of European debts—a burden that Europe had once encouraged—Britain, Germany, and Italy blockaded the country in 1902–3. While all the European powers threatened Venezuelan sovereignty, they also competed with each other (Ewell 27, 40–41). Although the warships dispersed, they had in effect staged a dress rehearsal for World War I. Thus the interruptions in Woolf's narration, from teacups to Venezuela, are only apparently ludicrous, for they call attention to absurdities in the social world. Abrupt breaks reveal the gap between "gallantry" in the drawing room and the hostility toward women that lies behind it, as ellipses expose the gap between "heroism" in South America and the territorial designs served by the arrival of the gunboats.

Because Brecht's audience has to keep assessing a larger social context, his discontinuous scenes give "a socialist direction to [the cubist] aesthetic: 'It is always desirable to have two notions—one to demolish the other'" (Lunn 122). Woolf also juxtaposes lines so that one can undercut the other. In *Between the Acts,* for example, Bart Oliver remembers his past tour of duty in India as he presently commands only a drooling Afghan hound (13, 17). The thin flanks of the dog diminish the size of his conquest. To Bart, moreover, Indians, Afghans, his daughter-in-law, and his sister all, more or less, are pets: subhuman. To juxtapose Bart's self-congratulation with the drool carries entertainment value, creating an explosive humor which has only recently received attention (Little, *Comedy* 22). Beyond entertainment, humor pushes readers to re-evaluate incongruous details. When Bart's memory of carrying a gun in India shows up next to a "blob of foam" on the dog's nostrils, the glory of Empire dissolves into froth (*Between the Acts* 13, 17).

Juxtaposed fragments thus frequently rename each other, as disparate items prove after all to be similar. When Peter Walsh in *Mrs. Dalloway* sits in a park next to a sleeping baby and dozes off, Peter, too, is shown up *as* the baby he is *next to* (88). He remains babyish: immature and unworthy to govern India. Woolf's technique here participates in a phenomenon described, for poetry, by Roman Jakobson: "In poetry not only the phonological sequence but in the same way any sequence of semantic units strives to build an equation. Similarity superimposed on contiguity imparts to poetry its thoroughgoing symbolic, multiplex, polysemantic essence . . . anything sequent is a simile" (111). He gives an example from Slavic folklore in which "the willow, under which a girl passes, serves at the same time as her image" (111). Likewise, Woolf allows the baby to serve as both environment to Peter and image of Peter. Her use of metonymy to build metaphor is one factor giving to her prose a polysemantic, poetic quality, as long as "poetry" is understood to include satire and not just "delicate" lyric.

Woolf consciously considered the satiric effects of juxtaposition, as several reflexive passages in her novels demonstrate. In *Between the Acts*, for example, the villagers who complain about Miss La Trobe's play obliquely point to Woolf's own techniques: "The tune changed; snapped; broke; jagged. . . . Nothing ended. So abrupt. And corrupt. Such an outrage; such an insult. And not plain. Very up to date, all the same" (183). Miss La Trobe's discontinuous cacophony resembles contemporary jazz, cubism, or the techniques of modern playwrights (Sears 229). As the audience grumbles, however, it also reveals the reason why modern artists might adopt such fragmentation: "What is her game? To disrupt? Jog and trot? Jerk and smirk? . . . what a yaffle . . . to reflect, presumably, ourselves?" (183). Although members of the audience might try to avoid facing their faults by charging that young artists "can't make, but only break," La Trobe "yaffles" or mocks the larger institutions of Empire, military, and marriage not only to destroy a society but rather to suggest ways of remaking and revising it (183).

Just as Woolf juxtaposes sensory impressions to convey coherent intellectual content, she uses emotion as a way to approach social problems. The lessons of Bloomsbury—"Personal relationships plus aesthetic sensibility equals the good life" (Holroyd 46)—were a starting point, not ends in themselves. Instead of adhering to a too-rigidly defined "Bloomsbury formula," which supposedly privileged only private relations, Woolf (as well as several other members of the group) actually, from the beginning of her career, was pursuing a public program which she formulated explicitly in 1929:

> The change which has turned the English woman from a nondescript influence, fluctuating and vague, to a voter, a wage-earner, a responsible citizen, has given her both in her life and in her art a turn toward the impersonal. Her relations now are not only emotional; they are intellectual, they are political . . . and her novels naturally become more critical of society, and less analytical of individual lives.
>
> We may expect that the office of gadfly to the state, which has been so far a male prerogative, will now be discharged by women also. Their novels will deal with social evils and remedies. Their men and women will not be observed wholly in relation to each other emotionally, but as they cohere and clash in groups and classes and races. (*Collected Essays* 2: 147)

Exercising her Socratic role as "gadfly to the state," Woolf employs the hit-and-run tactic of humorous juxtaposition and the often subliminal tactic of evocative, concrete detail.

As Woolf indicates in this essay on "Women and Fiction," when she presents personal relations of characters, she aims at delineating not so much unique individuals as representatives of a milieu and a time period. In her diary for June 1923, while she was composing *Mrs. Dalloway,* she characterized herself as "post-Dostoevsky," meaning that she and her moment in literary history had moved away from exploring psychology. She denies that she is writing "from deep feeling," according to a Dostoevskian prescription, or even from a purely aesthetic fascination with words, "loving them as I do" (*Diary* 2: 248). Instead of a psychological or sensuous motive, her chief goal, she declares, is "to criticise the social system, and to show it at work, at its most intense" (*Diary* 2: 248). Although many readers have felt that she does skillfully evoke internal states that add up to complex characters in her novels, she modestly makes that effect secondary. She already accepts cheerfully that "character is dissipated into shreds now" (*Diary* 2: 248).

When Woolf brushes aside a requirement to compose "from deep feeling," she is, in part, following the modernist turn away from romantic self-expression. This ideal is represented, for example, in T. S. Eliot's "Tradition and the Individual Talent." In addition to avoiding any direct confession of her own feeling to maintain the modernist impersonality of the artist, Woolf also bypasses, at least as a primary goal, naming any "deep feeling" of characters. She thus participates in a depersonalization of characters that is often taken to be another sign of modernism (Lunn 34). As Toril Moi observes, Woolf undermines "the notion of the unitary self" (7).

Illuminating this loss of self in modernism, Eugene Lunn helpfully distinguishes between a negatively felt "dehumanization" and a positively celebrated "stylization." The more optimistic stylization includes a "depersonalizing surrender to the ojectifying qualities of language, sight, and sound (as in symbolism or surrealism)" and an equally positive "'scientific' study of the object world, promising its intellectual or physical reconstruction (cubism)" (Lunn 61). Because Woolf's well-known pronouncement that "in or about December, 1910, human character changed" (*Collected Essays* 1: 320) coincides with the date of Roger Fry's First Post-Impressionist Exhibition in London (Rosenbaum 21), Woolf seems to draw on the liberating possibilities suggested by painters like Picasso and Matisse to lessen the importance of representation (Woolf, *Roger Fry* 172). She may have followed the further experimentation of these painters to decompose character into stylized fragments. Post-Impressionists, in turn, drew much of their inspiration from African art (Hughes). Appropriately, since Woolf's montages often include some reminder of modern Africa's place within the European empires, she also seems to have been affected by the aesthetic possibilities of African nonrealistic sculpture. In 1920, after attending a "show of Negro carvings," she speculates, "I dimly see that something in their style might be written" (*Letters* 2: 429). She disjoints fragments of selves and reassembles them, to reveal the social patterns that sketched such personalities in the first place.

Although Woolf's stylizations may well offer the aesthetic compensations of "language, sight, and sound," they thus also promise to recompose the social world. Sounding very much like Woolf herself, La Trobe, in *Between the Acts,* might be glad that her discontinuous pageant has touched Lucy personally, so that "You've stirred in me my unacted part" (153). Yet La Trobe is not satisfied that her art should only buoy Lucy's individual emotion, fantasy, and confidence. She protests that "she was not merely a twitcher of individual strings; she was one who seethes wandering bodies and floating voices in a cauldron, and makes rise up from its amorphous mass a re-created world" (153). Neither authors, characters, nor audience, therefore, can retreat into individuality and privacy. Instead, authors observe an intense impersonality, characters participate in a "floating" stylization, and the audience must take on the responsibility to re-create the social world. Like Medea throwing the fragments of her father-in-law into a cauldron, La Trobe wants to dismantle a patriarchy to make a new social order (Ovid 195, 197).

What Woolf was calling "the old post-Dostoevsky argument" (*Diary* 2: 248) might now be named a post-structuralist loss of belief in the "subject," which, in turn, grows out of some strands in modernism (Lunn 39). Peggy Kamuf argues that Michel Foucault gives an appropriate context for Woolf's turn "away from this historical preoccupation with the subject, closing the book on the 'I'" (11). Just as post-structuralists regard people as intersections of language and culture, Woolf views her characters not so much as isolated, autonomous individuals as linked consciousnesses, connected to each other and to their time and place. Clarissa Dalloway, for instance, warns that "to know her, or any one, one must seek out the people who completed them; even the places" (*Mrs. Dalloway* 231). Clarissa feels that she is "laid out like a mist between the people she knew best, who lifted her on their branches as she had seen the trees lift the mist"; she admits, moreover, to being a "part of people she had never met" (12). This image of human beings as dynamic space, a kind of social atmosphere, resembles the post-structuralist emphasis on a blending of people as interactive products of culture.

Several other novels by Woolf include lines which anticipate such a cultural emphasis. In *The Years,* the character Maggie muses, "Am I that, or am I this? Are we one or are we separate?" She keeps asking her sister, "What's 'I'?" (140). Similarly, when Peggy drives with her aunt Eleanor, she wonders, "Where does she begin, and where do I end?" (*Years* 334). As the most important unifying force, a common historical condition, rather than genes or mystical empathy, colors the characters: "We start transparent, and then the cloud thickens. All history backs our pane of glass. To escape is vain" (*Jacob* 49). When Jacob fills his pipe, sips his whisky, and checks his wallet, the narrator cautions the reader not to see an independent Jacob expressing only himself: "Moreover, part of this is not Jacob but Richard Bonamy—the room; the market carts; the hour; the very moment of history" (73). Peers and social expectations influence Jacob, even determining that he "prefers" whisky, whereas birth in a different sex or class would have prescribed a different beverage.

Woolf reflects this view of people as junctures of time and place in her narrative strategy, by moving constantly from one consciousness to the next. Rachel Blau Duplessis calls the result a "collective protagonist" ("Feminist" 329). Yet such a collectivity should not be taken to represent a homogenous community, nor even a healthily fragmented series of voices which tolerate individual differences (Cuddy-Keane 274, 279). Rather than validating all these multiple voices indiscriminately, Woolf usually undermines them. Whether she quotes characters directly or follows their thoughts through free indirect style, she lets characters condemn themselves. To encourage readers' "satiric and critical distance," she allows no consciousness to continue for too long, a technique that "distinguishes her use of stream of consciousness from Dorothy Richardson's or Joyce's or Faulkner's," for those authors foster more identification with characters (Zwerdling 53).

As Woolf rapidly shifts narrative point of view to encourage a skeptical, critical distance, she also again relies on incongruous juxtaposition as part of characterization. At a crucial point in "Mr. Bennett and Mrs. Brown," revised several times for printings and lectures in 1923 and 1924 (Daugherty 269, 278), she illustrates this technique of deliberate non sequitur. Distinguishing between "Georgians," such as herself, and "Edwardians," such as Arnold Bennett, Woolf criticizes Bennett for leaving his character Hilda Lessways looking out the window at houses, while he goes on to record rents, freehold, copyholds, and fines, in exhaustive detail (*Collected Essays* 1: 330). It may appear that Woolf rejects Bennett's social interests, an erroneous impression not lessened when she claims that her hypothetical character "Mrs. Brown is eternal, Mrs. Brown is human nature, Mrs. Brown changes only on the surface . . . not one of the Edwardian writers has so much as looked at her" (330). This frequently quoted line, implying a timeless soul, appears to contradict all Woolf's other statements, before and after, about history's backing and coloring an individual's "pane of glass" (*Jacob* 49) or about authors' protesting social ills and serving as "gadfly to the state" (*Collected Essays* 2: 147). Actually, Woolf does not suddenly abandon her long-standing concern for social issues in favor of an "essential" human nature. Instead, to reveal society, she simply advocates a method different from that of the Edwardians. She prefers concrete detail instead of abstract disquisition, economy instead of harangue, and implicit undercutting through suggestive metaphor instead of explicit lecturing with lists of rents.

"Mr. Bennett and Mrs. Brown" even illustrates Woolf's characteristic fictional methods by interrupting the story with a humorously incongruous remark: "Perhaps she was going to London to sign some document to make over some property. Obviously against her will she was in Mr. Smith's hands. I was beginning to feel a great deal of pity for her, when she said, suddenly and inconsequently: 'Can you tell me if an oak-tree dies when the leaves have been eaten for two years in succession by caterpillars?'" (323). While Mrs. Brown herself remains unaware of her resentments, her recollection of the attack of the caterpillars on the oak may parallel, indirectly, her instinctive resistance to an oak-hard patriarchal system which, beyond the immediate situation of mortgages held by one powerful man or worries over one son's debts, puts Mrs. Brown against her will into the hands of all men. Woolf raises the stakes beyond present rents and individual burly corn-chandlers like Mr. Smith, to larger issues of class and gender. The humor and the open-ended suggestiveness of the abrupt change of topic, from "some property" to "an oak-tree," operate almost in the style of Zen non sequiturs, which are supposed to shock students into realizing that they may not even have been asking the right questions. The word "caterpillars" affronts the serious consideration of "some document" and expands the topic, just as Clara's command to Troy, "Wait till we cross the road," both undercuts the dignity of the genteel outing and seriously comments on a larger issue, militarism.

Woolf may object to Bennett's style for some of the same reasons that Brecht rejects the "documentary montage" of Erwin Piscator (Lunn 123). Although Brecht learns from Piscator's "epic theater" and adopts many of its precepts as his own, he dislikes the way his teacher projects contemporary newsreels or quotes newspapers on the stage. Brecht judges these chunks of raw material "a poetically impoverished, mimetic reproducing of the outer world, instead of its parabolic reconstruction in the theatre" (Lunn 123). Nevertheless, if Brecht avoids Piscator's "documentary montage," he produces his own montages and presents fictional parables which still target social problems. Similarly, Woolf grows impatient with Bennett's minute documentation but retains his concern for the larger community.

As Woolf makes soul a function of society, she also satirizes society *through* characters. Although Zwerdling recognizes some satire of institutions, he thinks she must spare individuals: "Woolf's picture of Clarissa Dalloway's world is sharply critical, but . . . it cannot be called an indictment, because it deliberately looks at its object from the inside" (120). Whereas he assumes that Clarissa's "soul has survived" the corruption around her (128), *Mrs. Dalloway* thoroughly mocks Clarissa and every other character, as I will argue in chapter 1. In a letter of August 1923 to Gerald Brenan, Woolf admits that, while working on that novel, "my own view . . . of humanity in general, falls and falls. Some base perfidy set me off, and now I can see little good in the race, and would like to convey this in writing. I should like to make odious, mean, lying characters . . . but then, (this is my weakness) tolerance keeps breaking in, and I excuse the creatures instead of blighting them" (*Letters* 3: 65). Although she creates no single-hued villains, she indicts the situation in which they live. Her characters, all to some extent "odious," fail not as individuals who stray from a moral code, but as representatives of an immoral society, which fails them. No matter how distinctive, complex, and poignant Woolf might make a few of her characters, both they and more schematic ones still serve to expose how anyone, including the reader, under similar circumstances of class, gender, and race, is likely to become warped. Just as the compromised characters should not merely "adapt" better to their surroundings, so Woolf does not invite readers to dismiss satirized individuals, but to consider changing society—and ourselves.

In her indictment of a whole society, Woolf does not spare female characters, who thus cannot serve as strong role models. Sallie Sears, baffled that Lucy and Isa in *Between the Acts* flounder so much, still maintains that, "as in her other novels, Woolf places the burden of hope upon the women characters" (217). Sandra Gilbert and Susan Gubar likewise believe that Mrs. Dalloway can "regenerate" her peers with "divine grace" (*Sexchanges* 317). Woolf, however, satirizes Lucy, Isa, and Mrs. Dalloway along with the men. Admittedly, Woolf's tone is sometimes hard to catch, as she condemns a stupid society yet pities the character who is caught in that society, while still regretting how the character herself perpetuates social problems. The first page of *Jacob's Room* illustrates the complexity of this tone. As the widow Betty Flanders writes to Captain Barfoot, a tear obstructs her view—making a rather pretty blur, in fact. Betty seems superficial, easily distracted from her grief. Is Woolf mocking her? Yes and no. Although Betty may have felt real grief in the past, by now she is using emotion as a tool, to attract the captain. However, if she schemes, she personally is not at fault, for, as a widow, provided by her society with so few means of earning a living for herself and her children, she *has* to find a supporter. In a similar ambivalence, the book pities Betty as the mother of a son who dies, but also unsparingly shows that this oblivious woman has adopted the injustices of her milieu and in some ways actually has solicited the war that kills her own son. Betty is typical of the women in Woolf's books; none qualifies as a totally strong and likable role model or even as a completely innocent victim. Like the male characters, the women may admirably do the best they can under the circumstances, but those circumstances need revision.

Just as Woolf may individualize some characters less to serve broader indictments, so she focuses on mundane details in order to hint at world affairs, rather than praising "the significance to be found in everyday life" (Wheare 10). In the passage quoted from *Jacob's Room,* it is not because Clara has captured some timeless peacefulness unavailable to bustling diplomats that her everyday promenade receives more space than Sir Edward's policies. Instead, the dismal limitations of the young woman's era have captured her. It is true that Woolf advises, in "Modern Fiction," "Let us not take it for granted that life exists more fully in what is commonly thought big than what is commonly thought small" (*Collected Essays* 2: 107). She is arguing that if Joyce's *Ulysses,* which she had seen in manuscript (*Diary* 2: 188), at first appears confusing because of mundane detail, either dull or obscene, readers should persevere with an important book. Nevertheless, if she defends *Ulysses,* she finally judges it a "bright yet narrow room" (*Collected Essays* 2: 107). When Woolf herself furnishes Clara's narrow room with the mechanical brightness of "pretty china teacups," she exposes in all its tedium the only activity that Clara is permitted to undertake. Moreover, Woolf looks *through* that narrow drawing room to the larger vista of all middle-class women so thwarted.

Although Woolf constantly mapped historical currents, she grew impatient with the definition of history as battles, legislative bills, and the lives of famous men. She wished that historians would record more information about conditions affecting ordinary people. In *A Room of One's Own,* she called for more biographies of workers: "And there is the girl behind the counter too—I would as soon have her true history as the hundred and fiftieth life of Napoleon or seventieth study of Keats and his use of Miltonic inversion which old Professor Z and his like are now inditing" (94). Woolf had already followed this prescription, in fact, four years earlier in *Mrs. Dalloway.* There she introduces the prime minister but then neglects to record a single word out of his august mouth. Instead, she dwells on the effect of his presence at a party in making more work for the scullery maids (251). She evokes sympathy for Mrs. Walker, scouring endless tureens. Nevertheless, the cook experiences drudgery, not the "significance" of everyday life (Wheare 10). Her work weighs too heavily, as Clara's too lightly, while their society wastes the talents of both working-class and middle-class women. In addition to revealing the maid's plight, the passage pokes fun at the prime minister, by reducing him to just another item in the list of dishes, one more "chicken in aspic" (251). Although the prime minister cannot claim importance in the sense of glory and rectitude, the attitudes and values behind the policies carried out by such a cipher retain immense importance for Woolf, in their power to determine people's lives.

Woolf's eye for small detail testifies to her belief that material conditions create mental patterns. She insists, for example, in an early short story, "The Journal of Mistress Joan Martyn," that medieval stockings shed light on medieval brains (*Complete Shorter Fiction* 34). Orlando's "biographer" similarly remarks, not altogether facetiously, that if the streets were better drained, literary style would improve (113). To the extent that Woolf assumes a kind of base for every superstructure, Jane Marcus is right in calling Woolf "Marxist" (*Art and Anger* 77). Woolf does not interest herself in the softness of wool stockings or the glint of the puddles in the street for their sensuousness alone. At the same time that she can savor their aesthetic qualities, she also seeks fundamental connections, as do Marx and Engels in *The German Ideology* (1845–46): "Conceiving, thinking, the spiritual intercourse of men, appear here as the direct efflux of men's material behaviour" (quoted in Eagleton 4).

Woolf has created several reflexive passages in *Jacob's Room* and *A Room of One's Own* which define this technique of using mundane detail, such as Mrs. Walker's chicken jellied in aspic, to insinuate comparisons for topics of greater import, such as the prime minister's rigid conventionality. In *Jacob's Room,* the narrator pauses for a metafictional comment: "But who, save the nerve-worn and sleepless, or thinkers standing with hands to the eyes on some crag above the multitude, see things thus in skeleton outline, bare of flesh? In Surbiton the skeleton is wrapped in flesh" (162). In other words, as we go about our daily lives, we seldom notice social motives. Although Woolf laments the myopia that confines us to quotidian trivia, she multiplies this trivial detail, then tries to bring its oddity at last to attention through juxtaposition. Thus readers may become aware of the "skeleton," the articulation of ideologies making us what we are. As if to illustrate how to flesh out an ideology, the narrator leaves "some crag above the multitude" to launch into an introduction of characters replete with mundane detail: "'The kettle never boils so well on a sunny morning,' says Mrs. Grandage . . . a baby is deposited in her lap, and she must guard the sugar basin while Tom Grandage reads the golfing article in the *Times,* sips his coffee, wipes his moustaches, and is off to the office, where he is the greatest authority upon the foreign exchanges and marked for promotion" (162). The Grandages, who never reappear, seem to exist in their one paragraph solely to illustrate "fleshed out" ideologies in Surbiton. Indeed, the drive for money that fuels the foreign exchanges, the boredom of listening to platitudes about the kettle in a repressed society that never says what it feels, the inflexible division of labor into female baby-sitter and male climber of the corporate ladder, together articulate the materialism, competition, and frustration that help answer the question, "Why did Jacob have to die?" As she argues in *Three Guineas*, greed, combativeness, and an apocalyptic longing for release from boredom make wars more possible. Woolf, therefore, stands as the thinker, "with hands to the eyes on some crag," who can indicate that she and her peers and her readers—myself—are wrapped in ideologies, often dangerous ones.

A Room of One's Own contains other reflexive passages that advertise how Woolf plans to use close-up detail not only for its own aesthetic sake, but also to map social vistas. The fictional speaker decides that what she likes about a new novel by "Mary Carmichael" is that just when it seems that nothing momentous is happening—when "some one sewed or smoked a pipe"—the reader suddenly feels as if "one had gone to the top of the world and seen it laid out" (97), like the thinker on a crag overseeing multitudes in *Jacob's Room* (162). The speaker in *A Room of One's Own* agrees with Carmichael that the only way to catch "unrecorded gestures" is "to talk of something else, looking steadily out of the window" (88). Thus, if Woolf rejects Bennett's gaze out the window at prosaic buttons and factories, she herself focuses on the lowly kitchens of servants or a promenade with the dog Troy. She does so not to give exhaustive evidence from the foreground of social conditions, but to orient the gaze, through juxtaposition and metaphor, toward the background links among Empire, military, and gender relations, which together constitute a comprehensive imperial ideology.

Woolf's whole oeuvre, in fact, can be said to have as a central project what her short essay "Thunder at Wembley" (1924) attempts: to sweep away this imperialism. Under the pretext of describing a sudden shower at the British Empire Exhibition, Wembley Park, London, the essay warns that a political storm is brewing. The location of the exhibition outdoors, letting in raw nature, works against the artificial illusion of glory. Although the organizers hope "to show off to the best advantage snowy Palestine, ruddy Burma, sand-coloured Canada," they fail to notice that the "wind is rising" (*Collected Essays* 4: 186). The weather seems to presage revolutions: "Pagodas are dissolving in dust. Ferro-concrete is fallible. Colonies are perishing and dispersing" (186). Whereas the oblivious "Massed Bands of Empire," had they been able to detect the signs of collapse, certainly would regret the passing of the Empire, the narrator exults in its dissolution. She hopes that the arrogance of the puffed-out band members, "men like pouter pigeons," will not always impress the public. Although intellectuals of the time were likely to criticize the Wembley Exhibition, Britons in general were sufficiently captivated by its mystique to attend in record numbers: twenty-seven million (MacKenzie 101, 111). What, Woolf asks incredulously, "is the spell it [the show and the Empire] lays upon them? How, with all this dignity of their own, can they bring themselves to believe in that?" (*Collected Essays* 185).

Woolf facetiously attributes such doubts about the worthiness of Empire making to a bird, part of that nature which the organizers should never have admitted: "But this cynical reflection . . . was made, of course, by the thrush" (185). If the organizers of the Wembley Exhibition had anticipated the demystifying effects of "Nature," they would have taken steps to keep "her" out (184). For a female thrush, like the "outsider society" in *Three Guineas*, joins with a refreshing, if frightening, natural sky, to criticize the flimsy delusions of imperialism: "Clergy, schoolchildren, and invalids group themselves round the Prince of Wales in butter. Cracks like the white roots of trees spread themselves across the firmament. The Empire is perishing; the bands are playing; the Exhibition is in ruins. For that is what comes of letting in the sky" (187).

Although Woolf's books repeatedly let in a little "sky," a deflationary light on the ideologies of Empire, her message often has gone as undetected as that of the cynical thrush. Martin Green, for example, in *The English Novel in the Twentieth Century: The Doom of Empire,* mistakenly concludes that Peter Walsh, recently back from India in *Mrs. Dalloway,* and Bart Oliver, colonial retiree in *Between the Acts,* represent "all that is most genuine. . . . Usually in Woolf's work, men's sexual glamour is guaranteed by their [imperial] adventures" (xiii). Marcus and Carroll, on the other hand, recognize that Woolf refers to the overseas adventures of these men only to undercut them, damning not individuals so much as the system that trains them. However, no extended study has yet investigated how centrally Woolf condemns the Empire, indicting both worn-out values at home and their exportation abroad.

Woolf shared her dislike of the Empire with several of her friends.

Lytton Strachey's *Eminent Victorians* contains "an attack on imperialism and power politics" in the essay on Charles Gordon, who died at Khartoum (Annan 23). Although the British government claimed to have no designs on the Sudan, Strachey accuses the government of sending a reckless Gordon into North Africa because some officials hoped that he would *not* follow orders and thus would require a large rescuing force—which then could, as if by accident, remain as an occupying army (L. Strachey 285, 341). In *Mrs. Dalloway*, Peter Walsh stands under a statue of Gordon, which "achieved at length a marble stare" (77). The deflation of achievement into a "staring corpse" discredits both Gordon and Peter, who, like his idol, worships the discipline of "Boys in uniform" (76–77). Another of Woolf's friends, E. M. Forster, denounced the swagger of the British abroad and satirized Anglo-Indians in *A Passage to India*. Strachey and Forster are said to have drawn their condemnation of imperialism from nineteenth-century liberalism, which tried to combine social justice and individual liberty (Rosenbaum 13).

Among Woolf's associates, it was Leonard Woolf who, focusing less on individuals and more on political systems, worked most actively against the Empire—after serving as a colonial administrator himself. In *Growing*, the volume of his autobiography which covers his years in the Ceylon Civil Service (1904–11), he explains, "I had entered Ceylon as an imperialist, one of the white rulers of our Asiatic Empire. The curious thing is that I was not really aware of this. The horrible urgency of politics after the 1914 war, which forced every intelligent person to be passionately interested in them, was unknown to my generation at Cambridge" (25). Only gradually does he discover "how evil the system was beneath the surface for ordinary men and women" (159). Looking back, he is astounded "how long it took me to become fully conscious of my position as a ruler of subject peoples" (111). Leonard begins to question this position only after a respected Tamil lawyer accuses him of striking him with a riding whip. Although Leonard denies the charge and can figure only that, once when his horse skittered, he must have accidentally flicked the lawyer, he concludes, "perhaps for the first time I felt a twinge of doubt in my imperialist soul, a doubt whether we were not in the wrong, and the Jaffna Tamil Association and Mr. Sanderasekara in the right, not right in believing that I would and had hit him in the face, but right in feeling that my sitting on a horse arrogantly in the main street of their town was as good as a slap in the face" (113–14). Although Leonard did not write *Growing* until late in his life, he must have recounted a few of the incidents earlier to Virginia, for she appears to borrow from his experience for both *Mrs. Dalloway* and *The Years*. Whereas Leonard can admit ruefully to past harshness and obtuseness, Virginia's characters Peter, Martin, and Sir William, who mimic Leonard, retain an unflattering complacency.

Once Leonard Woolf began to see the destruction caused by "economic imperialism" and the arrogance of his own role as colonial administrator, he not only quit his Civil Service post but launched an active opposition. He argued against the Empire on Labour Party committees, in political journals, and in two books, *Empire and Commerce in Africa* (1920) and *Imperialism and Civilization* (1928). Virginia Woolf judged *Empire and Commerce* "masterly and brilliant" (*Letters* 2: 416). Selma Meyerowitz assesses this work: "Woolf argues that imperialism was morally wrong, culturally destructive, and economically impractical. In 1919, this position was radical. Yet events in Africa in the decades since Woolf's study have revealed that Woolf's analysis of the past and future relationships between Western imperial nations and African territories was both historically perceptive and prophetic" (78). He may have been not only perceptive but also practical. Duncan Wilson claims that the Labour Party's Advisory Committee on Imperial Affairs "was one of the most effective instruments for securing the freedom of the British colonies, and on this subject [Leonard] Woolf's was the most constant and powerful influence" (248).

Because Virginia Woolf also criticized European economic exploitation as early as *The Voyage Out*, completed in 1913, her ideas and Leonard's must have influenced and reinforced each other all along, in a fruitful intellectual exchange. In 1923 Woolf praises Leonard's company, unlike her other friends' "cheapening" talk: "He may refuse to kindle, but he never detracts; & so, when he does kindle, the glow is of the purest fiery red" (*Diary* 2: 235). This "fiery" Leonard may have considered Virginia as, in a way, even more incendiary socially than he was. In his fable "Fear and Politics: A Debate at the Zoo" (1925), he makes the mandril the most radical of the zoo creatures, a Bolshevik disliked by the rhinoceros of the piece, Conservative Prime Minister Baldwin. "Mandril" was Virginia's pet name between them at least as early as 1912 (Virginia Woolf, *Letters* 2: 12).

In any case, the Woolfs certainly inspired each other with their ideas about social change (Chapman and Manson 61). Both believed, for example, that political solutions to colonization and wars were not possible without prior economic and social changes. As Leonard cautions throughout *Empire and Commerce,* people have to change not just laws but "beliefs and desires" (368). Virginia also connects "private" lives, from the bedroom to the boardroom, with international repercussions. Whereas Leonard blasts imperialism through discursive prose, she satirizes it through juxtaposition and imagery. Indeed, she sometimes draws her images from Leonard's facts and figures. In ways that have not yet been noticed, *Empire and Commerce* in particular illuminates several of her novels. For example, Leonard's accusations about the "fraud" and "force" which support the British trade in African "frozen mutton" (*Empire and Commerce* 340, 353) give a context for her visual image of blood dripping from the underdone mutton served to the colonizer in *The Years* (321). Similarly, in *The Waves,* her description of Louis, the international shipper who dreams of pharaohs and shuts his "bony hands . . . like the sides of a dock closing" (275), gains point from Leonard's discussion in *Empire and Commerce* of the Suez Canal and the devastating rivalry to which it contributed.

Together Leonard and Virginia Woolf also tried to influence public opinion by publishing anti-imperialist books at their Hogarth Press. A cursory glance at the titles from Hogarth (in Woolmer) reveals a number of books on imperial subjects: Norman Leys's *Kenya* (1924); Lord Olivier, *The Anatomy of African Misery* (1927); G. S. Dutt, *A Woman of India: Being the Life of Saroj Nalini (Founder of the Women's Institute Movement in India)* (1929); Horace B. Samuel, *Beneath the Whitewash: A Critical Analysis of the Report of the Commission on the Palestine Disturbances of August, 1929* (1930); Denis Ireland, *Ulster To-day and To-morrow: Her Part in a Gaelic Civilization* (1931); Leonard Barnes, *The*

New Boer War (1932); C. L. R. James, *The Case for West Indian Self-Government* (1933); K. M. Panikkar, *Caste and Democracy* (1933); W. G. Bollinger, *Race and Economics in South Africa* (1934); Parmenas Githendu Mockerie, *An African Speaks for His People* (1934); and Leonard Barnes, *The Future of Colonies* (1936). Although Virginia or Leonard need not have agreed with every word of each individual author, the general tone against Empire certainly was planned: "The Woolfs set out deliberately to publish what they wanted—and never what they did not want" (Woolmer 6).

Virginia Woolf read manuscripts for the press (*Letters* 3: 78, Bell 2: 200), and some books on the Empire seem to have influenced imagery in her novels, just as *Empire and Commerce* did. In chapter 1, I argue that Edward Thompson's *The Other Side of the Medal* (1925), on the 1857 Indian Mutiny, illuminates an important scene in *The Years.* Similarly, William Plomer's *I Speak of Africa* (1927) may have confirmed some of Woolf's connections between Empire making and repressed sexuality. Plomer's book forms an important background to *Orlando,* where Orlando's eventual husband is a colonialist active in South Africa.

Although the Empire is a central topic in Woolf's books, she never directly portrays any of the colonized people as characters. Perhaps unwilling to speak for an experience outside her own, she does presume, from time to time, to label people of color with all the unpleasant prejudice of her contemporaries. References in Woolf's letters and diaries to colonized people fall disappointingly into a condescending tone. In one instance from 1919, her friend Janet Case, on Leonard's recommendation, had written to a Ceylonese editor, requesting his support in a campaign for leniency, after World War I, toward Germans and conscientious objectors. When the editor refused, Virginia consoles her friend by dismissing "little timid coffee coloured men . . . neither advanced nor philanthropic," who want to "keep in with" the government. She does record a moment of learning, when Leonard reads this page of the letter and objects that "he doesn't think it quite fair to say that the poor wretches aren't advanced, but they may feel that as they're going strong for self government in India and Ceylon and therefore are liable to be called disloyal by foolish people out there they shouldn't

run the risk of being also called disloyal by other silly people from another point of view" (*Letters* 2: 353–54). Although she accepts correction here and eventually condemns racism explicitly in *A Room of One's
Own* (52) and *Three Guineas* (66), she never entirely escapes a coolness
derived from her early training to feel "superior."

It also must be admitted that Leonard, despite his honesty in transferring the terms "uncivilized" and "savage" from the Africans to the
Europeans (*Empire and Commerce* 155), annoyingly refers to Africans as
"non-adult races" (364). Unlike many of his contemporaries, he argues
that the Africans could not have been called "non-adult" before the arrival of Europeans but had been rendered childishly dependent by the
loss of one culture and the denial of another:

> In this process of what Mr. Chamberlain called "convincing the native of the
> necessity and dignity of labour," the whole tribal organization, and the bonds
> which bound together the fabric of native social life, will necessarily be de-
> stroyed. The Government will be powerless to substitute, whether by education
> or otherwise, anything in their place; for any real education will unfit the native
> to take his place as a docile labourer on a penny a day in the scheme of eco-
> nomic imperialism. (*Empire and Commerce* 357)

Leonard Woolf scathingly condemns the destruction of African social
systems, the extortion of slave labor, and the refusal to provide Western education once the colonizers have dismantled traditional education. Economic imperialism, he says, thus reduces Africans, who had
been independent and mature, to the status of untutored dependents.
Nevertheless, if this argument correctly highlights the victimization
of the colonized, the phrase "non-adult races" still carries some of the
glib disdain of his era.

Despite Virginia Woolf's residual insensitivity to colonized people
and her lack of first-hand knowledge of the colonies, she felt strongly
that the English civilization which the British imposed on their subjects was not worth exporting. In a 1919 essay, "The Royal Academy,"
she judges that the patriotic paintings at an exhibition and the patrons
who view them display a revolting enthusiasm for the Empire. The

crowd outside the gallery admire "'The motor-cars of Empire—the bodyguard of Europe—the stainless knight of Belgium'—such is our English romance that nine out of ten of those passing . . . do homage to the embattled tyres and the kingly presence of Albert on his high-minded charger with some nonsense of this sort" (*Collected Essays* 4: 206). She lampoons a "bluff nobleman" who intones, she says, in the style of Kipling, "Clean between the eyes, eh what? . . . Damned foreigners. Post of duty. The Guard dies, but never surrenders. The ladies of our family—Up, Guards, and at them!" (4: 207). Leaving it ambiguous whether he charges at the foreigners or the ladies, the hypocritical nobleman is receptive to the imperial "illusions of all kinds [which] poured down upon us from the walls" (4: 210).

As so often is the case in Woolf's works, these glimpses of Empire in "The Royal Academy" lead to reminders of war. When she sees that a painting by Sargent overemphasizes and thus trivializes the bandaged eyes of a soldier, the cumulative sentimentality surrounding Empire making and war making overwhelm her:

> But Mr. Sargent was the last straw. Suddenly the great rooms rang like a par-rot-house with the intolerable vociferations of gaudy and brainless birds. How they shrieked and gibbered! How they danced and sidled! Honour, patriotism, chastity, wealth, success, importance, position, patronage, power—their cries rang and echoed from all quarters. "Anywhere, anywhere, out of this world!" was the only exclamation with which one could stave off the brazen din as one fled downstairs. . . . (4: 211)

The desire to flee "anywhere, out of this world," provoked by the false values of "patriotism, chastity, wealth," echoes Charles Baudelaire's prose poem which concludes, "N'importe où! pourvu que ce soit hors de ce monde!" (213). Unfortunately, the exotic lands to which both Baudelaire and Woolf's gallery-goer want to escape are already occupied, and the distant inhabitants do not remain unaffected by their visitors. Whereas conventionality initially may have propelled some of the European adventurers away from home, by the time Woolf's narrator wants to close out the parrot din, the hypocrisies and rationalizations of Empire have become just another oppressive convention; scarcely any shore remains beyond the reach of Western influence.

Woolf is aware that the desire to sail away from all problems can be dangerous. Although Rachel in *The Voyage Out* leaves England, she remains part of her father's commerce, which exploits its workers. When Rhoda in *The Waves* pretends to set her boats sailing, her need for refuge is poignant and innocent, yet her conspicuously white petals in a serviceable brown basin might entail others' misery: "The big blade is an emperor; the broken blade a Negro" (*Waves* 18–19). Orlando floats her toy boat ecstatically, but her husband, Shelmerdine, sails a real ship to South Africa destructively. Woolf mocks his participation in colonialism as the bullying of a boy, by having him arrange childish shells, like Rhoda's, as his blueprint for subduing South Africa (*Orlando* 257).

Just as Woolf's characters entertain fantasies of escape by sea but glimpse a much harsher reality on the invaded shores, she herself excitedly read Renaissance travel writings as a teenager but later revised her opinion of them (*Diary* 3: 271; Fox 45). Eventually she connected modern imperialism, which she had learned to hate, with its roots in Renaissance expansionism. In a 1917 review of Sir Walter Raleigh's prose, she admits her attraction to his "great zest in living" (*Collected Essays* 3: 30). Nevertheless, she quotes from his own mouth a strong condemnation of conquest and colonization, as Raleigh uneasily wonders what the Europeans (whom he now tries to distance as "they") actually have left behind them for others, along with their fame: "They themselves would then rather have wished, to have stolen out of the world without noise, than to be put in minde, that they have purchased the report of their actions in the world, by rapine, oppression, and crueltie, by giving in spoile the innocent and labouring soul to the idle and insolent, and by having emptied the cities of the world of their ancient Inhabitants, and filled them againe with so many and so variable sorts of sorrowes" (quoted in *Collected Essays* 3: 29). This passage questioning the whole civilizing mission puts in doubt her initial description of Raleigh the civilizer confronting "savages" (27). In both *The Voyage Out* and *Orlando*, she parallels modern imperialists to Renaissance explorers who are themselves savage.

If Woolf had to dampen her early enthusiasm for Elizabethan adventurers, she also had to confront her own family's involvement with the Empire. One ancestor, four generations back, "settled in the West Indies and prospered in the unpleasant trade of buying sickly slaves and then curing them sufficiently to make them fit for the market" (Bell 1: 1). A great-grandfather, on the other hand, lobbied the House of Commons against the slave trade and, when unsuccessful, worked with the Clapham Sect in its campaign against slavery (Bell 1: 3–4). Woolf's grandfather, Sir James Stephen, who argued against slavery but for colonization, was Permanent Under Secretary for the Colonies, and her conservative uncle Fitzjames Stephen codified Indian law (Marcus, *Patriarchy* 80, 83). Marcus reports of this uncle, "In *Liberty, Equality, Fraternity* he declares that women and the working class must be kept down forcibly in order to show the colonies how rebellion will be treated" (*Patriarchy* 90).

Woolf must have felt an acute sense of guilt when she realized that her own life-style depended to a certain extent on the fruits of an Empire exposed in her novels as unjustified. She broaches this complicity in *A Room of One's Own* when she wonders about the source of the income that will enable women to write. The speaker, who sounds like Woolf yet is fictionalized in important ways, encourages women to get jobs. She has to admit, however, that her own "room" and independence were made possible not by a salary but by a legacy: "Society gives me chicken and coffee, bed and lodging, in return for a certain number of pieces of paper which were left me by an aunt, for no other reason than that I share her name." She adds, "My aunt, Mary Beton, I must tell you, died by a fall from her horse when she was riding out to take the air in Bombay" (37). This death resembles that of Percival, the Anglo-Indian in *The Waves,* who is in some ways based on her brother Thoby (*Diary* 4: 10). Both falls interrupt the arrogant presence of Europeans on horseback which constituted a slap in the face to colonized people, as Leonard Woolf realized (*Growing* 114). The character Mary Beton's fatal fall is all the more striking because Woolf's own aunt, Caroline Emilia Stephen, from whom she inherited 2,500 pounds in 1909, died not in India, but in Cambridge, after years as an invalid

(McNeillie 1: 267). Caroline was, however, the daughter of Sir James Stephen, Under Secretary for the Colonies. Leonard reported that Woolf's legacies from Caroline and her brother Thoby yielded some 400 pounds a year, almost equivalent to the 500 pounds which Woolf decides a writer needs (Bell 2: 39). The fictional detail of the ride "to take the air in Bombay," like the fall of Percival, seems to acknowledge that Caroline and Thoby, though not colonists themselves, did derive at least part of their income indirectly from the Empire, a gigantic "taking" of somebody else's "air" and space.

Moreover, Woolf herself has to acknowledge a kinship with that rider in Bombay. At the end of *A Room of One's Own,* the speaker selects the name Mary Beton and identifies with the aunt (109). The speaker began by parodying a normal introduction—"call me Mary Beton, Mary Seton, Mary Carmichael or by any name you please"—and then letting the names migrate to other characters (5). These names come from a Scottish ballad (*Letters* 3: 487n), which Woolf could have known from several sources (Marcus, *Patriarchy* 179). The ballad "Mary Hamilton" is composed in the voice of a woman who, impregnated by a high official of the court, kills her baby and is condemned. In one version, she defiantly wears white to the scaffold; she tells the executioner, "Yestre'en the queen had four Maries / This nicht she'll hae but three; / There was Mary Beaton, an' Mary Seaton, / An' Mary Carmichael an' me" (Friedman 183, 219). Woolf may allude to this ballad to suggest that many women have been silenced: if not through the extreme of execution, then through slow killing by social systems that deny to women a public voice. Mary Hamilton or Shakespeare's hypothetical sister Judith, whom Woolf imagines committing suicide because pregnant, have not been heard. The speaker in *A Room of One's Own* modestly identifies with the more docile Marys left behind, waiting for a bolder Mary Hamilton or a creative sister equal to Shakespeare yet to be born.

This migration of names through *A Room of One's Own* produces several effects. It merges the rare woman who did manage a university education (Mary Seton) with the speaker, who feels uneducated (like Woolf). It unites in a single, on-going task the author who still writes stiffly (Mary Carmichael) with the writer known for her finesse (Woolf), thereby transmuting the accomplished author from an isolated "genius" into a product of others' lessons. Such sharing of names further identifies women thought of as victims, excluded from fulfilling work, with victimizers, albeit unconscious ones, like the aunt living off the colonies. The reader, too—some common Mary or Kathy—is implicated. Writer and reader share guilt for the blindnesses of the past and present, as they share responsibility to make the future different: less dependent on the hierarchies of men over women, colonizer over colonized, fighter over peacemaker, rich over poor.

1.
Devouring the Lamb:
Sex, Money, and War

Mrs. Dalloway

Despite differences in style, both *Mrs. Dalloway* (1925) and *The Years* (1937) scathingly depict British society as deadened and deadly. When the character Peter Walsh sees an ambulance carrying the body of the suicide Septimus and exclaims, "One of the triumphs of civilisation," the irony implies that the ruin of veterans like Septimus is indeed a product of what Peter accepts as enlightened living (*Dalloway* 229). Like the ambulance, English civilization carries death. First, it eventuates in World War I, which is presented in all Woolf's books not as an anomaly or an external threat to British society, but rather as its inevitable result. Second, Britain maintains the Empire, based on deadly drives for power and money. Both books extensively allude to the Empire to epitomize the folly and pretentiousness of exporting empty values abroad. In *Mrs. Dalloway*, Peter Walsh in 1923 has just returned after five years as a colonial administrator in India, and Lady Bruton wants the "superfluous" people of England to emigrate to the colonies (166). In *The Years,* Abel Pargiter, head of the Pargiter clan, has fought in the famous Indian Mutiny of 1857, and his children and grandchildren have raised sheep in Africa, ruled in India, and policed the Empire. Moreover, these novels expose gender roles shaped to fit imperial and commercial needs. Both books powerfully indict a system of dominance that operates at home and abroad.

Such a system pervades all areas of life. *Mrs. Dalloway* describes external detail and internal consciousness for a variety of characters, presenting a cross-section of many classes during an ordinary June day in London in 1923. As Woolf was beginning this novel in fall 1922, she was reading both Homer's *Odyssey* and James Joyce's *Ulysses* (1922) (*Diary* 2: 205).[1] Like Joyce, who presents an ordinary wanderer, Leopold Bloom, on a single June day in Dublin in 1904, Woolf deflates Odysseus's heroic efforts to get back home. She substitutes for Odysseus's trials the mock battles of an unremarkable person, Clarissa, who faces only the threat of a backfiring car. Parodying the conclusion of the *Odyssey,* she turns the scene of Odysseus's restoration to Penelope into Clarissa's half-hearted reunions at her party. Yet if Woolf seems to reduce the scope of the *Odyssey,* she does so only in denying the grandeur of the characters. Actually, *Mrs. Dalloway* ranges further even than Odysseus's circuit of the Mediterranean, as the book touches on parts of the British Empire from Canada to India, past and present.

In fact, Woolf may have been responding to Leonard Woolf's statement in 1920 that he could imagine "a wonderful new Odyssey in which the wanderers are States and nations, the characters national beliefs, desires, forlorn hopes, ambitions, greeds, and ideals, the background not men and cities, but races and continents" (*Empire and Commerce* 48). "National beliefs" operating over "continents" might indeed be said to be Virginia Woolf's real topic in *Mrs. Dalloway.* As she was composing the novel in 1923, she recorded her plan "to criticise the social system, and to show it at work, at its most intense" (*Diary* 2: 248). Her indirect approach to satire, however, misled critics for many decades to assume, with Jean Guiguet, that "the mechanical relations between individuals, such as are imposed by the social structure, dominated by concepts of class and wealth . . . are not her problem" (quoted in Zwerdling 120). Alex Zwerdling's "*Mrs. Dalloway* and the Social System," originally printed in 1977, was one of the first readings to underline Woolf's awareness in this novel of historical forces shaping individuals. Nevertheless, although Zwerdling admits that "Woolf's picture of Clarissa Dalloway's world is sharply critical," he concludes that the novel "cannot be called an indictment, because it deliberately looks at its object from the inside" (120). He believes that Clarissa's reactions, particularly to the news of Septimus's death, are "in marked contrast to the way her set usually deals with outsiders" (128). Satire, however, demolishes Clarissa along with the rest of her world, so that she remains representative of her set, not in contrast to it. She fails to break with convention, not as a particularly weak individual, but as an almost inevitable product of society, which remains Woolf's real target.

As the acknowledged "symbol of what they all stood for, English society," the never-named prime minister appropriately frames the book (262).[2] At the end, after he and Lady Bruton have consulted, Clarissa surveys the room: "Perhaps there was somebody there. But there was nobody. The chairs still kept the impress of the Prime Minister and Lady Bruton, she turned deferentially, he sitting four-square, authoritatively. They had been talking about India. There was nobody" (279). The repetition of the phrase "there was nobody" not only registers a current absence but also hints at the presence of a nullity a few minutes before. Nevertheless, if the officials stand revealed as insubstantial or shallow, they do possess power. Governmental opinions and social norms together carry enormous weight, affecting Septimus, Clarissa, and all the characters.

Matching his anticlimactic appearance at the end of the book, the prime minister contributes to the opening street scene—and to the world—nothing but backfiring (19). When the sound of his car pulls Clarissa up short in her self-congratulatory musings, the rude interruption is apt and funny. It is also ominous, for prime ministers have indeed commanded instances of the "pistol shot" which the shoppers at first assume the noise to be (19). The World War I veteran Septimus, "unable to pass" because of the present motorcade and because of the past policies of such leaders, accurately detects a "horror" just behind the drawn blinds (20–21). The prime minister's car generates adulation for the "dead," the "flag," and the "Empire," supposedly sacred goals, all smeared by the insouciance of exhaust fumes (25). For the sake of a vague, unifying emotion under the flag, not for any particular cause which could be named and argued, people are stupidly "ready to attend their Sovereign, if need be, to the cannon's mouth" (26).

Yet this scene with the prime minister's car further hints that the officials and citizens who think that mindless patriotism is a worthy goal should read the admonitory handwriting on the wall, here updated to skywriting. Humorously, the ordinary folk who have waited so patiently for the mysterious car to pass through the gates of Buckingham Palace actually miss its arrival when they stare at a circling airplane instead. The palace, enjoying "the heavenly life divinely bestowed upon Kings," now has its heavenly messages written by the plane's white smoke in an overarching sky (27). Indeed, the British kingdom would like its own piece of sky to extend into a worldwide Empire: "The clouds to which the letters E, G, or L had attached themselves moved freely, as if destined to cross from West to East on a mission of the greatest importance which would never be revealed, and yet certainly so it was—a mission of the greatest importance" (30). The "destined" imperial "mission" from West to East, of which Peter's assignment in India is representative, remains, however, an embarrassing blank or, worse, a dangerously garbled directive accepted by uncritical, babyish, sleepwalking citizens: "'Glaxo,' said Mrs. Coates in a strained, awe-stricken voice, gazing straight up, and her baby, lying stiff and white in her arms, gazed straight up. 'Kreemo,' murmured Mrs. Bletchley, like a sleep-walker" (29). When the exhaust smoke resolves itself finally into what is probably an advertisement for toffee, the candy trivializes both the government and the priorities of the citizens.

This advertisement reveals, moreover, the basis of the state in commerce. As Leonard Woolf emphasized in 1920, since the 1860s the British government had been openly declaring a philosophy long in effect, that governments exist to further commercial ends—a belief which "has caused more bloodshed than ever religion or dynasties caused in an equal number of years, when gods and kings, rather than commerce, were the 'greatest of political interests'" (*Empire and Commerce* 10). At about the same time, advertising became the watchword of the day. From the 1870s on, the "most aggressive and innovative advertisers" were companies "dependent on the imperial economic nexus" (including the sugar for toffee); such advertisers were "concerned to sell not just their own product, but also the world system which produced it" (MacKenzie 16). *Mrs. Dalloway* mocks both commercialism and imperialism in the skywriting scene, by reducing the West-East "mission of the greatest importance" to a nonsense word, "Glaxo."

Society, then, is the main character of *Mrs. Dalloway,* with individuals serving as microcosms of the cultural macrocosm. Clarissa, for example, is often described in terms that link her to social institutions, and these, in turn, parallel Clarissa; both she and the institution are described as a "hostess." The chauffeur's white pass that clears a way for the prime minister's sleek car "burnt its way through . . . to blaze among candelabras, glittering stars, breasts stiff with oak leaves, Hugh Whitbread and all his colleagues, the gentlemen of England, that night in Buckingham Palace. And Clarissa, too, gave a party. She stiffened a little; so she would stand at the top of her stairs" (25). If Clarissa's party resembles a royal reception, Buckingham Palace, in turn, looks "like an old prima donna facing the audience all in white" (177). Similarly, St. Margaret's, regulating the business hours, chimes "like a hostess who comes into her drawing-room on the very stroke of the hour and finds her guests there already" (74). A Marxist might call these parallels among royalty, church, business, and Clarissa herself examples of "homology" (Williams 104–5). In *Mrs. Dalloway,* such parallelism indicates that pervasive attitudes—materialism, class consciousness, complacency, repression—affect or "stiffen" the whole society in the same direction, whether one looks at government, Clarissa's upper middle class, the aristocracy as represented by Lady Bruton, or the patriotic poor who watch the skywriting. The comparisons to a hostess or a prima donna work in both directions, to shift attention from Clarissa to the larger public world that shapes her, and to show how attitudes formed in a drawing room can reverberate into policies implemented around the world.

Mrs. Dalloway steadily exposes the hollowness of the representative middle-class pair, Peter and Clarissa, despite a few likable traits. Although Peter can make fun of the English for "dressing up in gold lace and doing homage," he is not exempt from paying similar homage to rank and money (262). By 1923 he has abandoned any good impulses he may have had as a young man. Although thirty years ago he inclined to socialism, now he savors "the silver, the chairs," which are even more "delicious" than Clarissa herself (75, 61). Turned into a thorough capitalist, currently forgetting his old "abstract principles," he now praises only the game of cricket, Bartlett pears, and upward mobility (75, 247, 244). He has betrayed his idealism, yet even those early efforts, consisting only of reading on a peak in the Himalayas, look narcissistic. The books on philosophy and science sent out to him from London seem not to have benefited any Indians (76).

Clarissa too compromises her best impulses. Sally Seton long ago had seemed to reveal to Clarissa that the latter "knew nothing about sex—nothing about social problems" (49). Sally had inspired her to try to understand both sexuality and politics, but, despite Clarissa's initial longing, she has pursued neither physical passion nor her concern for world affairs. If once she went so far toward sapphism as to kiss Sally, now she will not even visit her (see Jensen 172). Clarissa has converted her feelings for people, whether Sally or Peter, into a "passion" for gloves and shoes (15). The only trait that redeems this superficiality is her occasional lucidity. She realizes, for example, that she has always wanted to impress people by spectacular entrances. Yet she reproaches herself without experiencing any real intention to reform. Although she is "annoyed" at herself and wishes she could live her life over again, it turns out that she would live a second life not to display herself with less vanity, but only to look more attractive, with "beautiful eyes" (13–14).

As for the awareness of "social problems" (which Clarissa attributes to Sally's youthful unconventionality), Clarissa's response to social issues began small and then shrank. Although she claims that she and Sally wanted to "reform the world" and "abolish private property," they never posted even their one letter of protest (49). On the day of her party, Clarissa gives away a cushion only because it is "bald-looking" and gushes gratitude to her servants only because their dependency enables her to feel generous (57–58). In her diary, Woolf says that in *Mrs. Dalloway* "I want to bring in the despicableness of people like Ott[oline]. I want to give the slipperiness of the soul" (*Diary* 2: 244). She criticizes Lady Ottoline for inviting someone whom she regards as lowly to her party and then being kind to her solely so that she can congratulate herself on her own magnanimity (cf. *Diary* 3: 32). Woolf assigns such subterfuges to Clarissa in her self-serving gift to the maid and her grudging invitation to drab Ellie Henderson (180).

Far from following social events, Clarissa cares more for her roses than "for the Albanians, or was it the Armenians?" (182). Although it might seem inevitable occasionally to confuse foreign names, the magnitude of the problem in Armenia makes it less likely and more insensitive that Clarissa would forget it. In 1915, between 600,000 and 1,000,000 Armenians died when the Ottoman Empire ordered the deportation of the Armenian population to Syria and Palestine. After a brief independence in 1920, Armenia was incorporated into the USSR in 1922, so the country would have been very much in the news at the time of the novel's setting ("Armenia").[3] Clarissa jumbles the names of distressed countries with no real care for who is suffering.

Clarissa is as ill-informed about other current events. Her knowledge of Empire is confined to the book cover *Big Game Shooting in Nigeria* (13). Treating Africa as a place for animals, not people, this book is tellingly displayed next to *Jaunts and Jollities,* a title suggesting that she can conceive of Empire only as a distant lark (13). Moreover, Clarissa's proprietary interest in the prime minister extends only to whether he will enhance her party; she is "prancing" as she escorts "her" prime minister (264). Although her musings inadvertently reveal him as a glorified but finally useless "nobody," Clarissa adopts him with pride (279). When she admits that she is glad her old friends are present solely so they can "envy" her high-placed connections, she finally has to judge her pride a "hollow" sentiment, as she once before wondered "if the whole panoply of content [of her life] were nothing but self love" (265, 17). Despite these moments of self-knowledge, however, she quickly fills that hollow place only by intensifying her hatred of the resentful, lower-class Miss Kilman (265).

Complementing Clarissa's emptiness, her whole crowd looks somnolent or moribund. Peter Walsh and Lady Bruton, for example, each end a scene by snoring; they fail to strike the dignified pose which their sense of self-importance would require (85, 170). Clarissa similarly is startled by Peter Walsh's unexpected visit "like a Queen whose guards have fallen asleep and left her unprotected . . . so that any one can stroll in and have a look at her where she lies with the brambles curving over her" (65). This allusion to the fairy tale of Sleeping Beauty makes Clarissa a Briar Rose. However, the Peter Walsh who praises primarily "the silver, the chairs" becomes a commercialized, tinsel Prince Charming (61). Similarly, "Queen" Clarissa never awakens from her decaying values, just as the real queens and prime ministers who might be in the motorcade remain oblivious for decades to their own dangerous, briar-sharp policies.

This glittering but false society in the drawing rooms, occupied by the compromised Clarissa and Peter, is displayed against grim references to Empire. Lady Bruton and Peter Walsh, supporters of Empire, mask their real motives, power and greed, behind a self-satisfied claim that they bring "justice" to the "hordes" (274). *Mrs. Dalloway* keeps insisting, however, that "civilizers" like Lady Bruton and Peter are merely exporting a dead civilization. Lady Bruton's luncheon to promote colonization, for example, is one of the main "events" (or non-events) of the book. She dawdles over food and chitchat but maneuvers the conversation around to her real reason for inviting Richard Dalloway and Hugh Whitbread: to solicit their help with her letter to the *Times* urging emigration to Canada. Seeking a cause, "half looking-glass, half precious stone," she wants to siphon off "the superfluous youth of our ever-increasing population [. . .] what we owe to the dead" (165–66; ellipses in brackets are Woolf's). Although she says that the emigrants must be "born of respectable parents," obviously they count less than she and her illustrious dead ancestors do (164). The expanding population might cut into her hefty share of the national wealth, so she tries to get rid of them. Woolf debunks Lady Bruton's disdain for "superfluous" people by saying caustically that Hugh, her amanuensis, "went on drafting sentiments in alphabetical order of the highest nobility" (167).

Lady Bruton, caricature that she seems, represents attitudes toward the indigent and toward the colonies that were widespread in the nineteenth century. A familiar apologist for the British Empire, Sir John Robert Seeley, argued in 1883 that the "superfluous population" of England could move to the colonies, which were, in his self-deluded view, all "so thinly peopled that our settlers took possession of them without conquest" (quoted in Snyder 118; see 108). Hundreds of thousands of the poor did emigrate from Great Britain; some colonies were also used as "dumping-ground[s] for convicts" (Thomson 94). Convicts, however, could include strikers. In 1830, starving field laborers "rioted in support of their demand for a wage of half-a-crown a day. Nineteen of them were hanged and 481 were deported to Australia: which serves to emphasize . . . the savagery of the laws and the penalties to which the working classes were subjected" (Thomson 16–17).

Carrying this savagery into the twentieth century, Lady Bruton exposes, behind her noble sentiments, their true basis in force. In a marvelously suggestive pose at her luncheon, she raises the red carnations from Hugh against her lace "with much the same attitude with which the General held the scroll in the picture behind her" (158). This juxtaposition has two implications. First, Lady Bruton holds her flowers in the stance of a military man because she would, in fact, prefer to be a commander. On the surface, she thinks that she has accepted her training that women must be passive and guided by men: "If Richard advised her, and Hugh wrote for her, she was sure of being somehow right" (166). Although she has, in effect, dictated to her guests exactly what to advise and compose, she assures herself of meeting all requirements for ladylike behavior, including a false self-deprecation. Nevertheless, while she masks her temperament by turning her chair "deferentially" to men (279), behind the façade she is not only forceful in business but likely to be combative on the field: "if ever a woman could have worn the helmet and shot the arrow, could have led troops to attack, ruled with indomitable justice barbarian hordes and lain under a shield noseless in a church, or made a green grass mound on some primeval hillside, that woman was Millicent Bruton" (274). Despite her mellifluent name, the hostess doubles as a militant brute. She worries, in 1923, about "the news from India" and obviously chafes to call in more troops against Indians, who for her qualify as "barbarian hordes" (168). The word "noseless," however, makes the desire to wage war comical as well as gruesome and stupid—nothing more than piling up skulls in crypts.

One thing the "barbarian hordes" in India were pursuing at the time was Gandhi's *satyagraha,* literally "holding on to truth," i.e., passive resistance (Snyder 417). Woolf may have learned of Gandhi's program when, in 1917, she helped Leonard do research on the British Empire (*Diary* 1: 229n). For many years Leonard maintained his interest in independence for India and Ceylon (Wilson 248). If he continued to discuss these matters with Woolf, she may have heard, for example, of "the most infamous act in the last decades of British rule," a massacre of Indians which occurred during Peter Walsh's tenure abroad (Moorhouse 226). After one of Mahatma Gandhi's *hartals* or general strikes in Amritsar in 1919, 1,500 Indians were killed or wounded when Brigadier-General Reginald Dyer ordered his troops to fire on an unarmed crowd. Although London forced Dyer into early retirement, "his disgrace was not acknowledged by all his fellow-countrymen. A debate in the House of Lords produced a majority of 121 to 86 in Dyer's favour" (Moorhouse 229). In contrast to the support which greeted Dyer, prison terms were meted out to Gandhi; in 1923, as Lady Bruton fulminates, he was in jail (Moorhouse 232).

Just as Woolf lets Lady Bruton's label "barbarian" boomerang against herself, when the hostess seeks only to ride down the "hordes" and lie "noseless," Leonard Woolf similarly uses the words "civilized" and "savage" sarcastically, to mean the reverse. In *Empire and Commerce in Africa,* he charges the words "uncivilized" and "civilized" with damning irony:

> As long as the uncivilized Africans were left to themselves in uncivilized Africa, the idea of blowing out rocks in the highlands of Abyssinia in order to allow the Nile to rush down and spread destruction and death over the plains of Egypt did not occur to the rulers of Egypt and Abyssinia. But, when civilized and Christian nations like France and Britain appeared in these regions as "rival Powers," this ingenious device had to be reckoned with as a practical possibility of strategy and policy. (155)

Leonard points out that, while destruction and greed seemed to be the operative European "ideals," the newspapers fed the British public false stories of the "barbarous habits" of non-Europeans. He recounts, for example, how no one informed Britons that the British had betrayed a treaty with the king of Abyssinia. Instead, the press lavishly reported that this king punished those who indulged in tobacco by cutting off their noses and lips:

> That the information was untrue [a few people were slightly scarified so that they could not smoke until healed] is perhaps not of any great importance, for the history of the dealings of all European States with African kings is one of almost unredeemed treachery and breach of faith. . . . An uncomfortable inference is easy that . . . breach of faith and treaties becomes in this way an almost holy weapon for the noble crusaders who are spreading European civilization through the "Dark Continent." (164–65)

Employing the same tactic that enables Leonard Woolf to undercut the words "noble," "Dark," and "not of any great importance," Virginia Woolf ironically reverses Lady Bruton's judgments. With Dyer praised for mowing down the crowd and Gandhi imprisoned despite nonviolence, the "indomitable justice" which Lady Bruton assumes looks more like domination than justice. By 1929 Woolf directly calls this "rage for acquisition," which drives people like Lady Bruton to "make frontiers and flags; battleships and poison gas," a "lack of civilisation" (*Room of One's Own* 38–39).

A second reason Woolf poses Lady Bruton with red carnations against a general's scroll, in addition to the need to show up Bruton's own militancy, is to suggest an important connection between chivalrous behavior toward women—bestowing delicate flowers on decorous ladies—and the aggressive behavior of her relative the general toward colonized territory. Woolf was very much aware how the requirement for chastity in women had been used as a justification for colonization. Thus, in *Mrs. Dalloway*, for example, she evocatively juxtaposes a colonizer who harangues a crowd and girls whose only characteristic is virginity: "In a public house in a back street a Colonial insulted the House of Windsor which led to words, broken beer glasses, and a general shindy, which echoed strangely across the way in the ears of girls buying white underlinen threaded with pure white ribbon for their weddings" (25–26). The rowdy man in the pub apparently wants his government to fight more vigorously to retain the colonies. He evades any discussion of markets, raw materials, cheap labor, and prestige; instead, the only motive for continued imperialism allowed into the national consciousness is the need to protect the "girls buying white underlinen threaded with pure white ribbon for their weddings." By repeating "white," "white," and "pure," Woolf magnifies the concept of purity to the point of absurdity, so that the passage mocks the colonials and their supposed need to protect girls.

Just as the virginal girls' purity is juxtaposed against the returned colonial's belligerence, the camera eye in *Mrs. Dalloway* discovers "sacred" motherhood positioned next to the military: "The mothers of Pimlico gave suck to their young. Messages were passing from the Fleet to the Admiralty" (9). The Admiralty does not sidle up to the mothers by accident, for the military needs an icon—threatened motherhood or beleaguered virginity—to prop up its mission. The mothers nursing their young and the girls threading pure white ribbon serve as appropriate backdrops for the Admiralty and the colonist because Europeans had, in fact, labeled their subjects as uncontrollably lascivious, like Caliban, making force necessary—just to protect women.

E. M. Forster recognized a similar ideology in *A Passage to India* (1924), which Woolf read while she was still working on *Mrs. Dalloway* (*Diary* 2: 304). When Forster's character Aziz is falsely accused of raping the British visitor Adela Quested, protective sentiment clots around chastity in the form of a "young mother—a brainless but most beautiful girl" with her baby in her arms (180). The woman, who "dared not return to her bungalow in case the 'niggers attacked,'" becomes, "with her abundant figure and masses of corn-gold hair," a symbol of "all that is worth fighting and dying for; more permanent a symbol, perhaps, than poor Adela" (181). Yet, as Woolf suggests by making the young girls so overly "white" and having the colonial rant in such a vulgar manner, purity may be a requirement imposed for ideological purposes, and the resort to troops may be as stupid as breaking bottles in a pub. Moreover, if chastity in women is not a value, and if women are not under constant threat from supposedly lustful colonized men, then what excuse do the Europeans have to keep those would-be rapists in the preventive detention of Empire?

As a matter of fact, swashbuckling commanders in the British Empire were using "threatened womanhood" to vindicate brutality during the period when Woolf's Peter Walsh was serving in India. When Brigadier-General Dyer in 1919 ordered his troops to fire on an unarmed assembly, the immediate provocation was that three Britons had been killed and especially that a Miss Marcia Sherwood had been assaulted by a mob (Moorhouse 227). Although Sherwood was pulled to safety by a Hindu family, Dyer commanded that uninvolved Indians who had to travel on the street where she had been mauled "must do so by crawling on all fours" (Moorhouse 230). Magnifying the attack on one British woman to brand all Indian men as beasts, Dyer and his defenders in England excused a massacre. With her red carnations, Lady Bruton appears to be a delicate lady for whom knights like Dyer are performing their deeds. Yet, beneath her veneer, she is as aggressive as the trigger-happy Dyer.

In addition to exposing the power-mongering of Lady Bruton, *Mrs. Dalloway* also reveals her greed. Falling asleep, the dowager dreams of protecting her own upper-class "carpet," her private turf that settles heavily to the important last position in both sentence and paragraph. Her hand is "curled upon some imaginary baton such as her grandfathers might have held, holding which she seemed, drowsy and heavy, to be commanding battalions marching to Canada, and those good fellows walking across London, that territory of theirs, that little bit of carpet, Mayfair" (169–70). Mayfair, the territory in London which she regards as hers, did indeed grow rich because of territories abroad. The "nabobs," or fantastically wealthy returned members of the East India Company, had first settled in Mayfair a century earlier (Moorhouse 51). As the twentieth-century descendant of Empire-builders, Lady Bruton exhibits a materialism, hypocrisy, and bloodthirstiness which undermine her self-proclaimed rectitude: "she had the thought of Empire always at hand, and had acquired from her association with that armoured goddess her ramrod bearing, her robustness of demeanour, so that one could not figure her even in death parted from the earth or roaming territories over which, in some spiritual shape, the Union Jack had ceased to fly. To be not English even among the dead—no, no! Impossible!" (275). Even her bearing makes her the embodiment of weaponry, the ramrod to prime a gun. Comically, Lady Bruton cannot imagine herself as anything but an English ghost, and, more seriously, she and her values—to amass property and exact homage—are already dead.

Peter Walsh, on the other hand, tries to distance himself from militaristic colonizers like Lady Bruton and from returned Anglo-Indians who sit "in the Oriental Club biliously summing up the ruin of the world" (246). The former civil servants in the club assume that ruin will surely ensue, if authorities do not apply more force to prevent the Empire from slipping away. Peter, however, despite his efforts, closely resembles these colonials in greed, inability to perceive as human beings the Indians whom he was governing, and aggression. His commercial motive, for example, surfaces when he saunters complacently through London: "And there he was, this fortunate man, himself, reflected in the plate-glass window of a motor-car manufacturer in Victoria Street. All India lay behind him; plains, mountains; epidemics of cholera; a district twice as big as Ireland; decisions he had come to alone—he, Peter Walsh" (72). The repetition of "he," "himself," and "Peter" emphasizes his solipsism. The scene identifies Peter with manufacturing power by superimposing his face on the glass of the car dealer in Victoria Street, as the Empress Victoria imposes herself on India. Though Peter owns no car here, he approves of ownership and thus resembles the prime minister and the arrogant doctor Sir William Bradshaw, who flaunt their expensive cars as status symbols. As the prime minister's car is mockingly said to carry "a face of the very greatest importance against the dove-grey upholstery" (19), Bradshaw's car is "low, powerful, grey" (142). Bradshaw is satirized as much as the prime minister, in part because of the "very large fee which Sir William very properly [in the view of his wife] charged for his advice": "Her ladyship waited with the rugs about her knees an hour or more, leaning back, thinking sometimes of the patient, sometimes, excusably, of the wall of gold, mounting minute by minute while she waited . . . until she felt wedged on a calm ocean, where only spice winds blow" (143). Lady Bradshaw's musings in this ostentatious car lead her to the "spice winds" of Empire, as Peter's identification with the manufacturing power of England sent him literally to India. Creating a typical cluster of materialism, complacency, and coercion (exhibited by Lady Bruton, Sir William Bradshaw, and Peter), Woolf insists that the attitudes of Empire making also permeate life at home, including her ladyship's apparently innocent wait in a car and Peter's casual walk along a London street.

Peter moves on from his pride in motor-cars to boast of his "turn for mechanics; had invented a plough in his district, had ordered wheelbarrows from England, but the coolies wouldn't use them" (73). In what appears to be a source for Peter's problems, Leonard Woolf introduced English ploughs and bulls in Ceylon to replace buffaloes depleted by rinderpest. Although Leonard claims that the yield was better in plowed fields than in those turned over by the trampling of buffaloes, the cultivators later abandoned the English ways. He admits that the bulls were poorly trained and therefore not worth the trouble (*Growing* 199–200). Because Peter gives no reason for the rejection of his inventions, he seems to assume that the coolies were too stupid to know how to use his wonderful innovations. Yet his self-absorption and self-satisfaction in the rest of the passage hint that in fact the colonizers have little to offer their subjects.

Peter protests that his "susceptibility" to emotion and weeping, a trait that seemingly sets him apart from the more coarse military men, "had been his undoing in Anglo-Indian society" (230). Peter, however, is not really sensitive to other people. He wants to go to the Dalloways' party "to ask Richard what they were doing in India—the conservative duffers," but India is not to him a place of real people affected by British policies but "mere gossip" with which to "brush, scrape, kindle" himself (244). Although Peter scorns the Conservatives, he fails to specify any alternative. Instead of analyzing politics, Peter derives a kind of masturbatory glow simply from advertising his exotic role as colonial administrator, without questioning the effect of that role on others.

Peter is, moreover, "susceptible" to sexual desire toward a person whose opinions and individuality he has no wish to discover. He plans to marry Daisy, the wife of a major in the British army in India, as soon as they can secure divorces from their present spouses (68). Nevertheless, he admits that jealousy, not love, is his main motive in courting her (121). He is not interested in an interactive relationship with a complex person who would sometimes exchange ideas and caresses with him and sometimes range away in a life of her own. He prefers a fantasy character who, "securely fastened to the back seat," would adore him, while remaining circumscribed in a secondary role: "in short it might be happier, as Mrs. Burgess said, that she [Daisy] should forget him, or merely remember him as he was in August 1922, like a figure standing at the cross roads at dusk, which grows more and more remote as the dog-cart spins away, carrying her securely fastened to the back seat, though her arms are outstretched, and as she sees the figure dwindle and disappear still she cries out how she would do anything in the world, anything, anything, anything" (240). The "dog-cart" to which Peter consigns Daisy may gain some of its indignity from Dr. Johnson's comment that women preaching are like dogs walking on their hind legs, a slur to which Woolf frequently alludes (*Voyage* 292; *Jacob* 32–33; *Room of Own* 56; cf. Blain 240). In Peter's view of marriage—or, easier yet, in his memory of an affair—Daisy in her constricted dog-cart has no positive work in the world except to prop up his ego and sacrifice an excessive "anything" to him.

In addition to yielding to the lure of an ideal which would eclipse the real woman, Peter is further "susceptible" to urges to follow unknown women through the streets of London, fantasizing a liaison (78–81). He uses his status as a colonial administrator to imagine that he is "an adventurer, reckless . . . swift, daring, indeed (landed as he was last night from India) a romantic buccaneer" (80). He thus indicates a parallel between obtaining a woman and dominating a compliant colony, a connection that Woolf most thoroughly investigates in *The Years*. Woolf shrewdly epitomizes this link between mistress and colony in Peter's characteristic gesture of opening and closing a large pocket knife (60, 250). Because he stealthily fingers the knife while following a woman on "Cockspur Street," the knife is blatantly phallic (79). In the same way that Joyce in *Ulysses* lets the reader infer Bloom's masturbation, while mentioning only Gerty MacDowell's sentimental description of Roman candles exploding (360), Woolf displaces Peter's sexuality onto the knife. The condensed imagery succinctly connects phallus and weapon. Indeed, he is more interested in power than love.

Just as Peter regards sexuality as a means of dominating, so he sanctions real weapons. Although he claims that he dislikes the army and the Empire (82), he does, in fact, approve of boys marching with guns (76). He respects their "fine training" and the way that "one will" appears to work the boys' arms and legs, as if "life, with its varieties, its irreticences, had been laid under a pavement of monuments and wreaths and drugged into a stiff yet staring corpse by discipline" (76–77). "Corpse" does not augur well for the future of boys beginning military exercises. Yet Peter can only admire "the exalted statues, Nelson, Gordon, Havelock, the black, the spectacular images of great soldiers . . . [who] achieved at length a marble stare" (77). Peter's idols include Horatio Nelson, naval commander against revolutionary and Napoleonic France; Henry Havelock, a general during the Indian Mutiny of 1857; and Charles Gordon, nineteenth-century hero who furthered the British Empire in China and the Sudan. According to the portrait of General Gordon in *Eminent Victorians*, by Woolf's friend Lytton Strachey, members of the British government purposely had sent Gordon, "a little off his head," on an impossible mission in the Sudan, in order to draw sympathy for a martyr and thereby justify annexation (341). In Woolf's treatment of Gordon, the blankness of the "marble stare" marvelously tumbles the expectation packed into "achieved" (77). The rigor mortis of corpse and monument debunks the achievements of the commemorated men, who may not be so "exalted" after all.

Doing homage to military men, Peter himself holds a knife, revealing force to be the basis of his tenure in India, despite his claims of emotional susceptibility to the supposedly softening influences of women. With his knife as both phallus and weapon, sexuality becomes for Peter an exercise in ego, practiced with a woman whose own personality must be unknown and idealized, while colonization yields a vicarious sexual thrill as power over weaker countries. In the light of Peter's ma-terialistic, egotistical, and violent motives, Septimus comically but appropriately calls Peter "the dead man in the grey suit," mistaking him for the spirit of his wounded comrade Evans (105).

Because Peter cannot recognize his own deadness, he masks his exploits in India as spreading British "civilization." He characterizes civilization in one morning's vision:

> Admirable butlers, tawny chow dogs. . . . there were moments when civilisation, even of this sort, seemed dear to him as a personal possession; moments of pride in England; in butlers; chows dogs; girls in their security. . . . And the doctors and men of business and capable women all going about their business, punctual, alert, robust, seemed to him wholly admirable, good fellows, to whom one would entrust one's life, companions in the art of living, who would see one through. (82–83)

These "doctors" and "capable women" invoke the satirized characters Dr. Bradshaw and Lady Bruton, hardly admirable leaders to whom Septimus or the "superfluous" poor should "entrust" their lives. In fact, the list to which Peter keeps returning—"admirable butlers," "tawny chow dogs," "girls in their security"—is dipped in sarcasm. This trilogy of Peter's creed wonderfully advertises those aspects of English society that Peter admires and that the book as a whole criticizes: wide class differences, hypocrisy hiding force, and oppression of women. Reliance on butlers is only "admirable" to people who foster, as Lady Bruton does at her luncheon, "this profound illusion in the first place about the food—how it is not paid for" (158). Peter further regards civilization as his "personal possession," a phrase that deflates his "pride in England" into complacent evidence that he and a few others privately have scrambled above the level of butler (82). What the rich Dr. Bradshaw calls Proportion is really disproportion, his ten thousand pounds a year against the pittance that Doris Kilman earns by tutoring (224, 187).

Just as the "admirable butlers" in Peter's glimpse of civilization serve a not-so-admirable class system, the "tawny chow dogs," originally a fighting breed, camouflage in their fluffiness an ability to bite, as their owners hypocritically mask force behind high-sounding ideals. Although Lady Bruton relishes the thought of riding down barbarian hordes, she affects prettiness with a chow dog behind her (168). Like Bradshaw, she worships "Conversion," a vicious desire to "stamp indelibly in the sanctuaries of others the image of herself," whether those sanctuaries be found "in the heat and sands of India, the mud and swamp of Africa, [or] the purlieus of London" (154, 151). Conversion "disguised as brotherly love . . . offers help, but desires power" (151). No matter how majestic and benign Conversion pretends to be, this "Goddess" which fuels the Empire "loves blood better than brick, and feasts most subtly on the human will" (152).[4]

Like the chow dogs, Clarissa's Aunt Helena Parry looks harmless enough, just wanting to grow delicate orchids. At the mention of India or Ceylon or Burma, the elderly Miss Parry

> beheld, not human beings—she had no tender memories, no proud illusions about Viceroys, Generals, Mutinies—it was orchids she saw, and mountain passes and herself carried on the backs of coolies in the 'sixties over solitary peaks . . . fretful if disturbed by the War, say, which dropped a bomb at her very door, from her deep meditation over orchids and her own figure journeying in the 'sixties in India—but here was Peter. . . .
> "Peter Walsh," said Clarissa.
> That meant nothing. (271)

Miss Parry's failure to recognize Peter comically reduces him to "nothing." Moreover, Miss Parry's inability to "behold" any human beings or to understand that they might suffer more than a "fretful" mood during World War I discredits her. Her certitude that she, the real god of her "meditation," deserves to be carried betrays a need for power that actually lets the wars and mutinies go on, no matter how much she disdains individual viceroys and generals. Septimus's hallucinations further link orchids with death: "The dead were in Thessaly, Evans sang, among the orchids" (105). In fact, in Woolf's short story "Kew Gardens" (1919), a character whose disorientation resembles that of Septimus murmurs, "Heaven was known to the ancients as Thessaly,

William, and now, with this war, the spirit matter is rolling between the hills like thunder" (*Complete Shorter Fiction* 92). Miss Parry, with her orchids, becomes deadly by association with Septimus's visions. Her beautiful flowers provide no haven from force but serve as a screen for it, as the chow dogs' prettiness hides their teeth.

Peter's third ingredient for civilization, "girls in their security," takes on irony from the episode immediately preceding, in which he ogles an unknown woman in the street. She cannot have felt very secure if she glanced back to discover a stranger trailing her for blocks. Peter is not unique in his salaciousness. Richard Dalloway similarly hopes for some "spark" by passing close to a "female vagrant" whom he otherwise deigns to pity (176). These men hypocritically expect excitement for themselves while insisting on chastity in their wives and daughters. They thereby ensure legitimacy for patrimony and provide an excuse for the dragoons, supposedly needed, in part, to protect English women from foreign men. Ironically, it is English men like Peter and Richard from whom the stranger and the vagrant might need protection.

The ambivalent attitude represented by Peter's and Richard's idealization of women and their contrasting leering behavior in the street emerges in a fascinating scene as Peter snores on a park bench. A hypothetical "solitary traveller," possibly a dream figure representing Peter himself, rides through a wood toward the gigantic figure of a woman. This dream quester, "haunter of lanes, disturber of ferns, and devastator of great hemlock plants," does not seem to care that his enterprises are wreaking havoc on the environment (85). Instead, he preoccupies himself with idealizing women: "But if he can conceive of her, then in some sort she exists, he thinks, and advancing down the path with his eyes upon sky and branches he rapidly endows them with womanhood" (85). Not only are trees like women to the dreaming Peter, but women are also treelike, inanimate, to his waking perception. That is, women are not quite human beings with opinions of their own, but are providers of soothing shade for him, as they "dispense with a dark flutter of the leaves charity, comprehension, absolution, and then, flinging themselves suddenly aloft, confound the piety of their aspect with a wild carouse" (86). Like Ovid's Daphne, who was turned into a tree to nod a "timid blessing on her lover's pleasure" (Ovid 47), Peter's ideal woman may play either of two carefully demarcated roles. She may comfort and forgive him, as a long-suffering Angel in the House (Woolf, *Pargiters* xxx). Or she may suddenly become a whore, stirring a "carouse." Both roles, emphasized in the nineteenth century and based on the much older Mary-Eve dichotomy, exclude women from public life and confine them to the drawing room or the bedroom, as surely as Peter's Ovidian tree confines a Daphne.

Peter, sitting beside a nurse who listens to his snoring and watches a baby, suddenly awakens with the phrase "the death of the soul" in his consciousness (88). He associates the words with Clarissa, because she has—inexplicably, he thinks—rejected *him*. The epitaph, however, could apply to both Peter and Clarissa, as babyish, benumbed people. With their endorsement of consumerism and force, and their willingness to dismiss whole groups of people—women or coolies in Peter's case, lower classes in Clarissa's—as inferior to themselves, their souls have already died. The line from Shakespeare that occurs to Clarissa all day, "Fear no more the heat o' the sun," reveals her spiritual lethargy (13, 283). Only those who are already dead need not fear. Because this eulogy in *Cymbeline* (4.2.258) is recited over the "corpse" of Imogen, who turns out still to be alive, the allusion has been interpreted to mean that Clarissa can resurrect her past at the party (Miller 71). Instead, the phrase targets the hostess and her guests as the walking dead. For if Clarissa is an Imogen who revives to meet her man, then Peter unfortunately resembles Imogen's grimly named idol, Posthumus Leonatus, who at several points in the play can scarcely be distinguished from the more obviously brutish villain, Cloten. Just as characters see Imogen's drugged body and think that she is dead, Imogen finds the headless body of Cloten and mistakes it for that of Posthumus. Because the latter does, in fact, slander and even hit her, the confusion of husband and brute is sadly appropriate. Woolf's Peter inherits Posthumus's violence to the extent of admiring a military tread; and, despite his gallantry, he would confine his belle to a dog-cart, duplicating Posthumus's hostility toward the woman whom he supposedly loves. Given their association with *Cymbeline,* then, both Clarissa and Peter make us suspect that they may be muddling through a repressed and morally restricted posthumous existence.

Moreover, the society worshipped by these two characters is as withered as they are. As Peter displays an inadequate vision of civilization in his focus on "admirable butlers," "tawny chow dogs," and "girls in their security," Clarissa admires a dangerous or superficial world: "King and Queen," "whirling young men, and laughing girls in their transparent muslins," "woolly dogs," "discreet old dowagers . . . shooting out in their motor cars on errands of mystery," and shopkeepers "fidgeting in their windows with their paste and diamonds" (6). While Clarissa pretends to have to "economise," in fact she has plenty of access to the shopkeepers' diamonds. The phrase "old dowagers" announces Lady Bruton on her "errands" to unleash the troops on people who will have to be displaced to make room for the Britons she wants to get rid of. The silly phrases "bouncing ponies" and "up they sprung," along with the weary phrase "cricket . . . and all the rest of it," already mock the pursuers of the games of Empire, from king and queen to Lady Bruton to the diamond-seeking merchants. Even the "woolly dogs" in the list become a code word for insensitivity. After Clarissa shuns a maid who was impregnated by and then married off to her employer, Clarissa hugs the dog instead of the person to prove to Peter that she has a heart. Although love of animals might be expected to signal a larger compassion, here Clarissa is substituting pets for people to obscure her disdain. Altogether, in her initial survey of London, she displays only suspect ideals. Indifference to the servant's plight, silliness, acquiescence in a dowager's brutish Empire, and the segregation of "girls in their transparent muslins" all indict Clarissa and her society.

Peter and Clarissa, then, assign the word *civilization* to lists whose vacuity the book exposes. Despite their youthful aspirations, the two main characters learn to revere what their class values: silver and diamonds, men marching to war, and women demure in their white dresses. Clarissa's daughter Elizabeth, too, follows her elders in capitulating to the norm. She briefly listens to Doris Kilman's subversive admonition that "Law, medicine, politics, all professions are open to women of your generation" and indulges in a short-lived fantasy of earning her own living (198). Impetuously boarding a bus unchaperoned, she lets the crowds of people, more than "any of the books Miss Kilman had lent her, stimulate what lay slumbrous, clumsy, and shy on the mind's sandy floor to break surface" (208). Yet even this suddenly awakened impulse to independence leads only to old-fashioned images of women nursing the sick and finally to dreams of imitating men in dominating others: "So she might be a doctor. She might be a farmer. Animals are often ill. She might own a thousand acres and have people under her. She would go and see them in their cottages" (206). Even the prospect of becoming a doctor fades into the more familiar vocation of playing Lady Bountiful in the cottages.

With no encouragement to question either her society or herself, Elizabeth falls into the fate that Woolf in *Three Guineas* predicts for women joining the professions. What if women move into respected jobs, only to acquire with their new positions the materialism, competitiveness, and desire for status that have made the professions such poor educators of men? Imagining that she would "become a doctor, a farmer [i.e., a big landowner], possibly go into Parliament, if she found it necessary" (207), Elizabeth would blithely "join that procession" without changing any of the terms of the march around "the mulberry tree . . . of property" (*Three Guineas* 62, 66). Instead of seeking the modest independence which Woolf recommends in *Three Guineas* under the name "poverty" (80), Elizabeth wants money and power: "a thousand acres" and "people under her" (206). This last phrase especially taints Elizabeth's hopes by making more freedom for her depend on less freedom for others.

For all this brief emergence of Elizabeth's "slumbrous" impulse to independence, "down again it went to the sandy floor. She must go home. She must dress for dinner" (208). She prefers in the end to be taken care of by a man. Although from time to time she chafes against being defined as a member of the weaker sex, her momentary rebellion against the customary relationship of a woman to a man remains as poorly thought out as her defiance of the usual assumptions concerning fulfilling work outside the home. At seventeen, she resents that "People were beginning to compare her to poplar trees, early dawn, hyacinths, fawns, running water, and garden lilies; and it made her life a burden to her" (204). These terms of comparison might sound tender and desirable, yet the compliments come with a price tag. The poplar trees recall the forest-women in Peter Walsh's dreams, severely restricted Daphnes who must silently nod sympathetic inspiration to men. If the trees start the classical allusions, the hyacinth may conjure up Hyacinthus and early death, poor portents for Elizabeth's future development. Fawns scamper off, and water trickles away; demure animals and weak water, like women, are not expected to have courage or power. The dawn blushes, and the virginal lilies advertise their purity. The conventional praise beginning to flow to Elizabeth entails specific costs: women's exclusion from work in the world and the denial of women's sexuality.

By the end of Clarissa's party, Elizabeth has capitulated to these conventions. When, on the last page, Richard Dalloway draws his daughter to him, after he has just appraised her as a sex object, he co-opts her into a system that does not allow her even so much sensuality or freedom as she enjoyed in the days when she tumbled with the sheep dogs: "He had looked at her, he said, and he had wondered, Who is that lovely girl? and it was his daughter! That did make her happy. But her poor dog was howling" (296). The description of the dog as "howling" becomes a code word to indicate how much Elizabeth must give up (204, 287, 296). As Simone de Beauvoir says, nineteenth- and early-twentieth-century European marriage is "supposed to lend ethical standing to woman's erotic life, [but] . . . is actually intended to suppress it" (436). Although Woolf's Elizabeth is now said to be "happy," she has retreated from her two feeble revolts, when she imagined riding to fulfilling work or resisted definition as a "womanly"—i.e., immobile—poplar.

Because Clarissa, her family, and her society are so empty, Clarissa's little odyssey around London ends not in a meeting of Odysseus and Penelope but in neglect and silence. The only two people she has ever loved, Peter and the now tamed Sally, unexpectedly arrive at her party. Nevertheless, she keeps postponing any talk until "later" (272, 275, 284). The last words of the book wonderfully parody the grand reunion, as Peter exclaims melodramatically: "What is this terror? what is this ecstasy? . . . It is Clarissa, he said. For there she was" (296). The curtain bangs down prematurely, not because their greeting is ineffable but because there is no scene to show. When Peter (Septimus's "dead man in the grey suit") and the walking dead woman (who needs "fear no more the heat of the sun") finally draw together, they bring to each other the insubstantiality of two ghosts (105, 283). The conjunction of an absence with an absence nets the blank that follows "THE END."

When Clarissa misses her grand restoration to either Sally or Peter, the expected denouement linking Odysseus and Penelope is played out instead by the only appropriate conjunction, that of Clarissa with Septimus— that is to say, of the deadened Clarissa with the news of Septimus's death. As Lady Bradshaw gossips about the suicide of a young man, Clarissa at first reacts with childish peevishness: "Oh! thought Clarissa, in the middle of my party. . . . What business had the Bradshaws to talk of death at her party?" (279–80). After worrying for two pages, not about the anguish that Septimus must have felt but only about the threat to the light tone of her gathering, she finally sobers enough to admit that she herself has "defaced, obscured . . . in corruption, lies, chatter" her earlier values, which Septimus perhaps has "preserved" by dying (280). Although she cannot name what it is that Septimus grasps better than she, he does know, for example, that World War I was not a glorious opportunity for heroism but only "that little shindy of schoolboys with gunpowder" (145). He also knows that learning not to feel at his friend's death was a crime (130). Although he blames himself, the pathos surrounding him implicates his society instead, because it teaches numbness as the only available self-defense. Nevertheless, if Septimus sees more clearly than Clarissa, he does not die "holding his treasure," as she romantically imagines (281). Her civilization has long since deprived Septimus of the spontaneous responses worth living for.

Clarissa may push her lucidity so far as to realize that Septimus's death is indeed "her disaster—her disgrace" (282). Or perhaps her lucidity amounts only to self-love, making the story of Septimus *her* disaster, not because she accepts any indirect responsibility but only because she draws everything into her own orbit. In any case, Clarissa immediately slips back into delusion. She comforts herself that, if she has lost her idealism, at least she has learned to appreciate the moment. She can at least savor, she tells herself, the roses and the sun. However, by the time that she decides to be "glad" of Septimus's suicide because he "made her feel the beauty; made her feel the fun," the hollowness of "fun," in light of her intense hatred for Doris Kilman, for example, undermines Clarissa's claim to have substituted any valuable intensity of the present "moment" for an earlier awareness of "social problems," in historical time (283–84).

The society gathered at Clarissa's party, then, has failed totally. It claims to spread light to colonies but instead uses Lady Bruton's brute force to increase darkness. It distributes wealth disproportionally while hypocritically worshipping Proportion. It hates the slightest divergence from a narrow norm, converting offenders by ostracism or violence, both at home and in the overseas Empire. It represses female sexuality, refusing to encourage Clarissa to stay with Sally or Peter, or Elizabeth with Doris Kilman. Meanwhile, it diverts male sexual energy into violence or into adulation of Daphnes confined to the home. Because this society is already so rotten, the unintelligible song of the beggar woman at the subway station seems to advocate letting the civilization return entirely to leaf mold, to start the social world over: "the passing generations—the pavement was crowded with bustling middle-class people—vanished, like leaves, to be trodden under, to be soaked and steeped and made mould of by that eternal spring— / ee um fah um so / foo swee too eem oo" (124). Language must be started over, too, once words like "civilization" and "life," in the mouths of people like Clarissa, Peter, and Lady Bruton, have been corrupted to mean barbarity and death.

The Years

Like *Mrs. Dalloway, The Years* portrays a deadened society. Through the fortunes of one family, the Pargiters, Woolf exposes the "abominable system" of middle-class family life, where "all those different people had lived, boxed up together, telling lies" (222–23). *The Years* also follows *Mrs. Dalloway* in punctuating an examination of England's empty values with constant references to the Empire. Many of the

Pargiters have lived in or visited the colonies, spreading their version of civilization. Yet the family's hypocrisy, loneliness, and dullness, typical of its class, represent nothing worth exporting. Repressed sexuality and emotion become distorted into money lust and militarism. These social goals turn the eminently "nice" Pargiters into the perpetuators of an Empire which *The Years* condemns. As Leonard Woolf says in *Empire and Commerce in Africa,* the "evil" of imperialism is carried out not by monsters, but by ordinary people under the sway of a destructive political dogma (352–53).

The first sign of emptiness in *The Years* is that people fail to communicate. Avoiding all emotional or controversial topics, the Pargiters talk only about water boiling or spring coming late up north. Understandably, family members lose interest in this drivel: "Eleanor's attention wandered"; "his mind slipped a few words" (201, 374). When characters finally do turn their attention to a revelation—when Maggie, for example, hints that she and her cousin Martin really may be half-sister and -brother—someone always interrupts (247). Servants with jam pots inhibit the conversation of their masters, and the servants themselves mask all reactions. Babies wake up or older family members intrude into the crowded drawing room, disrupting barely sketched tales of parents' affairs or a country's military buildup. If someone like Sara ventures into unpleasant honesty, relatives hustle her out of the restaurant where "people were listening" (232). Instead of expressing anything personal, characters "quote" the cooing of pigeons: "Take two coos, Taffy. Take two coos [. . .] Tak" (187). This conventionalized rendition of birdsong has as little meaning as the people's usual rote responses. On the first page, the pigeons' "lullaby that was always interrupted" announces the scarcely human babble that rocks the Pargiters into permanent somnolence (3). Fittingly, the Pargiters also end the book and their all-night reunion by listening, pathetically, to pigeons waking up (433). A whole society for sixty years has not amounted to much more than the gurgling of beasts.

The fact that several characters know the same syllables of pigeon speech has been read as a consoling sign of "unity," that value supposedly all-important to Woolf. She has been said to exploit "verbal repetitions and echoes in order to convey to the reading public her own sense that there is a pattern behind, and a significance to, human experience" (Wheare 140). Instead of praising repetition, however, Woolf exposes the lack of significance in this society, as she relentlessly records the dreariness not only of speech but also of thought, which only intermittently achieves self-awareness. In the process, she risks creating a tedious book. Certainly the satire in *The Years* is more diffuse than in the compressed juxtapositions of some of her earlier works. For example, in *Mrs. Dalloway* Woolf locates Peter Walsh's concern for "girls in their security" next to his own voyeurism and lets the irony quietly undercut his piety and patriotism (78–82). Similarly, in *To the Lighthouse* she mentions "great men" cogitating next to rabbits scampering and relies on the silliness of the rabbits to puncture the pretensions of the thinkers (108). In *The Years*, on the other hand, Woolf places Eleanor's dread that Celia will remark that bats "get into one's hair" next to Celia's sure-fire comment, "They get into one's hair" (208). Instead of dazzling with satiric humor, here Woolf insists on a lack of humor. Double doses of the same clichéd misinformation about bats evoke in the reader the frustration felt by the characters. Nevertheless, *The Years* criticizes the society, both at home and in the overseas Empire, as radically as the other books. Far from deflecting attention from aridity and wrongs with consoling unities, this late novel unsparingly documents monotony and injustice. Indeed, this effect bears out Woolf's hope that *The Years* and *Three Guineas* would be considered "one book" (*Diary* 5: 148).

Two topics that seldom break through the veneer of polite conversation are politics and sexuality. Just as Sally Seton had made Clarissa Dalloway at least momentarily dissatisfied that "She knew nothing about sex—nothing about social problems" (*Dalloway* 49), here, too, Woolf connects attitudes toward the body and the body politic. Having argued in *Three Guineas* that values in the home and the workplace prepare for relations among countries, in *The Years* Woolf shows the links among various exclusions: of women, homosexuals, servants, and colonized people. The characters, however, refuse to discuss any of these crucial subjects. Although Eleanor attends political meetings and is said on two occasions to see "the only point that was of any importance," she will not speak this opinion (178, 95). Disappointingly, the reader does not hear Eleanor's sudden insight any more than the committee does, either as an utterance or as a thought. Nor does the reader learn what kind of meetings Eleanor supports. Probably they are suffrage groups, like Mary Datchet's organization in *Night and Day,* but votes for women are nowhere named. The gap that follows Eleanor's claimed revelation as she sits through political discussions may put Eleanor's profundity in doubt. In any case, this withholding of information duplicates for the reader the experience of the characters, who are similarly excluded, stultified, or unconscious of their real problems.

Interruption characterizes not only the speech but also the actions of people who might be drawn to each other. Yet occasionally loners who never quite touch do manage to communicate, if only through a kind of symbolic gesturing. Solitary characters resort almost to mime and to elliptical language, while the narrator relies on visual imagery and word play. For example, when Rose Pargiter invites her cousin Sara to a political meeting, she may also be inviting sexual attention, although the women exchange no explicit words. Rose and Sara pass a flower seller whose violets, "tightly laced," seem as constricted by their frill of leaves as the two women are by social expectations:

> But he went on repeating his formula automatically. "Nice vilets [*sic*], fresh vilets," as if he scarcely expected anyone to buy. Then two ladies came; and he held out his violets, and he said once more, "Nice vilets, fresh vilets." One of them slapped down two coppers on his tray; and he looked up. The other lady [Sara] stopped, put her hand on the post, and said, "Here I leave you." Upon which the one who was short and stout [Rose], struck her on the shoulder and said, "Don't be such an ass!" And the tall lady gave a sudden cackle of laughter, took a bunch of violets from the tray as if she had paid for it; and off they walked. She's an odd customer, he thought—she took the violets though she hadn't paid for them. He watched them walking round the square; then he began muttering again, "Nice vilets, sweet vilets." (174)

When Sara later recounts this conversation to her sister, Maggie, she says that Rose also called her a "Damned liar" (187). Yet, despite the insults, Rose buys flowers, and Sara takes them. Woolf has borrowed a conventional heterosexual courting gesture and transferred it to women. The hawker's pronunciation "vilets" includes "vile," the judgment which he and most of his society would probably make if they recognized the transaction as a courtship between women. The harshness of the conversation contrasts with the saccharine dialogue usual in *The Years,* in a way that is both refreshing—provoking Sara's laughter—and hurtful. For Sara has to reckon not only with the prejudices contained in the word "vile," but also with the added sadness that Rose really prefers Maggie's company and perhaps does not admit her feelings for either sister. Nevertheless, Sara shows that she understands Rose's perhaps unconscious sexual solicitation and completes the symbolic exchange by picking up the bouquet from the tray.[5]

This scene with the violets, because of its eroticism between women, repetition, and obliquity through concrete language, seems to owe something to Gertrude Stein, whose work Woolf did know (Duplessis, "WOOLFENSTEIN" 100–101). The impression that the passage includes a Steinian, sapphic undertone is supported by Grace Radin's summaries and quotations from the holograph of *The Years.* Radin reports that when Sara (still called Elvira in the draft) hears that Rose loves women, she is temporarily shocked, whereas Maggie cannot see what difference it makes whether one loves a man or a woman (Radin 54). Jane Marcus further suggests that the scene with the violets recalls the combination of affection and violence which characterized the friendship of Woolf and the composer Ethel Smyth (*Patriarchy* 52). Although Radin regrets "the extent to which feminist, pacifist, and sexual themes have been deleted, obscured, or attenuated" between the holograph and the final version of *The Years* (148), the exchange of flowers between women nevertheless remains a powerful, erotically suggestive transaction. Woolf has not so much deleted these themes as transferred them from authorial commentary to symbolic representation.

In her essays on the Pargiters, Woolf specifies that *The Years* treats two topics, love and money (*Pargiters* 30–31). "Love" includes attitudes toward sexuality, such as these erotic undercurrents between Sara and Rose. "Money," Woolf explains, encompasses how little a maid earns, how much time the Pargiter girls have to spend with a dressmaker, and how arrogant and secretive Abel becomes when his control over the family income grants him power (*Pargiters* 107–8). Eleanor wonders tiredly if her father has been spending yet more time "Taking shares out of one company and putting them in another" (*Years* 104). Although she deprecates the narrow-mindedness of reading only the financial papers (92), Eleanor herself is preoccupied with returns on investments, when she uses her father's money to build houses for tenants. She avoids discussing her business with her father because "He had no sympathy with people who were foolish about money, and she never got a penny interest: it all went on repairs" (105). Nevertheless, whether she ever does pay enough to get the drains in her flats to stop their eternal stinking, she certainly prospers over the years; eventually she can afford to travel all over the world. By setting the final reunion of the Pargiters in a business office rented for the night, with hors d'oeuvres on typewriting tables and coats next to a house agent's placards, Woolf indicates that the family has indeed defined itself in terms of money and status.

One scene in which Woolf exposes the passion for money that has replaced any sexual passion occurs during Eleanor's visit to her brother Morris and her sister-in-law Celia in the countryside (206ff). Attending only intermittently to their "prattling," Eleanor hears Celia commenting on the drought, "'Oh, but there's quite enough for everybody at present'. . . . And for some reason she held the sentence suspended without a meaning in her mind's ear" (207). Whereas Eleanor repeats the sentence only for the euphony of the English syllables, parochially comforting after "all the foreign languages she had been hearing" on her travels, readers might well pause for the sense. *Is* there "quite enough for everybody at present"? Is there enough water, enough property, enough opportunity? As Celia has just been scorning foreigners and wondering suspiciously if stable-boys steal her hay, it is clear that "everybody" is a very small group including only her own upper middle class, jealously guarding its territory against all outsiders.

Generally more sensitive than Celia, Eleanor displays many good qualities. She welcomes the French more open-mindedly, and she achieves one real breakthrough beyond conventionality when she refuses to imitate her society's rejection of the homosexual Nicholas. Nevertheless, Eleanor, like her sister-in-law, treats the servants as subhuman, only belatedly noticing if there is "enough for everybody" or not. Going upstairs from Celia's drawing room, Eleanor finds a copy of Dante and skims, "For by so many more there are who say 'ours' / So much the more of good doth each possess" (212). Because she cannot even conceive that the working class might want a changed system, "the words did not give out their full meaning, but seemed to hold something furled up in the hard shell of the archaic Italian. I'll read it one of these days, she thought, shutting the book. When I've pensioned Crosby off" (213). The jump from Dante's line to the servant shows that, for Eleanor, Crosby remains part of "they" and "theirs," not "we" and "ours," the group that Dante urges his readers to expand (*Purgatory* xv, ll. 55–56). A few pages later, Eleanor indeed has pensioned Crosby to a single room in a boarding house. The servant must leave the only family she has known for forty years and the house that, in her cleaning, she has touched more intimately than its owners have. Nevertheless, Eleanor insensitively concludes that Crosby will be happy to go, because the employer, rather late, has deigned to notice how dingy Crosby's basement room is (216). Despite Eleanor's genial, likable character, the book constantly points to ordinary folk—ourselves—as the ones inadvertently perpetuating the problems of class and Empire.

Eleanor, for example, demonstrates her apparent virtue at Morris's country house by being "glad" to stoop down to the ninety-year-old and sit through game after game of cards (209). Although she patiently bears the boredom, perhaps she *should* mind the vapidity and acquisitiveness of a conversation that alternates between who has "won the pig" at the fair and who has won the silver salver (213). Whereas the mother-in-law has the excuse of age for her tediousness, Morris, Celia, Eleanor, and the rest can plead no such cause. In fact, the beginning scene, in which the Pargiters' invalid mother mutters in surreal disconnection, appropriately announces the book (21–25). From this impossible conversation with an invalid, through cards with Celia's complacent and dictatorial mother midway through the book, to Delia's party at the end, to which the Pargiters return deaf and forgetful, *The Years* provides images of this whole stratum of English society: deaf to each other when they are still in their prime, forgetful of the working classes and the colonized people on whom their prosperity depends, and disconnected from each other and their bodies.

Just as *Mrs. Dalloway* shows a sickened and contagious society, *The Years* insists that England is, via World War I and the colonies, tainting others. Except for one scene set during an air raid, references to the war are usually tangential, because the characters remain so superficial. The "situation in the Balkans"—a phrase which warns in 1907 that war will soon break out—is for the Pargiters just a "diversion," from which Eleanor's "attention wandered" (200–201). Partygoers in 1914 mention a son with the fleet at Malta but can conceive only their own present discomfort, not a larger hell: "'He's at Malta—' she began. . . . But the fire was too hot for Aunt Warburton. She raised her knobbed old hand. 'Priestly [the servant] wants to roast us all alive'" (257). As with the name "Bruton" in *Mrs. Dalloway,* an anagram for "brute" makes its way into the name of old Aunt Warburton, who appears harmless but actually furthers the war. Ignorance, self-centeredness, unacknowledged fear of a servants' revolution, and the acceptance of soldiering as elegant but essentially unrelated to oneself—all these render her and most of the characters accessories to violence.

Only Sara briefly protests the idealization of war. When Morris's son North announces his departure for the front, she mocks, "'How many lumps of sugar does a lieutenant in the Royal Rat-catchers require?' I asked. 'One. Two. Three. Four'" (285). Although Sara recognizes the gravity of North's decision, she refuses to praise him, because the need to appear big and brave can create wars whether causes exist or not. Woolf had observed this drive to do battle for its own sake in her nephew Julian Bell, eventually killed in the Spanish Civil War in 1937. Although she detested fascism as much as he did, Julian's open letter to E. M. Forster explaining his enlistment especially disturbed her, because of its enthusiasm for a pleasurable fight. With the need to fight Franco somehow becoming secondary, he detected in himself a "barbaric lust for action of which war is the type. It is this that makes me feel . . . that the soldier is admirable" (quoted in Zwerdling 266). Quentin Bell, implying that his brother Julian was right to take up arms, objects that Woolf could not "sympathise with the excited interest of one who saw in warfare itself an art form to be enjoyed for its own sake" (Bell 2: 202). Julian endorsed the paradox of putting down war "by force if necessary" (quoted in Zwerdling 266), as does Woolf's satirized character North.

None of the other characters share Sara's disdain for North's soldiering. Eleanor sentimentally insists that she would defend her country if she could, and Renny makes munitions. Rose supports the war and eventually receives some kind of decoration for efforts on the home front (359). She looks like a "military man" even when she is very old, and when someone throws a stone at her as she speaks at a by-election, "she had enjoyed it" (358, 157). In *The Cause,* a history of the women's movement (Woolf mentions this work in *A Room of One's Own* 21, 58), Ray Strachey comments on attacks after 1907 against suffragists, who learned "to keep their own tempers" (307). When Woolf alludes in *The Years* to a campaign in which Rose is hit by a stone, the statement that Rose "enjoyed" the battles stands out ominously (157). It might seem liberating to see Rose cross gender lines that have reserved enjoyment of the fray to men only; however, it is not comforting to find aggression in her, too. Stones can be thrown at the innocent and nonviolent, but only the violent throw bricks themselves, as Rose eventually does.

No one gives any direct explanation of Rose's cause, but when Sara pictures Rose in prison, "Sitting on a three-legged stool having meat crammed down her throat" (232), contemporary readers undoubtedly would think of the hunger-strikes and force-feedings that attended the campaigns of the militant wing of the suffrage movement (Strachey 314, 325). Apparently Rose is not just a "suffragist" working peaceably for women's votes, but a "suffragette," a militant supporter of the Women's Social and Political Union, associated with Sylvia Pankhurst and her daughter Christabel (Strachey 302). When Eleanor nonchalantly announces Rose's detention in police-court for throwing a few missiles, she refrains from commenting and simply watches an owl fly past with a mouse in its claws (204). The juxtaposition suggests that Rose herself is adopting the aggression of the carnivore. She is learning to appreciate the attack for its own sake, for the thrill of the swoop.

Unlike Rose, Sara implicitly condemns all retaliation, as she recalls Rose's pugnacity to her cousin: "'Crash came a brick!' she laughed, flourishing her fork. 'Roll up the map of Europe,' said the man to the flunky. 'I don't believe in force!' She brought down her fork. A plum-stone jumped. Martin looked round. People were listening. He got up. 'Shall we go?' he said, '—if you've had enough?'" (232). Sara points up the paradox of using force to repel force, a tactic that makes all crusaders—whether the militant suffragettes, Julian Bell in Spain, or the Allied soldiers in World War I—as much violent bullies as those they have opposed. Such ostensible valor comes down to nothing more noble than making the plum-stones jump. Instead of stopping at one target, force perpetuates itself for the sake of excitement and the display of bravery. The defender turns into the aggressor, the twin of her or his opponent. As Rose's brother later jeers, "She smashed his window . . . and then she helped him to smash other people's windows" (420).

This window smashing recalls one particular event in the suffrage movement. As yet another unsuccessful bill for women's votes was bogged down in Parliament in 1911, "Mrs. Pankhurst and two companions broke the windows of No. 10 Downing Street, and simultaneously hundreds of women in other parts of London smashed the plate-glass windows of shop fronts, post offices, and Government departments. One hundred and fifty women were marched off to Holloway for this exploit" (Strachey 322). Rose, too, is in prison for throwing a brick (231). She may have thought that she was smashing the opposition to women's suffrage, but by agreeing to break the prime minister's windows, she sanctions his own resort to force around the world. By adopting the tactics of destruction, Rose has swelled the ranks of those seeking dominance and using violence to get it. Instead of condemning militant resistance outright, in an authorial voice, Woolf relies on the pettiness of the plum-stones or the helplessness of the mouse in the owl's claws to convey her disapproval.

Because the characters deny sexuality, worship money, and resort to violence both for its own sake and to gain property, *The Years* portrays a pathetic society. Woolf counterpoints this portrayal by repeated references to Empire, as the Pargiters try to extend the dominance of this impoverished civilization. All three generations of Pargiters have spent time in the colonies, as military men, administrators, and ranchers. The book opens with Col. Abel Pargiter palavering at a club with "men of his own type," retired soldiers or civil servants from India, Africa, and Egypt (4). In the second generation, Martin serves with the army in India and Africa. His cousin Kitty is the wife of an official in India, perhaps the viceroy (393). In the third generation, Martin's nephew North has raised sheep in Africa long enough for children at home to realize the usual expectations: boys have grown from nursery age into college men, girls into mothers (309). Even at Delia's party, in the long concluding section depicting the reunion of second and third generations, an Indian in a pink turban stands out conspicuously (354). The narrator never records what the Indian says—the Pargiters really are not capable of hearing any opinion other than their own—but from time to time, characters watch someone speak to "Eleanor's Indian" (354). The Pargiters at least consider him worthy of attending their party, if only as a souvenir of Eleanor's trip to the East. Nevertheless, if the man in the turban merely decorates their reunion, his presence is appropriate, since Empire has been a source of the family's wealth and a reminder of the folly of exporting emptiness abroad. In the same way that the Pargiters define themselves in terms of money, by holding their reunion in a business office, they are imbued with Empire to the point of identity; Maggie, distracted, misunderstands North's proposal that they go "To Delia's party" as a suggestion that they go "To Africa" (348).

The Years undercuts the "glory" of Empire every time colonization is mentioned. Although Eleanor enjoys a letter from her brother Martin in India without criticizing him, the description of his escapades renders him ridiculous. Clearly romanticizing an episode that is not heroic, Martin reports having been lost in a jungle: "I climbed a tree [. . .] I saw the track [. . .] the sun was rising [. . . .] They had given me up for dead" (108). Martin's adventure seems to draw on details from Leonard Woolf's days as a colonial administrator in Ceylon, when he, too, thought himself lost in a jungle and lit a last match. Whereas Leonard can call himself "idiotic," Martin displays no such self-awareness (*Growing* 213–15). Neither he nor Eleanor remarks on the irony of finding the beaten track only a few yards away, yet the reader can see that the brave hero faced a much diminished danger. When a brother later uses the slang "Oh, he's at the top of his tree" to describe a third brother's career, the recollection of Martin perched like a treed kitten converts each of the Pargiter men's careers—whether as barrister, Oxford scholar, or colonial policeman—into a foolish scramble in a jungle (200).

If Martin, to concoct any story at all, has to dramatize his exploits and hide his own blindness in India, another character who gives a glimpse of himself in a colony affects humility but actually is preening:

> "Give Sir William some more wine," Celia whispered to the nervous parlourmaid. There was some juggling with decanters on the sideboard. Celia frowned nervously. A girl from the village who doesn't know her job, Eleanor reflected. The story was reaching its climax; but she had missed several links.
>
> "[. . .] and I found myself in an old pair of riding-breeches standing under a peacock umbrella; and all the good people were crouching with their heads to the ground. 'Good Lord,' I said to myself, 'if they only knew what a bally ass I feel!'" (201)

One of Sir William's talents is that he pretends to be self-effacing. Eleanor, however, firmly undercuts that pose, revealing that his stories "sailed serenely to his own advantage" (202). Nevertheless, if she detects his arrogance, she immediately excuses it as "natural" (201). She ignores the parallel between the cowed servant girl and an intimidated Indian populace, a connection that Woolf pursues elsewhere in the novel. Preferring to remain obtuse and admiring, Eleanor mutes her criticism, because Sir William praised the brightness of her eyes thirty years ago and also because she never really questions Empire. Without relying on Eleanor's only partially awakened consciousness, the passage leaves it to the reader to take Sir William at his word when he admits that he was a "bally ass."

To construct Sir William's anecdote, Woolf again seems to be drawing on an episode from Leonard's experience in Ceylon. Once when Leonard rode to the hill country around Kandy, he arrived after dark in a thunderstorm. Despite the weather, a procession of headmen and villagers with drums and dancers paraded out to meet their British overlord: "Then I had to stand in the rain for ten minutes while each member of the crowd came and prostrated himself, touching the ground with his forehead" (*Growing* 157). Leonard admits that, at the time, he tried to defend the scene in a letter to Lytton Strachey, arguing that the prostration belonged to local feudal observances, now transferred to the British, and that feudalism displayed, at least on the surface, "depth, harmony, beauty" (*Growing* 158). Yet Leonard also eventually recognized:

> I was up above in the feudal hierarchy, one of the super-Chiefs, the Princes, or the Boyars, and, however much one may dislike the fuss and ceremony of social systems—and I do hate them—one cannot be impervious to the flattery of being a top dog liked by the underdogs. I certainly, all through my time in Ceylon, enjoyed my position and the flattery of being the great man and the father of the people. That was why, as time went on, I became more and more ambivalent, politically schizophrenic, an anti-imperialist who enjoyed the fleshpots of imperialism, loved the subject peoples and their way of life, and knew from the inside how evil the system was beneath the surface for ordinary men and women. (158–59)

Whereas Leonard gradually became aware of the injustice of his position and returned from Ceylon to write strongly anti-imperialist books, Virginia Woolf's fictional Sir William complacently reconciles the persistence of the British Empire with only mild self-deprecation.

Much more important than Sir William as an Empire-builder—and more fully satirized—is Abel Pargiter, head of the family and veteran of the famous Indian Mutiny of 1857 (13). That mutiny had multiple causes. Both Hindus and Muslims resented the increased activity of Christian missionaries after 1813, the use of the English language in schools, the British monopoly on trade, and the recent annexation of land belonging to the traditional ruling classes (Embree viii, 1–3, 75–76). Hindus were further upset by threats to the caste system and by the extension of legal protection to widows and Christian converts. Because parts of the civilian population rebelled along with the sepoys (or *sipahis*, Indians in the British Army), some later Indian observers wondered if "war of independence" might be a more accurate label than "mutiny" (Embree vii, 4). Even if Indians did not yet use the concept of one Indian nation, which they came to prefer at the end of the nineteenth century, the uprising was important for the later nationalist movement, and it did testify to widespread discontent with British rule (Embree 84).

The Woolfs' Hogarth Press published in 1925 a book on the mutiny, Edward Thompson's *The Other Side of the Medal,* which was sharply critical of the British. For some seventy years, a "conspicuous feature" of British writing about the uprising had been a focus on atrocities committed by Indians against Europeans: "That the British soldiers had sometimes acted with great ferocity was well-known, but the explanation given was that they had been maddened by the deeds of the rebels, and that on the whole the British had behaved with remarkable magnanimity toward their enemies" (Embree 52). In *The Other Side of the Medal*, however, Thompson finally corrects this view. He documents in excruciating detail the torture and execution of "many thousands" of Indian citizens who had not participated in the mutiny at all (Thompson 83). He also documents the burning of villages of friends as well as foes "along hundreds of miles" (107). He is especially anxious to show that the two most notorious massacres of Europeans, at Cawnpore and Jhansi, occurred *after* the British had taken widespread, indiscriminate vengeance. Thompson maintains that the Indian cruelties were motivated in part by a feeling of hopelessness in the face of British retaliation. He urges that England stop hushing up its own atrocities against Indians and "make them [the Indians] free again" (107, 126).

In *The Years,* Woolf counters British claims to military glory in India more subtly but just as uncompromisingly as Thompson does in this book from the Woolfs' press. A few pages after imparting the information that Abel Pargiter was slightly maimed in the mutiny, she places a scene in which his child Rose pretends to defend a garrison, actually Lamley's toy shop (13, 27). The juxtaposition of Abel's past exploits and Rose's present games makes the desire for colonies look like childish bullying designed to acquire more goods, which then become nothing more than toys for the adults. Moreover, the reader first learns that Abel lacks two fingers when he slides his hand down the neck of his mistress, Mira (8). Abel's daughter Delia relates the two topics of mutiny and mistress when she innocently asks, "Had any adventures?" The colonel barks back his reply, "There aren't any adventures for an old fogy like me" (15). Abel feels that he cannot reveal his amorous "adventures," so he lets the word call up for his family the sort of military deeds that, as a young man, he used to pursue in India. In the process he conflates the two activities. Having a mistress and keeping a colony, in fact, resemble each other as relationships between unequal partners.

Although *The Years* expresses sympathy for Abel when he periodically longs to tell his family about Mira, who really is important to him, their arrangement is shown in a mocking light. This disapproval is occasioned not by the sexual intimacies between Abel and Mira but by the fact that he hides her existence, considers Mira unworthy of hearing about his family or club, and ties her income precariously to her ability to please him. The name Mira may perhaps recall Ovid's Myrrha, who turns herself into a tree to escape opprobrium for a love affair that transgresses social norms (Ovid 288). Myrrha thus resembles Daphne, the other Ovidian woman confined to a tree, to whom Woolf alludes in *Mrs. Dalloway* (85) and *Orlando* (171). This Mira, confined and hidden because she earns a decent income only in indecent dependency, learns to flatter out of "duty" (7). Similarly, colonized peoples, whom Abel subjugated during the mutiny, mask their feelings and tailor their behavior to please masters.

Usually Woolf censures colonization indirectly, by juxtaposing unflattering scenes, such as Abel's past with Rose's games, or by letting characters such as Martin and Sir William condemn themselves with their own words. The only character who speaks directly against Empire is Sara, whose susceptibility to wine, predilection for metaphorical language (lost on her denser relatives), and insight combine to make her the most outspoken character in the book. She exposes the use of force as nothing but cowardice or sexual fear. North recalls a letter that Sara sent him in Africa. She admitted that "we"—the family and the society—are in "Hell." He remembers her accusations: "'And I,' he said, as he took his plate, 'was among the damned.' He stuck his spoon into the quivering mass that she had given him. 'Coward; hypocrite, with your switch in your hand; and your cap on your head—' He seemed to quote from a letter that she had written him" (321). "Coward; hypocrite, with your switch in your hand" is the most direct criticism of Empire in the book.[6] The narrator's telling detail of a spoon in a quivering mass of pudding further burlesques the "heroism" of attacking quivering flesh with weapons, whether North's switch or Abel's bayonet (51). Apparently North harbors little resentment against Sara for what he calls an "angry" and "cruel" letter; nor did her criticism reform him.

Very few characters mention the force that secures the colonies. Sara alone not only mentions the whips and the weapons; she also connects them with a kind of displaced sexuality. When her father, Digby Pargiter, commands his wife to leave their daughters and rejoin him, Sara jeers at him for "Pirouetting up and down with his sword between his legs" (144). At the same time that Digby apparently admires his wife in her finery, he browbeats her for not getting a new lock from a Mr. Toye (more protection for adult toys). Digby displays her for his benefit, not hers, as if showing off a possession. His badgering and his obsessive concern with possible burglaries—"they'd melt it down; we should never get it back" (145)—could mean that Sara is right in situating Digby's sword where his genitals should be. Dominance and possessiveness, directed toward his wife and some meltable object, seem to substitute for assurance concerning his sexual attractiveness, which he must worry about, in light of hints about a past affair between his wife and his brother Abel (124, 247).

Just as Sara sees the sword between her father's legs as a substitute for sexual prowess, and Abel views Mira and the mutiny as parallel "adventures," Woolf again connects colonization with aggressive and dishonest sexuality in relation to Martin. In all three cases, domination shores up egos which seem unsure that they could ever attract a free partner. In 1914, Martin is courting at a party: "'I've thought of three subjects to talk about,' he began straight off, without thinking how the sentence was to end. 'Racing; the Russian ballet; and'—he hesitated for a moment—'Ireland. Which interests you?' He unfolded his napkin. . . . 'Don't let's talk of any of them,' he said. 'Let's talk of something interesting. Do you enjoy parties?'" (250–51). Martin obtusely dismisses Ireland, whose Home Rule was a topic of immense interest to the Irish, as a trivial misstep in conversation. Ireland occurs to him as he ogles white arms, a white dress, and a pearl necklace, further revealing how control in the two realms, private affairs and public policy, are related in his mind. He thinks of the debutante as "Purely virginal . . . and only an hour ago I was lying stark naked in my bath in Ebury Street" (250). He seems attracted to her not so much in spite of the vapidity of her conversation as because of it. His own dullness gets to flaunt itself as at least brighter than hers. This need to feel superior was keeping Ireland subjugated, too; Home Rule Acts which had passed in the House of Commons were soon to be stalled in the House of Lords and rather conveniently postponed by the war (Taylor 16).

Another case in which Woolf connects sexuality with colonization—in addition to the links between Mira and the mutiny, and the "virginal girl" and the Irish—occurs in a scene depicting Edward Pargiter as a student at Oxford. Woolf succinctly reveals the lessons that Abel has learned from his experience in India and passed on to Edward: "'You can't drive a bayonet through a chap's body in cold blood,' [Edward] remembered him saying. 'And you can't go in for an exam without drinking,' said Edward. He hesitated; he held the glass to the light in imitation of his father. Then he sipped" (51). Edward demonstrates that he has indeed learned this lesson in the use of artificial stimulants, whether wine or force, when he plays two male companions off against each other solely for the sake of flattering and stimulating himself. At least one of the men, Ashley, is erotically attracted to Edward, but again, as in Abel's relationship to Mira, it is not eroticism that taints the scene (56). Rather, Edward's vanity and his willingness to manipulate the other men show a self-gratifying brutality that extends along a continuum, from Edward's arousing Ashley and then locking the door on him, to Abel's running a bayonet through a body.

In her essay *The Pargiters,* about the characters in *The Years,* Woolf further clarifies the causes of Edward's irritation with Ashley. Edward has learned that masturbation is "wrong," so he is feeling both frustrated and overly proud that he has "conquered" himself. Ashley's homosexual attentions also remind Edward that he is supposed to be worshipping Kitty, a girl whom he idealizes. Edward can see Kitty only as an abstraction, because his society, gender-segregated and closely chaperoned, has denied him the freedom to get to know her as a person (*Pargiters* 81–82). Woolf thus suggests that a distorted sexuality, denied its natural satisfaction with either homosexual or heterosexual partners, is one motive for carrying bayonets into colonies.

Woolf finds a strong second motive in greed, as pernicious abroad as it is at home. *The Years* does not shy away from the role of money in colonization. When North gets back from Africa, his relatives speculate whether four or five thousand pounds in savings at 5 or 6 per cent interest will yield enough income to live on (382). Although Eleanor sees nothing wrong in North's means of supporting himself, the reader already knows that North carries a switch in Africa (321). The prelude to that revelation also undermines North and raises the question of whether the material prosperity he has gained from the colonies is really worth the sacrifices required of the colonized, working under North's lash or the threat of its use. Driving to Sara's flat through unaccustomed traffic, North sees in the shop windows goods which must come from the colonies: "All these years, he thought to himself, looking at a floating banner of transparent silk, he had been used to raw goods; hides and fleeces; here was the finished article. A dressing-case, of yellow leather fitted with silver bottles, caught his eye. But the light was green again. On he jerked" (308–9). When carts slow his automobile, "He dribbled up to the door" (311). The uncomplimentary verbs "jerked" and "dribbled," the superfluity of the dressing-case with silver bottles, and his petty impatience in hooting at the cart-horse, all discredit this entrepreneur in Africa.

The narrator then clinches the condemnation of North when she insistently notes that he and Sara, who, like so many vacuous characters in *The Years*, have little to say to each other, are reduced to watching the cut of mutton drip blood into the dish (319). The reader more than once hears that they stare at the "disagreeable object which was still bleeding into the well" (321). Leonard Woolf's *Empire and Commerce in Africa* throws light on what North's career as a rancher in Africa may have entailed. Expecting a "fortune before them in wool and frozen mutton," the English expropriated all the best grazing land in British East Africa: "By fraud or by force the native chiefs and rulers were swindled or robbed of their dominions" (340, 353). The English then forced the Africans to work for them by decreasing the African Reserves and levying a hut tax. Africans had to work for a wage in order to pay the tax; wages were fixed at between one and three pence per day (345–47). Leonard scathingly condemns this system as outright "slavery" (347). Virginia Woolf too condemns the British presence in Africa, through visual imagery. When North, this man who has raised sheep in Africa, is now forced to eat underdone mutton, he suffers a Dantesque punishment for his stance with the switch. Because Eleanor reads the *Inferno* elsewhere in *The Years,* the reader is prepared to think of Dante's *contrepasso* punishments (212). North's income in Africa is steeped in blood—not only of sheep but of Africans.

This powerful image, of the "disagreeable object which was still bleeding into the well," may resonate further from an incident in colonial history treated in Thompson's Hogarth Press book, *The Other Side of the Medal.* One of the Indian atrocities in the 1857 mutiny that the British could not forget was the massacre at Cawnpore of several hundred Europeans, including 125 women and children, whose bodies were pitched down a well. This terrible event at "the Well" was played up in the English and Anglo-Indian press, where it was mixed with other stories "demonstrably false" (Moorhouse 111). The massacre was often used as a justification for British retaliation (Embree 34). However, if the Indians had to accept guilt for the Cawnpore well incident, Thompson recalls that the British, before Cawnpore, had committed another atrocity at a well. After two Englishmen had been killed in Lahore, the deputy-commissioner of Amritsar, Frederick Cooper, shot or suffocated 500 unarmed Indian soldiers and threw their bodies into a dry well (63). Thompson argues not only that such excesses drove mutineers to desperate acts but also that the atrocities, hushed up in the English community, poisoned Indian feelings toward the English for many years. Thus, when Woolf shows that the relatives of the mutiny veteran Abel Pargiter cannot proceed past an object "still bleeding into the well," the phrase may register the unresolved hatreds of the past (321).

As North can retire comfortably from Africa, the whole Pargiter family has benefited from infusions of money from the colonies, starting with Abel's military pension. In focusing on the Pargiters, Woolf is not presenting an anomalous family. In the late eighteenth and the nineteenth centuries, when England was transforming itself from an agrarian to an industrial society, it based much of its phenomenal growth on overseas enterprise (David Thomson 14–15). By mid-century, advocates of free trade such as Richard Cobden were touting trade as a grand mission: "Commerce is the grand panacea, which, like a beneficent medical discovery, will serve to inoculate with the healthy and saving taste for civilization all the nations of the world. Not a bale of merchandise leaves our shores, but it bears the seeds of intelligence and fruitful thought to the members of some less enlightened community" (Thomson 32). In fact, "her new wealth and her world supremacy rested on foundations of harsh sweated labour, appalling slum conditions in her new towns, and immense human misery" (Thomson 32).

The Years draws parallels between the condition of British workers and that of colonized people, sympathizing with both exploited groups. The anecdote involving Sir William shows the similarity between a nervous servant at Celia's, trying to make a good impression, and the abject Indians, bowing their foreheads to the ground (201). In another example, the servant Crosby, whose inadequate basement room Eleanor has ignored, applies herself to the dinner gong "like a savage wreaking vengeance upon some brazen victim" (34). By the time Martin boasts, "I'm Crosby's God," however, it is clear that the prideful and petty masters are in no way superior to the people at home or abroad whom they view as savages (230). Martin has set himself up as an idol more dangerous than any made of brass. Despite his distaste for army life, he has served the Empire faithfully in Africa and India. The fact that he eats mundane Brussels sprouts while he claims to be a "God" further reduces Martin's claim to divinity.

Both Martin and his nephew North recall Colonel Kurtz in Joseph Conrad's *Heart of Darkness.* Woolf particularly admired Conrad (*Diary* 2: 49). Martin, like Kurtz, enjoys having people worship him (cf. Neuman 70). North, the man with the switch, thinks of himself as living in a "heart of darkness": "He surveyed the thin yellow liquid in which the bubbles rose more slowly, one by one. . . . He felt that he had been in the middle of a jungle; in the heart of darkness; cutting his way towards the light; but provided only with broken sentences, single words, with which to break through the briar-bush of human bodies, human wills and voices, that bent over him, binding him, blinding him" (411). Significantly, North glimpses how lost he is, not in Africa but in England, while listening to his relatives at the reunion. Woolf locates the heart of darkness in North and his society, not on the "dark continent" or in the societies of the colonized. Moreover, Martin's "Brussels" sprouts, when set beside North's "heart of darkness," may conjure up the Belgian capital from which Conrad's Marlow sets out for the Belgian Congo. Leonard Woolf thinks that in Africa the Belgians may have been more openly cruel than the British, but he judges the British just as destructive (*Empire and Commerce* 357).

If the men in *The Years* convert a kind of displaced sexuality into the strutting and money getting of Empire, most of the women, except for Sara, remain as unconscious of their own motives as the only partially self-aware North. Kitty, Delia, and Eleanor, second-generation Pargiters, all have some connection to colonization. At the reunion, North places Kitty high in the Anglo-Indian hierarchy: "He thought he remembered that she was the wife of one of our governors; or was it the Viceroy of India? . . . She might have looked very dashing in the eighties, he thought; in a tight riding-habit; worn a small hat, with a cock's feather in it; perhaps had an affair with an aide-de-camp; and then settled down, become dictatorial, and told stories about her past" (393). North may satirize Kitty only because her authority and her cock feather make her one of the "masculine old ladies" who encroach on his own virile prerogative of subjugating others. Nevertheless, he correctly intuits her use of the colonies to bolster her ego: "And I've three boys. I've been in Australia, I've been in India. . . . It exalted her; it cast a flattering light over herself, her past. But why did Martin laugh at me for having a car? she thought" (183). Power and money have motivated the domineering and boastful Kitty as much as these lures have goaded the men.

Delia's case is more complicated, because she appears to be hating Empire but actually is only romanticizing rebels without analyzing their motivations. At the reunion, her lifelong defiance is shown up as farce. Although the young Delia champions the Irish independence leader Charles Stewart Parnell, she does so mainly to annoy her father. Delia imagines herself actually speaking in a hall about Irish "Liberty" and "Justice" (23). What she most enjoys in the daydream, however, is the way Parnell would turn attentively to her. She seeks Romance, not Liberty, for herself or the Irish, and does not notice the contradiction in her politics when she "likes" listening to her father's stories of India. In those Indian scenarios, the Anglo officer hovering over his "huge silver trophy" looks more dashing to her than any Indian rebel, since, for her, these darker, poorer rebels do not possess the aura that Parnell has (36). Despite Delia's muddled thinking, sympathy for Ireland continues to shape her life. Her family's myth is that she married for the "Cause," by which they seem to mean Irish Home Rule. In fact, she probably married for abstract "Love" as her only cause, without any idea who a particular Irish suitor might be, or what Parnell stood for (357).

At the reunion, Delia's husband wonderfully pulls the rug out from under her idealizing. For all his quintessentially Irish name, Patrick hails from a family that, after three hundred years of colonizing in Ireland, still considers itself English. Now that the Irish Free State has finally, in 1922, become a coequal member of the British Commonwealth (Snyder 430), Patrick asserts that "our new freedom is a good deal worse than our old slavery" (399). The disgruntled Delia, former defender of Parnell, can only mutter shortly that it is "too early to tell" (400). However, Delia herself must assume the blame for her disappointment in Patrick: "Thinking to marry a wild rebel, she had married the most King-respecting, Empire-admiring of country gentlemen, and for that very reason partly—because he was, even now, such a magnificent figure of a man" (398). Ironically, she likes him because he embodies what she thinks she hates. Never questioning her society's definition of manhood as swagger and dominance, she chooses an admirer of Empire just like her father, despite her resentment of her father's domineering.

As a supporter of Empire, Patrick not only implicitly endorses the sword and the switch (Digby's and North's accouterments), but he also elevates money as his chief motive. At the party, the doddering Patrick is delighted to hear what a bargain the decorations are:

> "Roses are cheap today," said Delia. "Twopence a bunch off a barrow in Oxford Street," she said. She took up a red rose and held it under the light, so that it shone, veined, semi-transparent.
>
> "What a rich country England is!" she said, laying it down again. She took up her mug.
>
> "What I'm always telling you," said Patrick, wiping his mouth. "The only civilised country in the whole world," he added. (399)

Although Patrick can well afford to spend a few more pence for a bouquet, he rejoices that the huckster on the street must scrounge for a living. This "civilization" which he spreads from England to Ireland and the rest of the world means a tight-fisted capitalism, whereby a few people like himself thrive at the expense of the many. In a tactic that Woolf uses throughout her career, very small details, such as a bunch of roses, encapsulate global issues. For all the loving description of the veins in the petals, the latter gain their place in the narrative not only for their aesthetic qualities but also for their price and their political implications.

Although Eleanor is neither as romantic as Delia nor as boastful as Kitty, she has not thought much more clearly about the Empire. She never consciously questions the part played by her father's colonial pension in enabling her to build lodging houses and travel all over the world. After she visits India as a tourist, she admits that the natives, "half naked," are "beautiful" (337). While her words retain some condescension, she envies what she takes to be a freer attitude toward the body than her own Victorian training allows. Eleanor here adopts the familiar assumption—cause either for alarm or approbation—that "primitive" peoples are more "sexually volatile" than Europeans (Torgovnick 99). Eleanor's recognition of Indians' beauty at least contrasts with her brother Martin's scorn for alien bodies: "Each table had its pyramid of strawberries, its pale plump quail; and Martin, after India, after Africa, found it exciting to talk to a girl with bare shoulders" (130). Martin lists Caucasian women alongside plump quail, both morsels to satisfy a cultivated English appetite. Indian and African women, by contrast, fail to meet his standards for purchase. Eleanor might not analyze Empire any more than Martin does, but she does feel something "disappointing" in England after her first round of travels (199). Even India fails to satisfy her, probably because what she sees is Anglo-India. Instead, "what I want to see before I die" is "another kind of civilisation. Tibet, for instance" (335). If she could challenge more openly the imposition of the European ethic of acquisitiveness, force, and sexual repression on an Empire which instinctively she finds lacking, she might at last see "something different" (335).

Woolf's fear that the Empire simply meant exporting this ruinous ethic is borne out by the analyses of recent postcolonial critics, who argue that Indian nationalism, during its resistance to British political rule, adopted many British attitudes. The nationalists, for example, required Indian women to embody self-sacrifice, devotion, and chastity, in part because Victorian ladies, scorned but envied, also suffered this requirement (Chatterjee 249). Similarly, while countering British charges that Bengali men were "effeminate," nationalists began to absorb a Victorian martial ideal (Chakravarti 46). Thus Indians selectively validated values from the past, such as Kshatriya (warrior) and Aryan role models, and strategically transformed contemporary militant Marathas into heroes, although "sections left out from participating in the creation of such myths were still voicing their perception of the Marathas as marauders" (Chakravarti 49–50, 79). Once British prescriptions for fighting men and self-sacrificing women had spread to India, it is no wonder that Eleanor is disappointed by her travels.

At the reunion, Woolf abandons the method employed throughout most of *The Years,* that of letting vacuity speak for itself, and adopts humorous satire. North's thoughts sum up a civilization that puts its energies mainly into making money, colonizing, and segregating men and women into aggressive hunters and nurturing baby-makers:

> They were staying with Connie, [an aunt] went on, who was expecting Jimmy, who was home from Uganda . . . the next word he heard was "adenoids"— which is a good word, he said to himself, separating it from its context; wasp-waisted. . . . The men shot, and the women—he looked at his aunt as if she might be breaking into young even there, on that chair—the women broke off into innumerable babies. And those babies had other babies; and the other babies had—adenoids. (374–75)

The name Uganda briefly recalls the grazing lands of British East Africa, where North's sheep farm probably was located. Leonard Woolf slammed the British in his *Empire and Commerce in Africa* for misrepresenting a Ugandan king as a "semi-savage addicted to abominable cruelties," when actually it was a British expedition that savagely shot thousands of Waganda in retaliation for the murder of one Englishman, then used the occasion to steal land (283). Although North can criticize his relatives for doing nothing but reproducing themselves and their values and for shooting others (animals and humans), he himself is setting up "a garden, a room" in which to seduce a new girl, continuing the "hunt" for a quarry whose opinion does not interest him. He wants some kind of change, but he cannot conceive of his own role in bringing it about: "Could nothing be done about it? he asked himself. Nothing short of revolution, he thought. The idea of dynamite, exploding dumps of heavy earth, shooting earth up in a tree-shaped cloud, came to his mind from the War. But that's all poppy-cock . . . Sara's word 'poppy-cock' returned. So what remains?" (375).

What remains is for someone like Woolf to bring to consciousness, in readers if not characters, the links among sexual dishonesty, money lust, and colonization: the coordinates of both *The Years* and *Mrs. Dalloway.* As Woolf advises more explicitly in *Three Guineas,* the woman or man who wants to prevent war must puncture dangerous patriotism "by comparing French historians with English; German with French; the testimony of the ruled—the Indians or the Irish, say—with the claims made by their rulers. . . . [She will] absent herself from military displays, tournaments, tattoos, prize-givings and all such ceremonies as encourage the desire to impose 'our' civilization or 'our' dominion upon other people" (108–9).

2.
Staking a Territory: Marriage

The Voyage Out

In *The Voyage Out* (1915), Woolf began to study the links between the institution of marriage and capitalism, colonies, and militarism, connections that she would investigate further in *Night and Day, To the Lighthouse,* and *Freshwater.* In her first novel, a ship belonging to Willoughby Vinrace leaves London for South America sometime during the decade before World War I; he intends to sell dry goods and bring back rubber from the Amazon and hides from Argentina. On board are Willoughby's daughter Rachel and his in-laws, Helen and Ridley Ambrose. The politician Richard Dalloway and his wife, Clarissa (who later appear in *Mrs. Dalloway*), briefly travel on the same ship. At a coastal hotel in Brazil, Rachel becomes engaged to Terence Hewet. Nevertheless, when she anticipates married life, Rachel at moments hesitates, and Terence also expresses misgivings. Six of the Britons undertake an expedition up the river to visit a village in the jungle. When they return, Rachel develops a high fever and dies.

Rachel's travels on the ocean and then on the river have been interpreted metaphorically as her "voyage out of the social and sexual restrictions of her life," to discover her instinctual, sexual, or unconscious "'depths,' the primitive, communal flow of life" (Naremore 7, 29). As Rachel attempts to break free of her cramped training, the author is said to "voyage in," exploring "the subjective lives of her characters" as the only important topic (Naremore 7). Some critics suggest that Woolf may have borrowed the river trip from Joseph Conrad's *Heart of Darkness*, but they assume that she avoids Conrad's attention to European exploitation of foreign countries, to concentrate instead on one woman's personal problems, Rachel's "unwillingness to face the sexual implications of marriage" (Neuman 63). Woolf's adaptation of Conrad's plot about the Belgian Congo is judged, therefore, to be "comparatively limited": "The voyage into sexual knowledge and marriage, the heart of darkness in which we remain integral and separate even in our most intimate relationships: these do not yet gather in, in the manner of Marlow's introduction to his dark tale, the full moral reach of the history of Western civilization" (Neuman 64).

My reading of *The Voyage Out* reverses these conclusions. Instead of focusing on private psychology, the book subordinates personality to a range of historical and social determinants which Woolf believes shape individuals. Rather than depicting a fear of sexuality, the novel blames the social institution of marriage for threatening Rachel and Terence's relationship. As Christine Froula recognizes, the cause of Rachel's death lies "not in Rachel's psyche but in the culture that suppresses female authority" (89). The subsidiary wife role, on which Froula focuses, however, is examined in *The Voyage Out* within a larger context of economics and Empire. Far from neglecting Conrad's setting in a European colony, Woolf extends his investigation of the effects of commerce and colonization and condemns them even more scathingly than he.

Rather than plunging into a private unconscious, Woolf's South American river serves first as a literal conduit of trade. When it takes on metaphoric meanings, the river represents a whole social situation, built around commerce, which shapes unconscious reactions. Some of these associations begin to emerge when Terence unthinkingly praises a member of their group, the elderly Mrs. Thornbury: "Isn't she rather like a large old tree murmuring in the moonlight, or a river going on and on and on? By the way, Ralph's been made governor of the Carroway Islands—the youngest governor in the service; very good, isn't it?" (294). Following the river is, by connotation, going the route that British society has taken to produce its Mrs. Thornburys. "[S]weet but trivial," Mrs. Thornbury is not a villain (134). Nevertheless, as a person all too ordinary, she represents assumptions that the novel as a whole casts in doubt. First, Mrs. Thornbury raises a son to be colonial governor of an island; another son makes speeches to the "Union" (113), apparently the Unionist party which supported British Union with Ireland (Taylor 15). Whereas Mrs. Thornbury (along with Terence) approves her sons' imperial careers, other references undercut the supposed magnificence of European colonization. When the conversation shifts, for example, from politics to "the Empire in a less abstract form," the new topic turns out to be "dreadful accounts from England about the rats" (158). Although the gossip refers to real rodents, the discussion implicates a few metaphorical English rats ruling their Empire. Second, Mrs. Thornbury has other sons in the army and navy, implying that she believes force is justified in appropriating colonies (113). Third, Mrs. Thornbury and her friends assume that knowledge "isn't what women want," since she believes that the feminine mind is capable only of feelings, not thought (115). Mrs. Thornbury, then, following the stream of convention, accepts the confinement of women, guards her own financial privilege, and glories in the British Empire, which should be conquered and retained by her fighting sons.

These assumptions about personal privilege, international trade, colonization, militarism, and the subordination of women are shared by other characters. Woolf lays out the main knots of this network in the conversations of the Dalloways. Taking special favors for granted, the Dalloways manage to secure places on Willoughby's ship, which was not supposed to accept passengers, because they "came of a class where almost everything was specially arranged, or could be if necessary" (40). With his eye on international trade, Richard inquires about "the conditions of shipbuilding in the North" (50). He is not, however, talking only about merchant ships, which might visit foreign countries to trade with them on an equal basis. Instead, he and his wife admire warships, which participate in making other countries into English colonies (69). Richard, in fact, takes as his role models past and present imperialists. He exults that there have not been so many opportunities for young men "since the days of Pitt," and he praises Lord Salisbury for a policy like a "lasso that opened and caught things, enormous chunks of the habitable globe" (50–51). William Pitt the Elder

(1708–78) "secured the transformation of his country into an imperial power"; by the end of his career, Britain dominated North America and India and had acquired territory in Africa, the West Indies, and Minorca. William Pitt the Younger (1759–1806) introduced a bill to set up a government Board of Control over the East India Company ("Pitt"). Lord Salisbury (1830–1903) "presided over a wide expansion of Great Britain's colonial Empire." He believed that some form of "European, preferably British, rule [was] indispensable for the advancement of the 'backward' races and had no hesitation in imposing this rule by force, as he did in the Sudan (1896–99)" ("Salisbury"). After *The Voyage Out,* in 1922, Woolf reported that she was reading the life of Lord Salisbury: "I'm reminded, oddly, of my father" (*Letters* 2: 502).

Just as Leonard Woolf in 1920 criticized Lord Salisbury for partitioning East Africa between England and Germany on the basis of shaky treaties, bloodshed, and "flagrant international robbery" (*Empire and Commerce* 245–47), Virginia Woolf mocks Salisbury in her fiction by giving him vapid admirers, the Dalloways. As Richard is busy praising the imperialists, Clarissa sentimentalizes the Empire: "One thinks of all we've done, and our navies, and the people in India and Africa, and how we've gone on century after century, sending out boys from little country villages—and of men like you, Dick, and it makes one feel as if one couldn't bear *not* to be English!" (50–51). The smug excesses of the Dalloways undermine everything they stand for. Enraptured with being a wife, Clarissa exclaims, "We *must* have a son," and "Dick, you're better than I am" (50–51). She has internalized the message exemplified in Sarah Ellis's popular Victorian conduct books: "[You should remember] the superiority of your husband simply as a man" (quoted in Lilienfeld 151). In *The Voyage Out,* however, Richard shows this supposed superiority only by presuming to read, without her permission, a letter which his wife has been writing (50–51). Domination extends from the bedroom to India. The episode with the Dalloways succinctly traces the line of development from shipbuilding to colonization to the idealization of women as makers of babies to fill the ranks of future troops.

Although Mrs. Thornbury and the Dalloways unquestioningly ac-

cept the primacy of commerce, Empire, and marriage, Rachel begins
to resist the conventional responses. When she refers to an unmarried
woman caught "with one foot in the boat, and the other on shore," she
implies that she hesitates to join the social currents that would turn
her into the jingoistic Mrs. Thornbury, that "river going on and on
and on" (294, 298). Rachel wonders if she must follow her flood of feelings to the only sanctioned goal, marriage, and she will rebel against
assuming her role as privileged director of servants and inspiration to
gunboats.

In *The Voyage Out,* Woolf constantly foregrounds economic conditions. As Willoughby sends his ships out onto the ocean to trade, Mrs.
Flushing originally proposes the expedition on the river not in order to
"voyage inward" into the psyche or even to see the external sights, but
to make money. Indicating a pile of beautifully dyed and embroidered
cloth and exquisite jewelry made by Brazilians, Mrs. Flushing admits
that "they don't know what they're worth, so we get 'em cheap. And
we shall sell 'em to smart women in London" (235). Her unbridled
capitalist impulse to buy cheap and sell dear depends on duping the
peasants. Not only do these Britons cheat their trading partners, they
also deprecate them. Although the British visitors obviously admire
the crafts which Mrs. Flushing has amassed, they denigrate the people
who make them. Mrs. Thornbury protests, "I had no notion that the
peasants were so artistic—though of course in the past—" (197). Mrs.
Flushing's actions, however, quietly undercut her claims to British superiority. After announcing her plan to reap an exorbitant profit, she
carelessly flings her cloth samples around the room and, with a "superb
forefinger," commands that her servant Yarmouth clean up after her
(236). Beyond one finger joint, the inconsiderate Mrs. Flushing displays no superb qualities. Yet Woolf is not reproaching an unusual personal rudeness characteristic of Mrs. Flushing alone. Instead, this cloth
and trinket merchant participates in a public and usual system of ignoring the interests of both English maids and foreign peasants, who
must not be informed of the true value of their services and goods.

Because this reliance on "inferior" classes exists both at home and
abroad, Woolf parallels the Thames with the Amazon. Both rivers are

associated with a grasping form of trade and therefore with killing and death. The travelers choose to think that Rachel, merely a weak woman, caught her disease from the Amazon River: "You can't expect English-women to stand roughing it as the natives do who've been acclimatised" (361). Yet when they also insist, "It's absurd to say she caught it with us," they revealingly protest too much (359). They implicate the presence of the British themselves on the river as the element most lethal to South America.

The opening description of the Thames similarly associates this European river with death. When the Ambroses cross in a boat to their steamer, the ferryman becomes a Charon in a Dantesque underworld (13). This allusion to an underworldly guide, along with numerous other early references to death, prefigures Rachel's fatal illness (14, 15, 105, 111, 146–47). More importantly, the comparison of Helen, Ridley, Mr. Pepper, Aunt Emma, and Terence to corpses suggests that they inhabit an underworld already. Like the characters in *Mrs. Dalloway* and *The Years,* they become the walking dead. Illustrating this dead-ness, a tourist's diary entry reflects the barrenness of the environment back onto the Britons themselves: "Played lawn-tennis with Mr. Perrott and Evelyn M. Don't *like* Mr. P. Have a feeling that he is not 'quite,' though clever certainly. Beat them. Day splendid, view wonderful. One gets used to no trees, though much too bare at first. Cards after dinner. Aunt E. cheerful, though twingy, she says. Mem.: *ask about damp sheets*" (104–5). This whole crowd seems prematurely moldy with the grave because of their snobbishness (scorning someone not "quite" the right class), triviality (occupying themselves only with lawn-tennis and cards), and competitiveness (wanting to "Beat them").

Beneath the European travelers' apparent aimlessness and pettiness, from which Rachel tries to flee into music, Helen Ambrose detects a "profound and reasonless law . . . moulding them all to its liking" (263). This powerful law, which cannot be eluded through artistic diversions, might be termed capitalism spun out of control. At home, it threads "the richest city of the world" with long lines of the poor waiting "to receive a mug of greasy soup" (53). Abroad, it results in "economic imperialism" (Leonard Woolf, *Empire and Commerce* 24). When

Virginia Woolf locates a law of the jungle, hers is not the jungle of an ecologically untouched Amazon but the thicket of Willoughby's boardrooms. As the character St. John grumbles—petulantly, but apparently carrying Woolf's point of view here—the British are voracious, and "each beast holds a lump of raw meat in its paws" (177).

The character who most obviously represents this omnivorous capitalism is Willoughby, although he is by no means the only one imbued with its principles. His last name, Vinrace, reveals his overriding goal—to "win the race," in economic competition. When he is said to love, the object of the verb ostentatiously skips persons to seek out profits: he "loved his business and built his Empire" (23). The uppercase E extends his impact from the private family to international politics. With one of the "largest shipping businesses in Hull" (158), this merchant and financier boasts of his "triumphs over wretched little natives who went on strike and refused to load his ships, until he roared English oaths at them, 'popping my head out of the window just as I was, in my shirt sleeves. The beggars had the sense to scatter'" (196). His vulgarity signals a larger ruthlessness, for Willoughby's business dealings oppress others besides the workers whom he directly employs. The needs of financiers influence government policies that affect people all over the world. As Richard Dalloway predicts, "It's a business that won't stop with ships, I should say. We shall see him in Parliament, or I'm much mistaken" (73). The wording suggests that Parliament is itself a business. Once governments get involved with international markets, the use of force hinted at when Willoughby leans out his window escalates far beyond a few oaths. Government officials like Joseph Chamberlain, secretary of state for the colonies, embraced the nineteenth-century belief that the state should exercise its power over other countries for its own economic purposes. That belief, Leonard Woolf was to argue in 1920, "has caused more bloodshed than ever religion or dynasties" and "was the chief cause of the war [World War I] which we have just been fighting" (*Empire and Commerce* 10).

Finishing a draft of *The Voyage Out* in 1913, just before the war broke out, and publishing the book in 1915, Woolf already identifies a clear link between business and military force. Temporarily out of office at Parliament, Richard wants to go to Latin countries or the East "with a view to broadening Mr. Dalloway's mind" (39). That mind remains narrow, however; only the territory that he would like to annex for Great Britain grows to any breadth: "All seemed to favour the expansion of the British Empire, and had there been men like Richard Dalloway in the time of Charles the First, the map would undoubtedly be red where it is now an odious green" (89). Woolf's common practice of omitting quotation marks from paragraphs which express the opinions of successive characters, in free indirect style (Zwerdling 52), makes "odious" carry Richard's view, not that of an independent narrator. On their mind-broadening tour, the Dalloways observe "manufacturing centres" (39). When they inspect peasants in Spain—"Are they, for example, ripe for rebellion?"—the Dalloways certainly are not rooting for the peasants but instead likely are worrying whether the landlords can withstand protests in the same way Willoughby breaks strikes (39). Meanwhile, Clarissa looks at paintings. Despite this cultural veneer, the Dalloways' observation tour is hardly innocent: "Mr. Dalloway wished to look at certain guns" (40). The itinerary follows frighteningly from manufacturing centers to lethal force.

Although the Dalloways thus sanction military force to maintain material interests, they and other members of their society sugarcoat acquisitiveness with high-sounding ideals. Echoing Matthew Arnold, Richard claims to worship "the dispersion of the best ideas over the greatest area," "Unity," "dominion," and "progress" (64). Yet lawn-tennis and snobbishness hardly seem the "best" the world has to offer. "Unity" is also rendered suspect, as it will be in *The Waves.* Instead of referring to the comforting patterns of art, unity derives from the imposed union of Empire. "Dominion" is domination by guns. "Progress" means making money. Richard even congratulates himself, "I grant that the English seem, on the whole, whiter than most men, their records cleaner. But, good Lord, don't run away with the idea that I don't see the drawbacks—horrors—unmentionable things done in our very midst! I'm under no illusions" (64). Because he has gained for British seamstresses a work day one hour shorter, he thinks that he has done enough for them; nevertheless, wages for female textile workers remained low (Stearns 100, 111–15).

Furthermore, Richard's easy assumption that England's record toward workers and colonies is "whiter" betrays his racism and represents a widespread British view that Britain had a cleaner record in the colonies than other European powers. In *Empire and Commerce in Africa,* Leonard Woolf refutes this opinion, as Virginia Woolf demonstrates its falsity in fictional satire. Although Leonard grants that Belgium, Germany, or Portugal might use tactics in Africa that are more openly brutal than those of the British in their colonies, he goes on to condemn in the most scathing terms such British policies as the confinement of East Africans to reserves, the gradual reduction of even these paltry reserves, and the use of taxation to force Africans to work for the slave wage of a penny a day. Leonard concludes that the supposedly "milder"—"whiter," as Richard Dalloway says—British administrators turn out to be as destructive and barbaric as the rest (357). Although Richard claims to harbor no "illusions," he does delude himself about British grandeur and sanctity. Woolf pointedly undercuts his pretensions to superiority by assigning him the vocabulary of Conrad's Belgian colonizer in *Heart of Darkness*. Richard's insincere pronouncement, "horrors" (64), recalls Colonel Kurtz's famous summation for his own soul, "The horror! The horror!" (Conrad 68).

Another way in which British society sugarcoats its acquisitive and destructive colonizing is by enlisting the cooperation of the church. Rachel listens to a clergyman's opinion that British success in India derives from "the strict code of politeness which the English adopted towards the natives," a courtesy which can be practiced even by the "humblest" and "least important," i.e., by women (231). Yet Woolf has already made this very clergyman expose how radically impolite practice in the colonies is, and the doctrine from Psalms that supports it: "Break their teeth, O God, in their mouths" (227). Leonard Woolf similarly laments the way that church missionary societies in England become "the stalking-horse of economic imperialism" (*Empire and Commerce* 296). In one example, Leonard shows how the British East Africa

Company employed an unregulated adventurer named Captain Lugard, whose military forays in Uganda were "morally and legally wrong" (291). When Lugard arrived in England on a promotional tour, an ill-informed church lent him moral and financial support, supposedly on behalf of England and God but actually to benefit this one unscrupulous company. In *The Voyage Out,* Virginia Woolf satirizes the muzzy and sentimental rambling of the clergyman, which allows him to jumble contradictory ideas about politeness and military force, benign God and vindictive God.

With colonization an underlying topic of such importance in the novel, Woolf situates the British Empire in the context of antecedent colonizing, particularly that of the Roman Empire and the European expansionism of the sixteenth and seventeenth centuries, all of which receive some attention in Rachel's story. Frequent references to Edward Gibbon's *The Decline and Fall of the Roman Empire,* for example, implicitly compare the Roman Empire to the British Empire, with the result that both appear unjustified and doomed. *The Voyage Out* assigns Gibbon's history a role in the formation of the corrupt figures Mrs. Thornbury and Mrs. Flushing. The former praises it: "A very wonderful book, I know. My dear father was always quoting it at us" (200). Mrs. Flushing reminisces, in ludicrous hyperbole, about "some of the happiest hours of my life. We used to lie in bed and read Gibbon—about the massacres of the Christians, I remember" (200). Gibbon's Empire doubles as historical marker for the Romans and for the contemporary British Empire, supported by the exploitative river trade of these Gibbon admirers, and perhaps by a few massacres.

In another reference to this eighteenth-century historian, the character St. John makes an ability to appreciate Gibbon a test of Rachel's intellectual capacity (154). Ignoring content, he claims that only the author's style and wit count for him (201). But even the style, as St. John conceives it, betrays the militarism that makes up part of Gibbon's subject matter, since the sentences are said to go "marching" through St. John's brain like a "regiment" (106). This martial matter finally cannot be ignored, although at first Rachel tries to follow St. John's lead into some supposedly isolated aesthetic enjoyment. When she initially dips into her volume of the historian, she savors the words because they are "vivid" and "beautiful" (175). However, she soon grows disillusioned. The rhythms that had lulled her now go round "like a roll of oil-cloth" (201).

Even more important in Rachel's disillusionment than the predictability of the cadences is the fact that the melodious and exotic words— "Aethiopia," "Felix," "Arabia"—that originally had attracted her attention for their aesthetic quality form part of a subtle satire of the modern European imperialists. A passage about the Roman past, quoted from Gibbon, also conjures up the imperial present, as his vocabulary contains many reminders of contemporary world events:

> His generals, in the early part of his reign, attempted the reduction of Aethiopia and Arabia Felix. They marched near a thousand miles to the south of the tropic; but the heat of the climate soon repelled the invaders and protected the unwarlike natives of those sequestered regions. . . . The northern countries of Europe scarcely deserved the expense and labour of conquest. The forests and morasses of Germany were filled with a hardy race of barbarians, who despised life when it was separated from freedom. (174–75)

Gibbon adopts a complex attitude toward Roman conquest, seeming to admire the northerners' love of freedom and perhaps to feel sympathetic toward the southerners' unwarlike society. In *The Voyage Out*, however, his history serves as a foil for the modern European empires. Just as the Romans attempted to subjugate Aethiopia, the British and other Europeans had been trying, in the decades preceding the novel, to appropriate Ethiopia and the rest of North Africa (Leonard Woolf, *Empire and Commerce* 138–64). *The Voyage Out* several times alludes to the European appropriation of territory in this area. St. John, for example, shows off before Helen by explaining why England might make "a sudden move towards some unknown port on the coast of Morocco" (305). There had been two recent crises in Morocco, in 1905–6 and in 1911, provoked by the European scramble to control it. In the first crisis, France and Spain made a secret treaty partitioning Morocco and agreeing not to oppose Britain in Egypt. After a German gunboat appeared on the scene, a conference managed to hold the contenders apart.

In 1911, another German gunboat arrived, supposedly to protect Germans during an uprising but actually to intimidate the French. This "Agadir Incident" almost touched off a war among the European powers, but World War I was staved off for a few more years as France acquired a "protectorship" over Morocco, Germany got strips of territory in the French Congo, and Britain continued its acquisitions throughout North Africa ("Moroccan Crises").

This involvement of England in Morocco in 1911 may be what St. John has in mind. If so, the crisis helps to date the action of the novel. Helen enjoys it when St. John talks to her about "facts" such as the situation in Morocco, because such conversation "took her outside this little world of love and emotion" (304). Although Helen promisingly breaks out of the stereotype that women are concerned only with affairs of the heart and not with world affairs, she makes little progress in thinking about public events: "She respected their arguments [those of St. John and her husband] without always listening to them, much as she respected a solid brick wall" (305). Leonard Woolf, in *Empire and Commerce in Africa,* repeatedly objects to similarly slipshod use of the terms "fact" and "logic": "there is no logic of events and no logic of facts, there is only a logic of men's beliefs and ideals" (8). Leonard chides Chamberlain for claiming in 1895 that it is a "fact" that states exist in order to further commerce; Chamberlain is only promulgating an "opinion." Helen, too, trusts "facts" about "finance and the balance of power" and "stability," without really analyzing her information (305). In consequence, her facts turn into a "brick wall" which seems to impede as much as protect. Unlike her author, she totally misses the destabilizing effect that European gunboats have on the coast of Morocco, as they rehearse the squabbles soon to culminate in World War I.

If an arrogant St. John approves European domination of North Africa, Richard Dalloway seems an updated version of one of Gibbon's Romans attempting "the reduction of Aethiopia and Arabia Felix" (174). When he first reveals that on his broadening tour he mainly wants to inspect guns, he adds his opinion that "the African coast is far more unsettled than people at home were inclined to believe" (40). He could be referring to "Ethiopian Africa," as Leonard Woolf calls north-eastern Africa, or to the continent's eastern and western coasts—in all of these areas Britain had colonies (*Empire and Commerce* 154–55). Richard's belief in England's right to take guns to Africa, to pacify the latter's resistance, and to settle its highlands with Europeans, is undermined by the Dalloways' other behavior: their slyly using rank to break rules, his hypocritically idealizing his wife while sneaking kisses with Rachel, and Clarissa's smugly wondering how one can "*bear* not to be English" (51). These sterling English, as Leonard Woolf says, actually were engaged, along with other Europeans in Africa, in "the policy of grab" (*Empire and Commerce* 55). *The Voyage Out* satirizes that same commercialism in the Dickensian name of a salesman, "Grabb, to whom no piece of waste paper comes amiss" (12).

Woolf further condemns this forcible grabbing of territory—whether by English gunships in modern Africa or Roman troops in ancient Aethiopia—when she has the taciturn Mr. Thornbury, usually eclipsed by his wife, launch into a long tirade in which he claims that English ruins said to be remains of old Roman forts are really broken-down cattle pens (147). By extension, the passage mocks British fortifications as more prosaic than glorious. Mr. Thornbury further contends, "The argument that no one would keep his cattle in such exposed and inaccessible spots has no weight at all, if you reflect that in those days a man's cattle were his capital, his stock-in-trade, his daughter's dowries. Without his cattle he was a serf, another man's man" (147). In the context of references to contemporary Africa in *The Voyage Out*, Mr. Thornbury's observations recall that the British, in their colony in East Africa, had been appropriating grazing land from the Masai, for whom cattle were just such "stock-in-trade." The British then, by means of taxation, law, and starvation, forced the African herders to work for them. Subjected to what Leonard Woolf bluntly calls "a demand for slavery pure and simple" (*Empire and Commerce* 338, 347), the Masai cattle-breeder becomes the very "serf, another man's man" envisioned by Mr. Thornbury.

In light of such allusions to contemporary events, the passage quoted from Gibbon contains many ironies. The modern Empire glimpsed behind his "Aethiopia" and "Arabia Felix" is hardly likely to be "happy," once

Africa and the Middle East have been opened to theft and coercion. No wonder Rachel, through her reading of Gibbon, has become disillusioned. Although she does not consciously analyze the situation in this way, she instinctively reacts against her domineering companions. Gibbon's judgment that "the northern countries of Europe scarcely deserved the expense and labour of conquest" perhaps directs an additional criticism at England. Whereas Gibbon refers to the Germanic tribes, England also happened to be a "northern country of Europe" that Rome coveted. The passage, therefore, with its modern resonances, suggests that England has again become a savage place scarcely worth anyone's trouble.

While Woolf parallels the ancient Romans and the modern Britons only to reduce supposedly glorious fortifications to prosaic pens in which dung collects, the British imperialists pridefully modeled themselves on their Roman predecessors. Lord Palmerston, for example, who served as foreign secretary, home secretary, and prime minister between 1830 and 1865, delivered a famous speech in 1850 that opened the way to British intervention anywhere in the world by invoking a Roman conqueror's self-justification, "I am a Roman citizen." That Woolf knew Palmerston is clear from *Orlando,* in which the main character receives an invitation from Lady Palmerston (256). Leonard Woolf quotes Palmerston's speech: "As the Roman in days of old held himself free from indignity when he could say *civis Romanus sum,* so also a British subject, in whatever land he may be shall feel confident that the watchful eye and strong arm of England will protect him against injustice and wrong" (*Empire and Commerce* 150). Leonard objects in exasperation that the British government refused the task of curbing "irresponsible European adventurers" abroad, yet when these meddlers in foreign economic or religious matters inevitably provoked resentment, Britain suddenly assumed a self-righteous responsibility to protect its unrestrained citizens (150). Protection thus became a pretext for imperial control.

As *The Voyage Out* links the British Empire with one predecessor in the Roman Empire, it also compares the rapid nineteenth-century expansion of the Empire with sixteenth- and seventeenth-century European mercantilism. The novel mocks the supposedly heroic Renaissance explorers and colonists by describing the English and Spanish sailors as "drinking," "itching for gold," "greedy for flesh," and finally "churning up the sand, and driving each other into the surf"—hardly a distinguished record (89). Woolf traces twentieth-century attitudes back to the Renaissance when she assigns Rachel's father the name of Sir Hugh Willoughby, an Elizabethan explorer she had read about in her youth (*Collected Essays* 2: 18). Britain may not have managed to secure much of Latin America for the British Empire, a fact that Richard Dalloway regrets, but his contemporaries were doing their best to establish a new hegemony through trade. As Mary Louise Pratt argues, when nineteenth-century travel writers in Spanish America "reduce[d] America to landscape and marginalize[d] its inhabitants," they gave Europe the myth of an empty land awaiting its developer, and created an "ideological framework for the rush of European (notably British) capital that would take over the region once it gained independence from Spain" (147). Woolf, in fact, describes the British in *The Voyage Out* as founding "a small colony within the last ten years" (89).

It is not possible, then, to glorify the creation of Empire by invoking the Roman or Elizabethan pasts, nor can that activity be assigned solely to a few active colonizers. Instead, in *The Voyage Out,* all the characters are implicated, in that they draw both income and outlook from a capitalism revealed as tainted. Although Willoughby as financier and Richard as member of Parliament most directly pursue policies that exploit the "lower orders" and give rise to foreign spheres of influence or outright colonies, none of the other characters can claim to be uninvolved. Though at the time a Cambridge man interested in philosophy, history, and law, St. John probably will run a corporation someday, as Terence predicts; already he is on the road to becoming another Willoughby (307). Nor is Rachel, though seemingly opposed to St. John in every way, exempt from participation in her father's commerce. When she commiserates with "poor little goats," her father reminds her sharply, "If it weren't for the goats there'd be no music, my dear; music depends upon goats" (23). Although she has no desire to harm any creature, her pampered lifestyle depends on slaughtering animals for their hides and exploiting workers in foreign lands who, by Willoughby's own admission, must be kept "beggars" (196).

Many of the other travelers benefit from the British Empire. Mr. Pepper, for example, congratulates himself that he has "done good work in India" as a minor civil servant (26). His other accomplishments, enumerated in the same paragraph, amount to never taking a ticket without noting the number, devoting January to the study of Petronius and February to Catullus, and repeating "no" to women "on principle, for he never yielded to a woman on account of her sex" (25). The superstitious triviality, rigidity, and prejudice of these present attainments make it doubtful that he has made any real contribution to India in the past.

Like Mr. Pepper, Miss Allan has a financial link with colonial ventures that is less lucrative than Willoughby's but nonetheless real. Unusual for her time as an unmarried woman making her own way by teaching, indirectly she owes some of her modest independence to a brother in New Zealand:

> The letters brought her news of the failure of last year's fruit crop in New Zealand, which was a serious matter, for Hubert, her only brother, made his living on a fruit farm, and if it failed again, of course he would throw up his place, come back to England, and what were they to do with him this time? The journey out here, which meant the loss of a term's work, became an extravagance and not the just and wonderful holiday due to her after fifteen years of punctual lecturing and correcting essays upon English literature. (178–79)

Both this troublesome brother, sent out to New Zealand, and Mr. Pepper, "condemned to pass the susceptible years of youth in a railway station in Bombay," reveal that not all colonizers are enthusiastic adventurers (25). These two somewhat unwilling colonizers from the middle class apparently have been pushed by their ambitious families to take advantage of opportunities abroad. Yet, if they do not really want to undertake the tedium or hard work far from home, neither do they condemn Empire. Individuals like Mr. Pepper only grow more self-satisfied.

Each of the British travelers draws some kind of income—whether spectacular in the case of Willoughby or precarious in the case of Miss

Allan's brother—from worldwide business connections that contribute to informal European influence or outright annexation. In addition, each derives from such connections an often unconscious set of values. These values endorse competition, domination of persons regarded as inferior, and the use of force. Ridley, for example, though a scholar translating Pindar, has not peaceably retreated to an ivory tower. Instead, he is described as "a Viking or a stricken Nelson" (12). If Ridley does not personally subdue territory, apparently he does not object to such conquest, as he readily imitates the harassing and colonizing Vikings. Like Horatio Nelson, the eighteenth-century British naval commander who jeopardized his career for a love affair, Ridley is at heart a military man, despite his gallantry toward Helen and his delicate and disinterested scholarship.

Other men in *The Voyage Out* also glorify militarism, and this attitude permeates every aspect of their lives, including love. As soon as Terence invites seven or eight people on a picnic "to make the ascent of Monte Rosa," he starts thinking of himself as "Wellington . . . on the field of Waterloo" (125–26). Terence's transformation into a general when he sets out to court Rachel, like Ridley's resemblance to a commander when he walks with his wife, does not bode well for the equality of the two partners in each relationship. The phrase "ascent of Monte Rosa" may owe something to the tradition of the rose as a female genital symbol. (In *Jacob's Room,* a character renames herself Florinda "to signify that the flower of her maidenhead was still unplucked" [77].) For Terence, wooing on a South American mountainside becomes conflated with climbing the *mons veneris;* and the need to conquer and command spoils the possibility of a friendship or sexual exchange existing between equals.

Like Terence Hewet comparing himself to Wellington, Richard Dalloway confuses the images of soldier and lover. Indulging in a little flirtation with Rachel, he swaggers around the deck as if facing an enemy far stronger than the brisk winds actually being encountered. Acting like an admiral on his ship (or an exhibitionist), Richard "stood firm," "strode upright," and "met the blast"—that is, he conveniently collides with Rachel (75). After he kisses her, Rachel admits that she both likes his kiss and hates men as "brutes" (82). Her baffled Aunt

Helen concludes that "there must be something wrong in this confusion between politics and kissing politicians" (83). Yet Woolf, from one end of her career to the other, repeatedly insists on just such a linkage between the relations of countries and those of men and women. At the moment when Richard is confiding melodramatically to Rachel that his life has afforded him two revelations, about the "misery of the poor" and about "love," his wife, unaware of the dalliance, gushes:

> "Warships, Dick! Over there! Look!"
>
> Clarissa, released from Mr. Grice, appreciative of all his seaweeds, skimmed towards them, gesticulating.
>
> She had sighted two sinister grey vessels, low in the water, and bald as bone, one closely following the other with the look of eyeless beasts seeking their prey. Consciousness returned to Richard instantly.
>
> "By George!" he exclaimed, and stood shielding his eyes.
>
> "Ours, Dick?" said Clarissa.
>
> "The Mediterranean Fleet," he answered.
>
> The *Euphrosyne* was slowly dipping her flag. Richard raised his hat. Convulsively Clarissa squeezed Rachel's hand.
>
> "Aren't you glad to be English!" she said. (69)

The text mocks Clarissa as superficial when she "skimmed" toward her husband, cooing her extravagant self-satisfaction. "To be English" is to maintain the army and navy that will soon be waging World War I, culling weed and bone. At the same time that the ships are gearing up for war, Richard and Clarissa enact a kind of symbolic sexual intercourse, when Richard raises (his hat) and Clarissa convulsively squeezes. Meanwhile, the *Euphrosyne*, named after the female graces, must dip, bow, and defer. Men learn that they must kill "enemies" to impress women, and women learn that they must lower their own profiles in the world.

This constricted picture of men and women—as those who command and those who yield—apparently benefits men, because power resides with them. Yet such a system dupes men, too, consigning them to death on battlefields. *The Voyage Out* not only acknowledges the imminence of World War I but also analyzes some of its causes. The state's obsession with holding onto colonies, as well as the requirement that men be "manly" (i.e., deadly—to participate in homicidal and suicidal charges), makes belligerence the inevitable product of the characters' competitiveness, materialism, and domineering pride. When warships on the horizon elicit uncritical patriotic fervor, only Helen Ambrose objects to the maintenance of military forces, as she mutters that "it seemed to her as wrong to keep sailors as to keep a Zoo" (69).

Richard, Terence, and Ridley, then, all associate themselves with militarism, despite their apparently peaceful occupations as politician, would-be novelist, and scholar. Another, perhaps unexpected, participant in this glorification of force is Evelyn Murgatroyd, the hotel guest who avoids setting a wedding date while continuing to solicit multiple proposals. Confused by her own ambivalence toward domestic life, she fantasizes herself as a past adventurer in foreign lands—a role traditionally reserved for men. She wishes she could have been a colonist in Elizabethan times, "to cut down trees and make laws and all that, instead of fooling about with all these people who think one's just a pretty young lady" (192; cf. 264). Certainly Woolf sympathizes with Evelyn for wanting to "*do* something" rather than take a feminine role as passive art object (192). Yet Woolf also satirizes Evelyn as a woman meeting unsatisfactorily the dilemma posed in *Three Guineas*: the need to choose between remaining passive or breaking into the available professions, all of which reward aggressiveness. Already in *The Voyage Out*, Woolf derides these professions when she has Terence scorn the callings revered by his upper middle class: "What a miracle the masculine conception of life is—judges, civil servants, army, navy, Houses of Parliament, lord mayors—what a world we've made of it!" (213). Although Terence is lying to impress Rachel, he admits that women might try their hand at running public life. Nevertheless, Woolf asks in *Three Guineas*, should women just duplicate the professions as they already exist, "wear a judge's wig . . . speak from a pulpit . . . dress in military uniform, with gold lace on our breasts, swords at our sides, and something like the old family coal-scuttle on our heads, save that that venerable object was never decorated with plumes of white horsehair" (61–

62)? Evelyn, unfortunately, opts for the "coal-scuttle." If she could, she would wear the regalia and do the violent deeds of an acquisitive general, the butt of Woolf's derision.

As part of her muddled thinking, Evelyn does envision a vague, improved society. She wants to "conquer some great territory and make it splendid. You'd want women for that . . . But you—you only like Law Courts!" (136) Her suitor Mr. Perrott wonders how she can put these utopian dreams into practice: "Conquer a territory? They're all conquered already, aren't they?" (136). Evelyn revealingly protests, "It's not any territory in particular. . . . It's the idea, don't you see? We lead such tame lives" (137). Recalling the infamous battle cry of the writer Théophile Gautier, "Plutôt la barbarie que l'ennui," Evelyn prefers violence to boredom (Steiner 11). George Steiner blames the apocalyptic longings of Gautier's fellow writers of the nineteenth and twentieth centuries for inducing lethargy and preventing reaction against the militarism that led to the world wars. Woolf similarly shows that Evelyn, in failing to formulate a conscious understanding of her resentments, allows them to be directed into a dangerous enthusiasm for colonial adventures. Although Evelyn believes that she can safely entertain an "idea" that has nothing to do with "any territory in particular," her desire to conquer is, in fact, being rigorously enacted in her country's imperialism. Instead of reforming British life, restless malcontents like Evelyn unconsciously sanction violent conquest abroad, contributing to the spread of the very forms of British society that they claim to dislike. For all her legitimate frustrations, Evelyn has to take some responsibility for the "navies and armies" that precede and dominate the discussion of "political parties, natives and mineral products" that is reported on the same page as her utopian vaporings (136).

The Empire and its underlying values thus set their stamp on all the individuals in the novel and on their relations as couples. The South American river, as a main conduit for trade, shapes everyone's vision: "A few miles of this river were visible from the top of the mountain where some weeks before the party from the hotel had picnicked. Susan and Arthur had seen it as they kissed each other, and Terence and Rachel as they sat talking about Richmond, and Evelyn and Perrott as they strolled about, imagining that they were great captains sent to colonise the world" (264). The reiteration of pairs who even in intimate moments see this river emphasizes that scarcely anyone can escape the dominant outlook, social as much as topological. An invisible guidebook prescribes who may be considered an acceptable couple, the times when they may be together, the duration of the relationship (which is expected to last for life), and their attitudes toward each other. Even Evelyn, who resists the marriage expected of her, cannot make a clean break with tradition; rather, she stalls with multiple engagements that only torment her suitors and herself. She cannot give up a definition of womanhood that says she must prove herself desirable by parading her beaux.

Rachel, too, much more sincere and direct than Evelyn, finds that her engagement is a melody accompanied by the inevitable bass of dominant mercantile values. When she pronounces, "Terrible—terrible" to Terence's statement, "We love each other," she is thinking "as much of the persistent churning of the water as of her own feeling. On and on it went in the distance, the senseless and cruel churning of the water" (272–73). Rachel might well be imagining steamboats churning in the service of commerce, one of the main currents of her time that determine the forms taken by people's loves. Willoughby's harsh reaction at the temerity of workers who seek higher wages could explain her judgment: "cruel churning." A wedding cannot provide an escape from her father's house, since prevailing capitalist values sketch the parameters for marriage and, indeed, for all relations between men and women.

Women in such a society are expected silently to inspire their men. Willoughby, for example, tells himself that he is building his factories at Hull and his shipping lines solely as an offering to his dead wife, Theresa. According to Helen, he was not particularly kind to Theresa while she lived, but now that her memory has faded to an abstraction, he trusts that she must be blessing him from heaven (85). Richard applies to the living this philosophy of woman as inspiration. When Rachel apologizes that she has nothing to contribute to the conversation, Richard admits that he prefers women to act ignorant, since he can fill that void with a projected image of nurturing angels. Like Conrad's Marlow assuming that Kurtz's "Intended" in *Heart of Darkness* is happier with a lie, Richard believes that, because Clarissa stays at home, her "illusions have not been destroyed" (65). Condescendingly, he judges her deluded but claims, nevertheless, that this sweet naiveté "gives [him] courage to go on" (65). As the lives of nineteenth-century middle-class women became less arduous, they had more and more need of a "mission": hence the attractiveness to women of the mission to inspire men (Perkin 244). Thus, as Richard inspects the gunboats, Clarissa must convince him of his superiority, both to support his ego and to bolster her own sense of having some purpose, if only as animator behind the scenes.

This polarization of women and men into inspiring life-givers and brave death-dealers is reiterated in the South American village reached by the Britons at the end of their river voyage. Instead of providing a contrast to London, this village exhibits the same gender-based division of labor: one man with a weapon, many women with bowls and babies (284). When the Londoners find the country like "an English park," they reveal, first of all, that they are incapable of seeing anything other than a scene with which they are already familiar (279). The Brazilian roles actually do mirror their own, however, either because patriarchy characterizes the indigenous culture, too, or because the village already has been exposed to European ways. The gun, for example, is a European import. The village, with its "strange wooden nests," becomes "the goal of their journey," suggesting that Terence and Rachel have learned to regard the institution of marriage, the nest, as the only possible goal of love (284). Yet here that goal suddenly seems "strange." The "signs of human habitation," in a culture that recognizes such blighting gender divisions, can only be grim "blackened grass" and "charred tree-stumps," just as, to the travelers, London looked like "a circumscribed mound, eternally burnt, eternally scarred" (284, 18).

In addition to providing inspiration and babies, in the London-based economic system women also supply cheap labor. When Mrs. Flushing first proposes the trip to the village to buy cloth and crafts, she emphasizes her argument by "piercing the bed again and again with a long golden pin" (235). The conjunction of gold and bed might signal that marriage is as much a monetary arrangement as the river trip, a connection which Woolf makes again later in *To the Lighthouse,* when she associates the acquisition of a wife with the possession of a gold watch (175–76). The "piercing" of the bed hints that, in the institution of marriage, sexuality becomes a means of pinning women down socially, just as the terms of trade hurt the local inhabitants. In Mrs. Flushing's emphatic gesture, gold serves as a pecuniary emblem of the engagement which the expedition is designed to foster. Women do indeed provide cheap labor, as Richard's catalogue of his wife's activities indicates; Clarissa plays with the children and performs domestic duties, free (65).

The social definition of a middle-class woman as caretaker of children, hostess, and demure inspirer of a fighting man gives rise to several other assumptions about women, usually unspoken, which Woolf articulates in this novel. Less misogynistic than St. John, Terence still agrees that women have weak minds. He accuses his fiancée, "You've no respect for facts, Rachel; you're essentially feminine" (295). Yet Terence's discussion reveals contradictory gender expectations. The same woman who is thought incapable of respecting facts is considered more capable than Terence of handling domestic facts. The woman who has been elevated to the status of heavenly ideal muse is also painted as "less idealistic than men," with "no sense of honour" (291).

Paradoxically, this disembodied angel also must serve as the incarnation of sexuality, which is defined as evil. This last transformation appears in Richard's muddled thinking. When he touts "the age we live in, with its opportunities and possibilities," Rachel objects simply, "You see, I'm a woman"; his opportunities to follow careers in diplomacy and law do not exist for her (76). Richard counters that "a young and beautiful woman" does not need professional opportunities, because she has "the whole world [i.e., himself] at her feet" (76). Adding that she has "an inestimable power—for good or for evil," he kisses her. His language suggests that, while he judges it evil to kiss a woman other than his wife, he projects this supposed evil onto Rachel and all women, so that he may blame them and spare himself.

Among all these impossibly contradictory gender requirements exists a central expectation that lovers will marry. One of Rachel's acquaintances prescribes a wedding as the cure for any problem: "restlessness, eccentricity, taking things up and dropping them again, public speaking, and philanthropic activity" (180). *The Voyage Out,* however, satirizes the matrimonial solution to all ills. Instead of ending symptoms, marriage produces its own. The suggestion is that the institution is itself a disease or a death. After Rachel reads of the medieval Tristan's "corpse-like Bride," she throws down such a "senseless" book (35). When Helen appraises her niece "aesthetically," Rachel looks like "a victim dropped from the claws of a bird of prey" (37). Helen thus invokes the nineteenth-century tradition that sees women as beautiful, silent art objects: Snow White "dead and self-less in her glass coffin" (Gilbert and Gubar, *Madwoman* 40–41). Mrs. Thornbury, who spent "six weeks on my honeymoon in having typhoid at Venice," still comically calls them "some of the happiest weeks in my life," again linking honeymoon with disease (318).

These blatant associations of marriage with corpses, illness, or wounding usually are read as either prefiguring Rachel's death or betraying a warped fear of sexuality. Although Virginia Blain rightly denies that *The Voyage Out* is "manifestly prudish," as if Woolf were projecting her own unconscious fears, she still mistakenly understands Woolf to be consciously depicting Rachel as beset by private inhibitions (238, 240). Rachel, however, is not a pathologically timid woman who fears sexuality, but rather is an individual actively resisting specific oppressions in a sick institution. These "symptoms" are already evident in Rachel's engagement, indicating that both it and the type of marriage it heralds are deadening for women, by denying them economic opportunities and a range of fulfilling work.

As a first drawback to marriage, Rachel will be taking her place in a system of economic exploitation that she has begun to question. She will live off Terence's six or seven hundred pounds a year, while other women, servants or perhaps prostitutes, "die with bugs crawling across their faces" (213, 301). Immediately after the hotel crowd hears the announcement of Rachel's engagement, they learn of the suicide of a parlourmaid (306). Rachel and Terence cannot inhabit an isolated, blissful world but participate in a larger economic and social system, in which parlourmaids wait on luckier middle-class brides. Rachel already has recognized that "the whole system" which at half-past ten in the morning sets a housemaid mechanically brushing the stairs is "inexplicable" (36). To be "the Angel in the House," Rachel will have to supervise the "lower orders" (*Pargiters* xxx), and Terence, to receive an income while he produces no more than a few imitative paragraphs of an otherwise unwritten novel, will have to overlook the way that men like Willoughby keep their workers beggars.

As a second stultifying requirement of marriage, Rachel will have to renounce any public voice and give up her own work. She thinks that Terence and St. John at the courtship picnic are like "the ants who stole the tongue," implying perhaps that these men who take for granted their own superiority inhibit women's public voice, just as pests steal the gourmet food (293). As soon as they are engaged, Terence interferes with Rachel's work, her music. Although she exaggerates amiably, she seriously warns Terence not to presume to occupy her whole life: "Here I am, the best musician in South America, not to speak of Europe and Asia, and I can't play a note because of you in the room interrupting me every other second" (292). Instead of taking the hint, Terence compares her "tunes" to "an unfortunate old dog going around on its hind legs in the rain" (292). Woolf alludes to Samuel Johnson's likening women preachers to dogs walking on their hind legs (Blain 240). By considering his own novel-writing worthwhile but deprecating her music, Terence adopts a double standard concerning fulfilling work for men and women.

Even in Terence's case, marriage might compromise his work to some extent. He pictures domestic relations as people "walled up" (241) and imagines confessing to Rachel, "I worship you, but I loathe marriage, I hate its smugness, its safety, its compromise, and the thought of you interfering in my work, hindering me" (243). Nevertheless, if marriage constricts both partners, it will detract more from women's creative work, as Terence himself admits: "Marriage seemed to be worse for them than it was for men" (241). He can go out alone, or, if he stays in to write his novel, he can always shut the door. A woman, on the contrary, is not supposed to shut out the children; a "room of her own, let alone a quiet room or a sound-proof room," is even less likely (*Room of One's Own* 54). Even when Mrs. Thornbury approves younger women's "going out and doing things that we should not have thought it possible to do," she insists that "they give a great deal to their children," with no similar injunction for fathers (319).

In keeping a woman from a range of fulfilling work other than caring for children, middle-class matrimony becomes a kind of death. In denying the happily-ever-after ending, *The Voyage Out* caustically implies that it might be better to kill the bride at once, rather than submit her to the slow suffocation of wifehood. Throughout the novel, Woolf announces this sardonic conclusion in three descriptions of moths, whose struggles make people wonder if they ought to put the creatures out of their misery. In the first description:

> The sound [of the clock] slightly disturbed certain somnolent merchants, government officials, and men of independent means who . . . had the appearance of crocodiles so fully gorged by their last meal that the future of the world gives them no anxiety whatever. The only disturbance in the placid bright room was caused by a large moth which shot from light to light, whizzing over elaborate heads of hair, and causing several young women to raise their hands nervously and exclaim, "Some one ought to kill it!" (183)

The moth here is associated with young women, like Rachel, while the hotel's clientele, oblivious to the insect's plight, recall the merchant Willoughby Vinrace and the government official Richard Dalloway. These men are dangerous not through personal villainy, but rather as representatives of a larger, predatory economic system.

The second description of a distressed moth occurs in the passage in which Mrs. Flushing is reminiscing about reading Gibbon under a night-light: "Then there were the moths—tiger moths, yellow moths, and horrid cockchafers. Louisa, my sister, would have the window open. I wanted it shut. We fought every night of our lives over that window. Have you ever seen a moth dyin' in a night-light?" (200). Because her "happiest hours" are occupied by reading in bed about "massacres," the clash of these unexpected juxtapositions, near the word "cockchafer," perhaps associates what should be the happiest bed, wedlock, with violence. Woolf thus implies that the slow massacre, matrimony, might better be forestalled by a preemptive halt to the usual romance plot.

In the third description of a moth, after Rachel has died, her society feels no need to make any changes in the status quo: "The chessboard was brought out. . . . Round them gathered a group of ladies with pieces of needlework . . . much as if they were in charge of two small boys playing marbles. Every now and then they looked at the board and made some encouraging remark to the gentlemen. . . . Every now and then the moth, which was now grey of wing and shiny of thorax, whizzed over their heads, and hit the lamps with a thud" (370). At this point a young woman decides, "Poor creature! it would be kinder to kill it" (370). Social training keeps these males as eternally needy boys, much as it consigns the females to eternal motherhood and inspiration. The repetition of the phrase "every now and then" connects the subjects: the moths whose flight is painfully interrupted, the women whose only role is to encourage men, and Rachel, who has followed the "kinder" path to a quick death.

The three descriptions of moths together neatly sum up the English social system, as presented in *The Voyage Out*. While the moths engage in their futile struggles, the merchants are making money. The British emulators of Gibbon's Romans are building their Empire. The women, as Angels in the House, meanwhile soothe the men. The moths stand for anyone who does not fare well under this system: the parlourmaids on their knees at 10:30 A.M., the South American residents duped by Mr. and Mrs. Flushing, the strikers thwarted by Willoughby, the middle-class wives reduced to flattering men at their games. Woolf might be able to spare one fictional woman, Rachel, the traditional ending, as a way of calling attention to the deadliness already inherent in a marriage supposedly lived "happily ever after." At the same time, the sadness of the new ending asks readers to rouse themselves from their torpor under the old rules of the game and revise a battered system of commercialism, Empire, and prejudice.

Night and Day

The Voyage Out presents nineteenth- and early twentieth-century marriage as deadly because it deprives women of voice, a variety of work, and economic independence. *Night and Day* (1919) continues to explore women's longings for meaningful work, while also examining women's desire for sexual expression—a desire likely to be thwarted rather than fulfilled in the behavior expected of wives. The novel convincingly portrays passion for both intellectual work and people, while also communicating the sad perception that in "romance," the lover often idolizes a person he or she does not really see and may even prefer absent. The four major characters—Mary Datchet, Ralph Denham, Katharine Hilbery, and William Rodney—mistake their own emotions, temporarily pair off, and then realign themselves, in a modern *Midsummer Night's Dream.* Yet if Woolf imitates Shakespeare in the symmetries and ironies of an intricate love plot, she uses this traditional story of sorting out couples to undermine the socially sanctioned pairings, which are only apparently righted at the end.

To Shakespeare's "night" of erotic revels, *Night and Day* adds the "day" of creative work previously denied to women. Whereas Katharine's mother reverently visits Shakespeare's tomb, Woolf seems to want to bury a few of his time-honored plots: "[Mrs. Hilbery] did nothing but talk about Shakespeare's tomb . . . of great poets, and the unchanged spirit of noble loving which they had taught, so that nothing changes, and one age is linked with another, and no one dies, and we all meet in spirit, until she appeared oblivious of any one in the room" (496–97). The fact that Mrs. Hilbery clearly is fantasizing when she declares that "no one dies" places in doubt, too, her assertion that "loving" never changes. Forms of loving, including the role of loving wife, are open to question in *Night and Day,* as they were in *The Voyage Out.* Although the earlier novel more frequently shows the British Empire looming behind the institution of marriage, at a few crucial moments *Night and Day* depicts England's domination of other nations as a dangerous parallel to the domination of women.

Because upper middle-class Katharine Hilbery seems to feel only polite respect for her fiancé William Rodney, the reader is led to wish that she would accept instead the lower-middle-class Ralph Denham, who consciously admires her, as she unconsciously inclines toward him. The reader, however, cannot wholeheartedly endorse power-hungry Ralph as a suitor either. Although Ralph believes that Katharine captivates him despite her membership in a higher class, in fact he is drawn to her *because* of this standing. His resentment of her rank goads him to substitute her person for the money and status he lacks. When he first notices her, he thinks of her as a possession: "She'll do. . . . Yes, Katharine Hilbery'll do. . . . I'll take Katharine Hilbery" (24). Critics often misinterpret Ralph in a completely positive light; Judy Little calls him "the major speaker for truth" (*Comedy* 36), while Jane Marcus judges that he "seeks knowledge, not power" and "has no stake in preserving patriarchy" (*Patriarchy* 29, 31). Instead, he unattractively expects Katharine to "obey" and imagines that he has "conquered" her interest (61). As a tribute to his "will-power" (61), she must applaud him, even as she must simultaneously abase herself, "swooped from her eminence" (24–25). Depressingly, his dreams distort her, as both of them recognize (93, 381). Even late in the novel, he admits that he is happier when he can part from her and instead hug his daydream (423). Only twenty pages from the end of their story, he insists that there be no "states of mind in which he was unrepresented. He wished to dominate, to possess her" (489). While England stifles Ralph's desire for economic power with its rigid class system, society encourages his exercise of power over women.

This socially fostered trait of dominance, which threatens Katharine, also drives the Empire. Mary, who is attracted to Ralph as much as Katharine is, broaches the subject of colonies when she imagines "a scene of herself on a camel's back, in the desert, while Ralph commanded a whole tribe of natives" (83). Walking through the British Museum, she conjures up an exotic scenario to support her belief that he is "not in the least conventional, like most clever men" (83). Ralph, however, already has proven himself thoroughly conventional in one regard, his expectation that women must obey and flatter him. Similarly, Mary's view that he could command "a whole tribe of natives" follows the conventions of Kipling, whose plots, style, and premises Woolf later mocks openly in *A Room of One's Own* (106). Already *Night and Day* conveys scorn for the conquering hero. While Mary at first fails to question the heroism that supposedly would motivate Ralph in the desert, by the end of her stroll through the museum she is dissatisfied with her "amateurish" fantasy (83).

Mary's daydream in fact calls into question a familiar literary and cultural paradigm of quest and conquest, as seen in a long-running battle of male warrior and (often female) monster. The setting for Mary's thoughts on her lunch hour includes two rooms of the British Museum. In the first, she gazes at a statue of Ulysses. In a sly comment, the narrator supposes that Mary's "emotions were not purely esthetic," connecting the nudity of the statues with the young woman's physical desire for Ralph (82). That Mary is almost tempted to address a confession of love to a statue, not a person, creates pathos, while at the same time her homage hints that live people who mold themselves in ideal images, such as the room represents, might also prove unsatisfactory. For "solitude and chill and silence" underlie and finally undermine the solemnity and beauty of the gallery (82). In fact, it could be said that the power of the marble statues to isolate, chill, and silence Mary derives from the cultural acceptance of Ulysses as the ideal Western man.

Woolf knew Ulysses's story from the *Odyssey*, which she read at least as early as 1907–9 (Silver 133, 166); in April 1918, she also was reading the manuscript of James Joyce's *Ulysses* for possible publication by the Hogarth Press (Bishop 43). Mary does not immediately define what it is about the classical Ulysses that simultaneously attracts and repels her. She might resent the gender stereotypes of passive wife and active quester that keep Penelope at home while her husband sees the sights—no camel rides for her. Or Mary might sense the double standard according to which Penelope, if not Joyce's Molly, must repulse all suitors, while Odysseus can enjoy sexual affairs with Circe and Calypso. Or she might denounce his entrepreneurship—a motive so strong, he admits to Penelope, that he could have been home many years earlier but for his desire to amass yet more silver cauldrons (Homer 295). Although Mary does not name the sword and the sacks of loot that prop up

Ulysses's manhood, elsewhere *Night and Day* faults these same institutionally sanctioned desires for conquest and wealth. Even the gentle William Rodney conforms to the vogue for the hunt: "I don't care much for shooting . . . but one has to do it, unless one wants to be altogether out of things" (204). And Ralph's attraction to Katharine resolves itself into a craving for material goods. On the same page in which he declares "I love you," he also elaborates, with only "half-humorous gravity," "I should advise you to let me keep it [your ruby ring] for you" (423).

The paradigmatic male warrior, violent and acquisitive, fights enemies whom he can admit not as equal human beings but only as subhuman creatures or monsters. Mary moves from the room in which Ulysses is located to a gallery displaying "engraved obelisks and winged Assyrian bulls" (83). This art, with its phallic columns and potent fertility animals, supports her sexual fantasies by means of mythological images from the past. Yet in order to include her twentieth-century self in the scenario, she must also imagine the contemporary sands of Empire. Mary's train of thought runs, in fact, from Assyrian bulls to "monsters . . . couchant in the sand" to the "tribe of natives" that evokes the British Empire, all within ten lines (83). At the time the book was published, desert mandates belonging to Britain existed in Egypt, Palestine, and Mesopotamia, then called Irak (Taylor 152). Deserts also had passed into British control in North Africa, as Leonard Woolf documents in *Empire and Commerce in Africa,* written while Virginia was composing *Night and Day.* The "tribe" as humans fades and is replaced by the animal or chimerical categories of bulls and monsters.

As soon as Mary mentions "natives," she immediately observes, "That is what you can do. . . . You always make people do what you want" (83). As Ralph would make colonized people obey him, he seems able to make her entertain erotic thoughts. The command that she ascribes to him is the pull of sexual attraction, actually her own sexuality projected onto him. The only patterns according to which her society allows her to express and understand this sexuality require an alarming degree of masochism, seen in the phrase "monsters couchant." A heraldic animal *couchant* is lying down, crouching, backing into a corner, even fawning. At best it is waiting for an opportunity to retaliate, while for the moment it appears conquered by the knight with his sword. A heraldic animal is also aristocratic, implying that, even in her daydream, Mary acknowledges that Ralph is more likely to choose Katharine than herself. Moreover, *se coucher,* in French, also means to go to bed, to copulate. Indeed, in *Jacob's Room,* the narrator associates the word *couchant* with sexual attraction, especially between people who are temperamentally incompatible: "Male beauty in association with female beauty breeds in the onlooker a sense of fear . . . have you ever watched fine collie dogs couchant at twenty yards' distance? As she passed him his cup there was that quiver in her flanks" (96). When Mary names the "monsters couchant," she in part identifies with them, as if to say, "Conquer me, take me, think me a monster, but touch me!"

When Mary momentarily accepts such identifications, she evokes a whole tradition in the West that associates women with monsters. In examples that Woolf would have known, Odysseus meets female monsters, including Scylla, Charybdis, Circe, and the Sirens, who are either threateningly violent or dangerously alluring. Oedipus answers a female sphinx, whose image in the sand epitomizes silence. Spenser's Redcrosse stabs Errour, a monstrous woman: "Halfe like a serpent horribly displaide, / But th' other halfe did womans [*sic*] shape retaine, / Most lothsom, filthie, foule, and full of vile disdaine" (1: 552). Woolf refers to Spenser's "monsters of allegory" in a 1907 essay (McNeillie 1: 145). The description of the allegorical Errour in *The Faerie Queene* implies that women themselves are filthy. Mary's movement from sexual desire to "monsters couchant," therefore, seems to reflect her internalization of a Western assimilation of women's bodies to monstrosity and a condemnation of their minds to silence. The drift of her thought—from sexual and desiring to despairing and masochistic—is disturbing, as she herself recognizes by the end of the page: "She was, indeed, rather annoyed with herself for having allowed such an ill-considered breach of her reserve" (83). Actually, Mary proves bold enough, not "reserved," when she moves to her own flat despite her father's protests, takes a job from ten till six, and invites men to visit her at home. She is even bolder when she courageously faces Ralph's stony indifference. Instead of breaching reserve, the fantasy at the museum is unsatisfactory because it betrays some of her deepest goals. Such a low self-image is inconsistent with her objectives at the suffrage office, and also with her later efforts, when she quits this first office to work for greater economic equality for all people.

Is the image of Ralph astride a camel entirely a figment of Mary's reverie, or is there really a chance that he might go to the colonies? His sister Joan fears that his "gambling" nature, a "perversity in his temperament," might make him give up his dull but safe job as a solicitor's clerk, to pursue instead "beauty" or a "cause": "She suspected the East also, and always fidgeted herself when she saw him with a book of Indian travels in his hand, as though he were sucking contagion from the page" (125). In seeking a field for his energies, Ralph may want to benefit "natives," as Joan tries to tell herself, but it is just as likely that he may hope to glorify himself, as she really suspects. Joan pictures Ralph tiring of "the discipline and the drudgery" of his plodding clerkship, "only to put himself under harsher constraint; she figured him toiling through sandy deserts under a tropical sun to find the source of some river or the haunt of some fly" (126). To the extent that Joan sees Ralph as a benefactor, perhaps finding cures for disease, she justifies European expansionism. *Empire and Commerce in Africa*, however, linked the European search for the headwaters of the Nile, for example, with self-serving greed and cruelty (155). Woolf would have known, therefore, that Joan's statements about the altruism of finding "the source of some river" are naive. Joan romanticizes a hypothetical trip by Ralph to Africa or India somewhat less than Mary does, in that she takes into account the actual risk and hardship that such an adventure might entail for her brother. As much as Mary, however, she fails to recognize the hardship and cultural disintegration that the presence of people like Ralph would mean for the inhabitants of desert and tropics.

If Ralph's family has a possible future stake in the Empire, Katharine's milieu and her relatives possess extensive past and present connections with the colonies. A "sugar king" resides in the Hilberys' neighborhood (203). An Uncle John worked in the Indian civil service because he could not pass more strenuous examinations (151). Another uncle, Sir Francis Otway, has retired from the government of India with less money than he thinks he deserves. In reality he leads a comfortable life, despite a worn carpet (208), but his disappointment has soured him to the point of mentally abusing his wife and children for the rest of their lives. Sir Francis serves as a kind of rough sketch for Abel Pargiter in *The Years*; both return from India and sacrifice a daughter named Eleanor, who must forego marriage or independence to keep a father company. Otway and Pargiter thus continue at home the tyrannies they have engaged in overseas, indicating the continuum between family and Empire insistently pointed out in Woolf's books.

The Hilberys themselves identify with the Empire so closely that they convert a tour of their house into a display of "relics" from the conquest of India (15). To introduce Ralph to her family, Katharine hands him a sword in an ornamental sheath, said to have belonged to Robert Clive (18). Clive, "a name the British would hero-worship as long as they contemplated India," was an eighteenth-century East India Company employee and soldier who reaped a fantastic fortune in "presents" from Indian officials (Moorhouse 44, 48). In contrast to his idealized reputation, however, Clive's career was rife with disobedience to company orders, swashbuckling, and bribery. He ignored company directives, instead fighting with an Indian faction in Madras against another faction supported by the French. He later participated in similar maverick alliances and military victories in Bengal: "Although no-one had yet grasped the fact that an Empire was being built, the structure of the British Raj was starting to rise from the trenching dug by Robert Clive" (Moorhouse 57). In addition to Clive's sword, the Hilberys' other prized Indian souvenir is a malaccca cane that belonged to a great-uncle: "he was Sir Richard Warburton, you know, and rode with Havelock to the Relief of Lucknow," during the Mutiny of 1857 (16). The Hilberys' family mementos thus commemorate both the founding of the Raj and, prophetically for Katharine's own rebellion, the first important threat to the Empire, the mutiny.

Although Katharine does not openly criticize her family, including its Empire making, she begins silently to question everything it stands for. Whereas her relatives regard the relics as sacred, Katharine dismisses the objects as dead and pretentious. She holds them out for Ralph's inspection "automatically," not reverently (19). When he later telephones to arrange an outing, she decides instantly to accept but makes a dignified show of consulting her engagement book; while the mouthpiece dangles, she "looked fixedly at the print of the great-uncle who had not ceased to gaze, with an air of amiable authority, into a world which, as yet, beheld no symptoms of the Indian Mutiny. And yet, gently swinging against the wall, within the black tube, was a voice which recked nothing of Uncle James, of China teapots, or of red velvet curtains" (310). The pause announces her own personal mutiny, as she resists her family's definition of women as conquered territory.

Just as Katharine Hilbery in her personal rebellion begins to iden-tify with Indians in their mutiny, Cassandra Otway's private insurrec-tion against her Anglo-Indian parents takes the form of filling her room with mulberry leaves, silkworm cages, and "home-made machines for the manufacture of silk dresses" (210). To some extent, her room re-calls Gandhi's India, filled with spinning wheels to make homemade cloth and so lessen India's dependence on English cotton mills. Gandhi called for such a program in "Indian Home Rule" in 1909 (Jack 118). Woolf may have known about these developments; she reports in Janu-ary 1915 that, after Leonard spent a late evening reviewing Indian Blue Books, they talked over hot chocolate, possibly about his reading (Di-ary 1: 31). In Night and Day, however, Cassandra's self-reliance is even more tentative than Katharine's. Despite her youthful eccentricity, Cassandra will settle into complacent conventionality, as the perfect wife for William. Her machines, after all, spin silk for upper-class dresses, not simple cotton ones.

Although Katharine seems not to grasp the specific hardships of colonized people any more than Mary, Joan, or Cassandra does, she is clearly groping toward such a realization. Just the mention of an In-dian man-servant brought back to England by an uncle makes Katharine "very angry" (115). She soon swerves away from consideration of his lot as perpetual servant, however, to chafe at her own position as a daugh-ter whose time is always available to—and wasted by—her family. Because her resentment toward her mother induces guilt, this fear of offending her parents on a personal level forestalls condemnation of the society on a public level.

The one indication that Katharine harbors more anger than she usually expresses against society is her outburst to Mary: "I want to trample upon their prostrate bodies!" (59). Mary replies quietly that "One doesn't necessarily trample upon people's bodies because one runs an office" (59). To some extent, Mary may be lamenting the futility of meetings which seem to accomplish nothing at all. However, she is also guarding against a desire to trample people, as opposed to destroying attitudes. Working in the peaceful wing of the suffrage movement, Mary warns that protesters and reformers must not turn into the bullies whom they oppose, as Evelyn Murgatroyd, in *The Voyage Out,* pursued her muddled rebellion against marriage only to the extent of imagining herself a Renaissance conquistador. In *Three Guineas,* Woolf explicitly rejects Evelyn's unhelpful reaction: opponents of tyranny resorting to tyranny. If self-proclaimed antifascists in England enjoy the use of force and regard whole groups as inferior, then they too are fascists: "we cannot dissociate ourselves from that figure [Führer or Duce] but are ourselves that figure" (*Three Guineas* 142).

Although Katharine does not join Mary at the suffrage office, she does try to revise the roles deemed acceptable for women. Without really articulating to others her resistance, any more than Rachel does in *The Voyage Out,* Katharine doggedly pursues two goals: meaningful work and expression of affection and physical desire in multiple directions. By work, she means intellectual and creative endeavors. While Mary Datchet reminds her listeners that "No one works harder than a woman with little children," Katharine argues for supplementing that vocation with other important jobs: "you can't limit work" (357). Although the responsibilities of a father to some extent also may curtail the time men can devote to creative work, as Mr. Ramsay's friends note in *To the Lighthouse* (37), husbands still renounce less than wives. William Rodney believes that he would not need marriage at all if he were a better writer; he insists, however, that Katharine and "all women" are "nothing at all without it; you're only half alive; using only half your faculties" (66). Keeping silent, Katharine nevertheless deeply disagrees that wifehood and motherhood are the essential and indeed the only callings for women.

The kind of work that Katharine craves requires education. As she laments, middle-class women have had training through their service at home only in psychology: "all that part of life which is conspicuously without order . . . moods and wishes, degrees of liking or disliking . . . she had been forced to deny herself any contemplation of that other part of life where thought constructs a destiny" (331). That is, she envies Ralph's "constructed" botany and speculative sciences. Woolf criticized this limitation of women's educational experience from her earliest story, written in 1906, in which she praises Rosamond's insight into personality yet also bemoans the fact that this young woman, "possessed of shrewd and capable brains, had been driven to feed them exclusively upon the human character" (*Complete Shorter Fiction* 22). By *A Room of One's Own,* Woolf credits the nineteenth century's confinement of middle-class women to the "common sitting-room" with making them adept at the novel, with its "observation of character" and "analysis of emotion" (70). Yet she simultaneously regrets that such training shunted off into fiction some talents that could perhaps have better served history or biography. In *Night and Day,* Katharine wants to study not psychological nuances at the tea-table but math and astronomy at the university.

By Katharine's generation, in the early twentieth century, it was not completely impossible for women to go to college. Indeed, Ralph's sister Hester hopes to go to Newnham, founded at Cambridge in 1872 (376). However, no one is encouraging Katharine to apply, and Hester, with less opposition from her family, will face other struggles. Ray Strachey's *The Cause,* which Woolf recommends in *A Room of One's Own* (21, 58), documents the experience of a woman at Newnham who sat for the Mathematics Tripos in 1890 and placed "'above the senior [male] wrangler,' thus winning the most famous mathematics honour in the world. . . . In spite of these resounding successes the degree question was not raised again at Cambridge" (260). In *Three Guineas,* Woolf blasts Cambridge for still not allowing its women graduating from Newnham and Girton to put a B.A. after their names, even though they had passed the same examinations as the male students. The few university-educated women in England consequently remained at a disadvantage in obtaining appointments (29, 153). As Woolf knew by 1919 and kept documenting for the rest of her career, Katharine could do as well at mathematics as a man and still not receive equal recognition or opportunities.

Night and Day shows that women need to acquire both more education and better chances of using it: in on-going research in mathematics, such as Katharine dreams of, or in social criticism and reform, as Mary prefers. An enormous amount of women's longing in this novel flows toward work. Although Mary loves Ralph (or, as she ruefully suspects, loves the "haze" of sexuality around him) and feels pain at his loss, she discovers "another love," love of work, which is not so much compensatory as additive (447, 451). This other goal, "a point distant as a low star upon the horizon," recalls Katharine's fascination with astronomy (451). The image of work as a star registers both the remoteness of such freedom for women and the similarity of the longing which unites the two women. When Katharine looks up at Mary's apartment, she sees that "the light was not moved. It signaled to her across the dark street; it was a sign of triumph shining there for ever, not to be extinguished this side of the grave" (505). Such emphatic language declares a passion for work that neither woman will give up.

Thus, when Katharine feels "secure" of all that meant anything to her, "figures, love, truth," the mathematical figures come first in the list, needing to be guarded because they had so often been denied to women (502). Then, as a desire second to her work with numbers, she needs "love," including intellectual, emotional, and sexual exchanges. Although Katharine's dislike of marriage sometimes is mistaken for rejection of a sexual relationship with Ralph (Leonardi 154), she expresses to Ralph her desire not only to "see each other" but also to "stay together. It's only marriage that's out of the question" (472). She similarly informs her mother that the couple want to "live together without being married" (482). The older woman reacts with horror to this confidence: "And you won't think those ugly thoughts again, will you, Katharine?" (484). Significantly, Mrs. Hilbery judges mathematics and cohabitation equally "ugly."

Critics often have sainted Mrs. Hilbery as "the magician-fool who . . . offers her renewing vision . . . , guiding and encouraging the chosen couple in their initiatory confrontation with the old order as represented by Katharine's father" (Little, *Comedy* 35). Marcus similarly elevates Mrs. Hilbery as a force bringing "order out of chaos": "Katharine is blessed and helped by her mother" (*Patriarchy* 25, 29). On the contrary, Mrs. Hilbery, though well-meaning, endorses patriarchy and obstructs Katharine's search for a new order. If Katharine were not engaged to Ralph but still walking with him—let alone sleeping with him—then, in the eyes of her conventional mother as much as in those of her blustering father, "Civilization" would be "overthrown" (477). Despite her refusal to debate her parents, Katharine covertly would like to overthrow many of the "civilized" expectations for women.[1]

Another radical proposal alluded to in *Night and Day,* in addition to meaningful work for women and copulation outside marriage, is the expression of affection and physical desire in multiple directions (cf. Radin 73 for similar proposals in the draft of *The Years*). Whereas the traditional romance plot recognizes only one "right" partner, a person of the opposite sex, this novel hints at many forms of love—some without sexual exchange, some heterosexual with many partners, some with partners of the same sex. When Ralph weeps outside Mary's house and Katharine weeps as William is accusing himself of selfishness, both express strong feelings for persons other than those with whom they are supposedly paired (506, 497). To explain that Ralph does not "really love" Mary or that Katharine does not "really love" William is putting too fine a point on feelings that remain intense and valuable. In fact, Ralph might have been physically drawn to Mary as much as to Katharine, had his training not taught him to dissociate affection and intellect from passion. His lively conversations with Mary derive their stimulation in part from the intellectual subject matter and in part from fondness and "muscularity"— perhaps indicating some physical bond between them (219).

For Ralph to accept Mary in physical terms, however, she would have to assume the place of ivy twining around his directing elm, as Milton says of Eve, alluding to a classical tradition depicting women as pliant and dependent (Sammons 117). Woolf was reading *Paradise Lost* in 1918: "I scarcely feel that Milton lived or knew men and women; except for the peevish personalities about marriage and the women's duties. He was the first of the masculinists" (*Diary* 1: 193). Although Mary Datchet, following Eve, might bestow trust on Ralph as she winds "her ivy spray round her ash-plant," she soon realizes that she cannot abnegate her own will and abase herself before him (226). To indicate her determination to find a new independence for women, despite some lingering "sentimental" attachment to the old model of ivy twining, "she picked two leaves from the ivy and put them in her pocket before she disencumbered her stick of the rest of it" (226, 232). Although Katharine does not want to be clinging ivy or "ornamental sheath" (18) any more than her friend does, the former's habitual silence, in contrast to Mary's outspokenness, enables Ralph to crystallize passion around the appearance of Katharine's greater subservience.

In addition to presenting the possibility of an intellectual, emotional, and physical relationship between Mary and Ralph (which he does not recognize), the novel portrays strong feeling and perhaps sexual desire between women (Marcus, *Patriarchy* 35). When Mary, despite her own love for Ralph, decides to tell Katharine of his preference for Katharine, she exhibits much generosity. Moreover, the two women experience a physical togetherness as Mary silently fingers the fur on her friend's skirt, feeling "bereft" yet "beloved" (278). Similarly, Katharine generously gives Cassandra, William's new fiancée, a ring. Whereas traditionally a man bestows a ring on a woman as a step in their courtship, here Woolf subversively lets a woman offer the token to another woman (495). Thus the book tacitly endorses forms of relationship other than the traditional heterosexual couple: affection without sexuality, bisexuality, and what today would be called homosexuality (in Woolf's day, buggery and sapphism).

Woolf may avoid these terms, as Ellen Rosenman persuasively argues, not out of prudery but because the few available labels still carried unacceptable connotations, such as "mannishness" and "perversion" in lesbianism ("Sexual Identity" 643, 649). Instead, Woolf lets concrete scenes like the presentation of a ring point the way toward wide-ranging experimentation in human relationships. As she defiantly asserts in *A Room of One's Own*, "if an explorer should come back and bring word of other sexes looking through the branches of other trees at other skies, nothing would be of greater service to humanity" (92). Although this image does draw somewhat on the common European assumption that "primitives" were "sexually volatile" (Torgovnick 99), Woolf casts her sympathies and identifications with the non-European people looking through the branches. When she sardonically predicts that, along with the "service to humanity," "we should have the immense pleasure into the bargain of watching Professor X rush for his measuring-rods to prove himself 'superior'" (*Room of Own* 92), she further expresses her solidarity with the unsuspected and certainly not inferior races/sexes.

Katharine's gift of the ring signals not only an exchange between women but also an attempt to escape from her high class. At times Ralph resents her rubies because they advertise her class, which he claims to hate (332). Yet he really wishes not to abolish special privileges but to gain them for himself, as we see when he advises her to let him keep her ring (423). Katharine, who has slipped off the rubies during this conversation, at least wants to divest herself of class determinants, although no doubt she will remain affected by them. Ralph, in contrast, wants to possess private prerogatives of his own—rings, gilt volumes of Dante, India, and a Katharine exclusively devoted to him (95).

If Ralph, who hopes "to dominate her, to possess her," does not tolerate spaces in Katharine's mind where he is "unrepresented" (489), so that she can pursue mathematical research and maintain other friendships, then he will be duplicating a division of labor that Mrs. Hilbery sanctions and Katharine rejects. In an evocation of the past that embarrasses her daughter, Mrs. Hilbery tries to convince her: "What is nobler . . . than to be a woman to whom every one turns, in sorrow or difficulty? How have the young women of your generation improved upon that, Katharine? I can see them now, sweeping over the lawns at Melbury House, in their flounces and furbelows, so calm and stately and imperial (and the monkey and the little black dwarf following behind), as if nothing mattered in the world but to be beautiful and kind" (116). Mrs. Hilbery accepts the lower status of both blacks and women. Although she does not mention the bedrooms beyond the lawns, her description resembles nineteenth-century paintings in which blacks appear in the background as signs of sexualized females (Gilman 240). Or, as Mary suspects, women are cast as "monsters couchant." Drawing on an even earlier artistic tradition, Mrs. Hilbery pictures both blacks and women as childlike dependents kept on leashes. Indeed, in a painting from 1775, after Clive's victories had made the British into rulers of Bengal, an Indian servant is depicted as "somewhere between the stature of the officer and that of his pet dog" (Moorhouse 47). The deferential Bengali artist, apparently trying to please the East India Company employees who commissioned such paintings, thus makes the adult Indian resemble a child: the dwarf to whom Mrs. Hilbery implicitly compares all colonized people.

Mrs. Hilbery's perfect woman, having nothing to do but look beautiful and listen to others' recitations of woe, corresponds to the flattering Angel in the House, the old-fashioned ideal whose destruction Woolf openly advocated in a 1931 speech: "Whenever I felt the shadow of her wings or the radiance of her halo upon the page I took up the inkpot and flung it at her" (*Pargiters* xxxii). Mild-mannered Katharine throws no inkpots. She does, however, try to "interrupt" her mother's distasteful "discourse" about angelic furbelows and subservient dwarves (116). And, as we saw before, she notices the contradiction between "kind" and "imperial" when she becomes "angry" at the mention of an Indian servant (115–16).

If middle-class marriage requires that women renounce meaningful work and other loves, as it encourages men to dominate others, then Katharine and Ralph's eventual engagement appears to be a disappointing capitulation to convention (500). Yet the novel ends on a subversive note. After the engagement, one might expect wedding bells and assurances that the spouses will live "happily ever after." Instead, the last lines record, "Good night . . . Good night" (508). The couple's parting is not ominous, however, as they need times apart. If Katharine does not utter temporary good-byes to Ralph, how can she solve mathematical problems? When can she sit with Mary, or visit William? Ralph too needs privacy to work on his history of the English village, to engage in "muscular" conversations with Mary, and to go for late-night walks with William. To be totally consonant with its premises, the plot should climax with Katharine's admission to Cambridge as a researcher in astronomy, perhaps sleeping with Ralph on weekends; at the end, the black dwarves should have been increased to full size and allowed to take their places on the faculty. In 1919, however, *Night and Day* cannot conclude but only pause, with women still rarities at Oxbridge and the colonies still on leashes, despite a few stirrings of protest, including Woolf's.

To the Lighthouse

Apparently, in *To the Lighthouse* (1927), nothing happens. Mrs. Ramsay knits part of a reddish-brown, hairy stocking. Lily moves a salt cellar across a tablecloth. Just as Woolf omits any grand events, she rigorously holds the conversation to platitudes: "Yes, of course, if it's fine. . . . But . . . it won't be fine" (9–10). She thus parodies two staples of the nineteenth-century novel, plot and dialogue, at the same time that she is satirizing society. Although a mood of mourning and loss cuts through the book, this satire ensures that *To the Lighthouse* achieves at points a rollicking humor, while simultaneously suggesting which aspects of society have to change.

In fact, this novel in which "nothing" happens casually overturns four pillars of English society. First, the book belittles the British Empire, established on an untenable claim of superiority. Second, like *The Voyage Out* and *Night and Day*, *To the Lighthouse* criticizes the institution of marriage as it existed in the nineteenth and early twentieth centuries. Third, the book questions the class system, built on private property. And, finally, it rejects the militarism that props up the Empire.

Moreover, *To the Lighthouse* exposes intricate interrelationships among colonialism, gender relations, property, and the use of force, by describing each metaphorically in terms of the others. Important juxtapositions compare acquiring a wife to stocking up on goods or staking claim to a colony. The book further lampoons "scientific" (i.e., commercial) expeditions and "heroic" (i.e., barbaric) battles by describing these public activities in terms of the most trivial childhood games in the private house.

One of the most interesting correspondences pointed out—and then mocked—in *To the Lighthouse* is the affinity between the Victorian ideal of saintly womanhood and that of glorious Empire. The novel indicates such a link by posing Mrs. Ramsay in two "tableaux," once as the Madonna and once as Queen Victoria. In her Madonna role, Mrs. Ramsay sits with her young son James, "outlined absurdly by the gilt frame" of an "authenticated masterpiece by Michael Angelo" (48). Meanwhile, a shadowy father paces up and down the terrace, just outside the picture. World views from the Christian to the Freudian have privileged a trio of mother, son, and spiritual or rational father. To worship the Madonna, however, is to omit daughters and single women (Rosenman 99) and, to a lesser extent, single men (the absent father may recoup the freedoms of bachelorhood).[2] Although Lily, in painting this scene from the lawn, acknowledges the familiar icon, she is trying to frame human relationships in a new way. Mr. Bankes at first is shocked that Lily would reduce "Mother and child," those "objects of universal veneration," to a "triangular purple shape" (81). By comically refusing to represent a famous beauty, Lily scores a small revenge. At the same time, she seriously prepares for new social definitions. Mrs. Ramsay, however, cannot credit either Lily's talent or the social revisions implied in her painting (29). She cannot take seriously Lily's new sketch of a life in which creative work and not a family might come first for a woman.

To the Lighthouse adds a companion piece for this tableau of the Madonna when Mrs. Ramsay ends a walk with Charles Tansley by stationing herself "quite motionless for a moment against a picture of Queen Victoria wearing the blue ribbon of the Garter" (25). Knights of the Garter pay homage to ladies, whose tokens knights wear. Mrs. Ramsay endorses both her apotheoses, as Madonna and as Victoria. To use Louis Althusser's terms, she has accepted the way her society "interpellates" her as "subject" (170–71). That is, her society calls her and all middle-class women both saint (whether Madonna or Angel in the House) and inspirer of Empire. Mrs. Ramsay responds to the call because men have been taught to pay homage to these myths, and she hears their allegiance to the myths as personal praise. This ideology is in turn useful to the state because it allows the colonizers to mask radical impoliteness to the colonized—"Break their teeth, O God, in their mouths," as the missionary in *The Voyage Out* says (227)—by means of politeness to ladies. The Angel in the House thus neutralizes any "deviltry" involved in the acquisition of territory.

A few years after writing *To the Lighthouse*, Woolf explicitly links the Angel in the House with the supposedly "civilizing" imperial presence of England. In a remarkable speech to the London/National Society for Women's Service on January 21, 1931, she first describes how the Angel learned to be self-sacrificing, soothing, asexual, and unthinking. She then analyzes the origin of this ideological Angel:

> Now this creature—it was one of her most annoying characteristics—never had any real existence. She had—what is much more difficult to deal with—an ideal existence, a fictitious existence. She was a dream, a phantom—a kind of mirage like the pools and the palm trees which nature places in the desert to lure the caravan across. The Angel in the house was the ideal of womanhood created by the imaginations of men and women at a certain stage of their pilgrimage to lure them across a very dusty stretch <of the journey>. They agreed to accept this ideal, because for reasons I cannot now go into—they have to do with the British Empire, our colonies, Queen Victoria, Lord Tennyson, the growth of the middle class and so on—[*reality*] <a real relationship> between men and women was then unattainable. (*Pargiters* xxx)

This speech, edited by about a third, was published after Woolf's death as "Professions for Women" in *The Death of the Moth* and again in *Collected Essays* (2: 284–89). The suggestive passage about the Angel, the middle class, and the Empire does not appear in the essay as printed by Leonard. (For reasons why Tennyson might appear in the quotation, see the discussion of *Freshwater*.) Although in the speech Woolf only outlines the idea, she axiomatically associates the middle class with the chastity assigned to the Angel. This connection might be explained by the growing concern of the middle class with legitimate male heirs. As Bridget Hill reports, the virginity of brides became more important toward the end of the eighteenth century, when more people entered the bourgeoisie, for "It was on women's chastity, [Samuel] Johnson claimed, that 'all the property in the world depends'" (180).

For the further connection of Angel with Empire, Woolf could have learned from her grandfather James Stephen just how explicitly the political thinking of the nineteenth century linked colonies and women. In 1850, while he was advocating greater autonomy for Canada, James Stephen insisted that England "ought never to give up" any of the other colonies. They were "wretched burdens to this country, which in an evil hour we assumed, but which we have no right to lay down again. We emancipate our grown-up sons, but keep our unmarried daughters, and our children who may chance to be ricketty, in domestic bonds. The analogy is a very close one" (quoted in Marcus, *Patriarchy* 83). Just as unmarried daughters are equated with invalids, unable to take care of themselves, the people of the colonies are seen as eternal children, unable to govern themselves. Because Woolf first realized and chafed at her own constricted situation as one of the "daughters of educated men" (*Three Guineas* 4), she came to recognize and sympathize with the oppression of the colonies.

Whereas Woolf says she "cannot now go into" the affinity between patriarchal family and paternalistic imperial state in her speech of 1931, in *To the Lighthouse* Woolf does examine this kinship, in a ludicrous scene in which a dinner party is breaking up. Mrs. Ramsay hears her husband reciting, "Come out and climb the garden path, Luriana Lurilee. / The China rose is all abloom and buzzing with the yellow bee" (166). Not listening to the words, she settles into the reverential atmosphere: "The sudden bursts of laughter and then one voice (Minta's) speaking alone, reminded her of men and boys crying out the Latin words of a service in some Roman Catholic cathedral" (166). At first reading, the cathedral hush might seem to lend beauty to the scene, hallowing the secular. However, when one becomes aware of Woolf's resentment of the patriarchal church, the predominance of men's and boys' voices appears more ominous. In *Three Guineas*, Woolf bluntly describes St. Paul as "the virile or dominant type, so familiar at present in Germany, for whose gratification a subject race or sex is essential" (167). In fact, she railed against the Christian church and its clergy throughout her career (Schlack 61–62). In *To the Lighthouse,* the cathedral serves only to surround and co-opt Minta's voice. The dinner party after Minta's engagement is the ceremony to consecrate the new Madonna, the new Angel in the House.

As Mrs. Ramsay makes sure that other women will take her place in the Victorian family, the scene also reaffirms the Angel's function in the public world of the Empire. While Mrs. Ramsay nods her approval of this induction of Minta into the vocation of serving men, Mr. Carmichael rises to pay homage to the old "queen." Although he has been to India, he is not one of the chivalrous knights whom Mrs. Ramsay pictures—polite to ladies and fierce to enemies—but rather is a murmuring mound usually "basking with his yellow cat's eyes ajar" (19). Mrs. Ramsay does not note that the opium which dyes his mustache yellow must have been introduced to him during his stay in India; Great Britain even fought the Opium War (1839–42) to force China to accept the opium that British merchants acquired in India (Leonard Woolf, *Empire and Commerce* 15 and *Imperialism* 78; Snyder 6). In his habitual somnolence, Carmichael reverses the stereotypes that assigned passivity to Asians and activity—entrepreneurial and military—to Europeans. Thomas Babington Macaulay, for example, expects energy of Englishmen and femininity and laziness of Bengalis, even concluding incongruously that such peaceful (and therefore civilized?) Indians are "thoroughly fitted by nature and by habit for a foreign yoke" (47). Mrs. Ramsay accepts this dichotomization into strong European and weak Asian when she assumes that only Englishmen properly "negotiated treaties, ruled India, controlled finance" (13). While the Angel in the House continues to back the Empire, Mr. Carmichael has "gone native" and adopted the repose supposedly characteristic of the East.

Normally Mr. Carmichael, the unchivalrous knight, does not bow to Mrs. Ramsay as the others do, but here at the dinner party he plays along with her expectations. As a preposterous priest, cavorting with his table napkin "so that it looked like a long white robe" (167), he antiphonally answers Mr. Ramsay's recitation: "To see the Kings go riding by / Over lawn and daisy lea / With their palm leaves and cedar sheaves, Luriana, Lurilee" (167). Elizabeth Boyd says that these lines come from a poem by Charles Elton (380). Leonard Woolf recalled that, when he moved to Ceylon, "over and over . . . my surroundings would suddenly remind me of that verse in Elton's poem" about "Luriana" and the "changing leaves" (*Growing* 27). Although he wrote *Growing* at the end of his life, he may have reported to Virginia these lines that remained for him a refrain of his days as a colonial administrator. To Mrs. Ramsay, the words are just "music," and she does not care to "know what they meant" (166). Actually, the topic is conquest. The kings, mentioned right after the Roman Catholic cathedral, go riding by with their "palm leaves and cedar sheaves," suggesting Jerusalem, Lebanon, a vague hint of the Crusades. If the two stanzas are put side by side, they say that "the China rose is all abloom and buzzing with the yellow bee . . . To see the Kings go riding by" (166–67). That the kings are riding seems to make the flowers bloom, to uphold the natural world, because it has come to seem "natural" to conquer. The world from China to India to Palestine must hop for those kings and foreign conquerors.

Although the kings (if not such functionaries as Carmichael) are no doubt growing rich from the cedar and other goods, their palm leaves suggest that officially they ride for Palm Sunday religion. In addition, imperial knights justify their exploits as deeds done in honor of a lady, the Luriana Lurilee of the poem. Her double-barreled name, however, makes her silly. Nevertheless, Mrs. Ramsay accepts that the kings should go out on quests because of her, receiving Mr. Carmichael's bow with "relief and gratitude" (167). Because her society defines her only as an inspiring beauty, she is not so much succumbing to "conceit" as grasping the only validation available.

Mrs. Ramsay, needing men's adoration, internalizes the patriarchal view of herself. Mrs. Ramsay's daughters, on the other hand, pursue "a mute questioning of deference and chivalry, of the Bank of England and the Indian Empire" (14). The silently rebellious daughters also entertain "infidel ideas" about "not always taking care of some man" (14).

Woolf, too, in this novel questions the Indian Empire, the Bank of England, and the current rules governing gender relations—an enormously subversive program.

Of Woolf's targets in *To the Lighthouse,* her dissatisfaction with the institution of marriage probably is best known (Lilienfeld). Woolf criticizes marriage and the relations between men and women leading to it on a number of counts. First, marriage divides labor and assigns traits in dangerous ways. When society expects child-rearing always of women and assigns intellectual labor or business to men, then caring and emotion are left to women and reason to men. Although brawn becomes less important in modern public life, an archaic rhetoric still allocates physical strength as well as courage to men, frailty and timidity to women. A vestigial chivalry asks men to save women from dangers and women to praise and inspire men's strength and intellect. Thus Lily Briscoe knows that Charles Tansley is supposed to save her, if "the Tube were to burst into flames," while she is supposed to "go to the help of the young man opposite so that he may expose and relieve the thigh bones, the ribs, of his vanity, of his urgent desire to assert himself . . . . But how would it be, she thought, if neither of us did either of these things?" (137). The burning Tube burlesques the medieval dragon, not to mention Tansley's sexuality. Under Mrs. Ramsay's influence, Lily succumbs and flatters Tansley: "but what haven't I [Lily] paid to get it for you? She [Lily] had not been sincere" (139).

A second trouble with this prescribed insincerity and these dichotomized attributes, which artificially set reason against feeling, is that such a system keeps both women and men eternally children. They cannot treat each other as equal adults. Women learn to present themselves as naive girls: "afterwards she [Minta] got on perfectly, and made herself out even more ignorant than she was, because he liked telling her she was a fool" (148). Similarly, Mr. Ramsay has to convince himself that his wife does not understand what she reads in order to perceive her as beautiful (182). No wonder that more is lost than a grandmother's brooch on the evening Minta Doyle becomes engaged to Paul Rayley: "yet Nancy felt, it might be true that [Minta] minded losing her brooch, but she wasn't crying only for that" (117). Whereas the Ramsays' daugh-

ter Nancy cannot articulate the ways in which both loss of independence and loss of any claim to adult reasoning power follow upon losing the clasp that holds one's clothes together, the scene as a whole
graphically introduces the subject of property rights, whose arrangement in marriage made women more dependent. When Paul and Andrew, hunting for the brooch before the tide comes in, decide to "plant
Rayley's stick where they had sat" (117), that phallic marker stakes out
territory. Like colonizers planting their flagpole, the two young men
have learned to define virility as ownership. Women, like colonized
peoples, are looked upon either as children or as property—the mute,
passive earth itself.

Another scene that shows men defining virility as ownership occurs when Paul communicates his engagement to Mrs. Ramsay: "He
was saying to her as he showed her the watch, 'I've done it, Mrs. Ramsay. I
owe it all to you.' And seeing the gold watch lying in his hand, Mrs.
Ramsay felt, How extraordinarily lucky Minta is! She is marrying a
man who has a gold watch in a wash-leather bag!" (175). Mrs. Ramsay
even reports the engagement to her husband in these same absurd, ma-
terialistic terms: "'How nice it would be to marry a man with a wash-
leather bag for his watch,' she said, for that was the sort of joke they
had together" (183). The "joke" sounds faintly obscene, the penis in
the vagina paralleled and outdone by the gold in the bag. A few lines
later, Mr. Ramsay is "swinging the compass on his watch-chain to and
fro"; for all the attractive intimacy of this older couple, "she could feel
his mind like a raised hand shadowing her mind" (184). The raised
hand suggests threat as much as protection. Thus, for both Paul Rayley
and Mr. Ramsay, the relationship of men to women becomes, through
training, a matter of possessiveness, status, control, and economic con-
venience.

When Woolf draws attention to Rayley's watch and Mr. Ramsay's
watch-chain as emblems of marital relations, she may allude to a passage in Charlotte Brontë's *Jane Eyre* in which Rochester laments that
Jane is escaping his grasp: "unfortunately I have neither my cigar-case,
nor my snuff-box. But listen—whisper—it is your time now, little tyrant, but it will be mine presently; and when once I have fairly seized

you, to have and to hold, I'll just—figuratively speaking—attach you to a chain like this (touching his watch-guard)" (273). Rochester is longing for a comforting "cigar-case" for a phallic "cigar." Yet he seems so uncertain that Jane would ever receive him of her own free will that he insists she give up her job as governess to become totally dependent on him. Jane, however, refuses to be financially and bodily attached to a "chain." The ending of the novel reinforces her resistance by once more bringing a watch into question. After his blinding and maiming, he has to transfer his watch to her: "Fasten it into your girdle, Janet, and keep it henceforward" (451). Whereas Rochester had wanted Jane's willpower and her source of funds to disappear into his pocket, by the end of the book she controls her own income and marries on her own terms. (Of course, because Jane's legacy comes from a colonizing relative, her freedom unfortunately implies somebody else's unfreedom.) In 1916, in an essay on *"Jane Eyre* and *Wuthering Heights,"* Woolf referred to "the genius, the vehemence, the indignation of Charlotte Brontë" (*Collected Essays* 1: 186). Woolf seems to have borrowed Bronte's watch from *Jane Eyre* to express, in *To the Lighthouse,* her own indignation at the transfer of women's property to men, the exchange of women *as* property, and the assumption that women cannot read scientific instruments or direct their own lives.

Because of such attitudes, fixed in nineteenth-century and early twentieth-century marriage, Lily begins to suspect "love." In the Grimms' fairy tale read by Mrs. Ramsay to her son, the Flounder asks, "Well, what does she want then?" (87). Like baffled men from the quester in the Wife of Bath's tale to Freud, the Flounder asks a crucial question about women. Lily knows, in direct answer to the Flounder's wording, what women *do not* want: "if you asked nine people out of ten they would say they wanted nothing but this—love; while the women, judging from her own experience, would all the time be feeling, This is not what we want; there is nothing more tedious, puerile, and inhumane than this; yet it is also beautiful and necessary. . . . So she listened again to what they were saying in case they should throw any light upon the question of love. 'Then,' said Mr. Bankes, 'there is that liquid the English call coffee'" (155). The leaps in the conversation comically reduce a romantic love potion to bad coffee. Yet when Lily thinks that women do not want "love," she is not denigrating sexuality, merely the only respectable form of it in her day, marriage. The "reddish light" of physical attraction that she feels from Paul Rayley "intoxicated her," and "for a glory it surpassed everything in her experience" (261–62). Nevertheless, Lily realizes that marriage requires women to make other sacrifices—of income, independence, sincerity—so that the fire "fed on the treasure of the house, greedily" (261). Although on some days Lily longs for the domestic scene (32), she has to keep mocking physical lures to remind herself that sexuality, glorious as it is, does not outweigh such costs as having to pretend to be all feeling and no mind: "Time after time the same thrill had passed between them—obviously it had, Lily thought, smoothing a way for her ants" (295). The toilsome ants in the sentence miniaturize Mr. and Mrs. Ramsay's married love to the most mechanized socialization.

In fact, marriage seems to have tamed sexuality itself into a tourist landscape of uniformity for all. Nancy, for example, refuses to praise Minta's engagement "as if it were Constantinople seen through a mist, and then, however heavy-eyed one might be, one must needs ask, 'Is that Santa Sofia?' 'Is that the Golden Horn?'" (112). Ten years before *To the Lighthouse,* Leonard Woolf, in *The Future of Constantinople,* had focused on the rivalry for that city as typical of the dangerous competition among imperial powers. In Virginia Woolf's allusion to "Constantinople seen through a mist," both colonial acquisitions and fiancées become delusive economic plums. The phrase "Golden Horn" seems to afford a glow to the phallic horn, yet the accompanying "Santa Sofia" unpleasantly puts women on pedestals as asexual beings, as Saint Wisdom or Angel in the House. Thus Nancy finds the matrimonial prospect tedious despite its attractiveness.

Similarly, when Mr. Bankes occasionally envies his married friends, his language quickly trivializes a landscape all too well known: "it would have been pleasant if Cam had stuck a flower in his coat or clambered over his shoulder, to look at a picture of Vesuvius in eruption" (37). Although Woolf sometimes has been accused of shying away from any mention of the bedroom (Lilienfeld 169n), her leaping fires, golden horns, and erupting Vesuvius are as blatant as D. H. Lawrence's sun rays, icicles, and "columns of blood," for example, in *The Woman Who Rode Away* (89) and *The Plumed Serpent* (446). But where Lawrence thinks that the phallic answer is enough, Woolf often caricatures the images. She does so not because she cannot recognize a "glory" in sexuality but because she detects a desire to keep those sainted Sofias both mute and inactive—the same hostility that lets Lawrence imagine a flint blade killing the woman just as the phallic ray of the sun penetrates the cave (Lawrence, *Woman* 89).

Men appear to benefit from the Victorian system, because they can claim to be smarter and stronger and altogether more golden. Actually, men also lose a great deal in such constructions of gender. The sentimental picture that Mr. Ramsay conjures up of men working in the public world and women in the private house has a corollary of sacrifice for men, too: "He liked that men should labour and sweat on the windy beach at night; pitting muscle and brain against the waves and the wind; he liked men to work like that, and women to keep house, and sit beside sleeping children indoors, while men were drowned, out there in a storm" (245). In a strategy typical of *To the Lighthouse*, "clunker" words ridicule the surrounding claims. Thus the phrase "while men were drowned" falls out of the sentence, tearing the habitual assumptions which do not even let Mr. Ramsay notice that he "liked" men to drown.

If the "drowning" of Minta's brooch is a sign that she will lose a part of herself when she becomes Mrs. Rayley, men metaphorically "drown" by approaching women not as intellectual partners but as nurturers only. Men give up equal adulthood when they seek women as pillows, as much as the women remain children when they pretend to be ignorant. Thus Mrs. Ramsay treats Tansley as a boy needing her "protection" (13). Her husband uses her to bolster his self-confidence, "like a child who drops off satisfied" (60). Normally, the radical sacrifice that Mr. Ramsay implies for men is only figurative. Nevertheless, to be manly, his son Andrew must become a soldier and be blown up in France.

Mr. Ramsay, safe at home, might like to think of his intellectual endeavor "to reach R" as equivalent to battling enemies or leading a Polar expedition in a storm, but really he can forego dying in the snow to slip indoors for whisky and wifely sympathy (54–57). On one level, Woolf's satire of this imaginary storm pokes fun at Mr. Ramsay personally, for inflating philosophical struggles on the lawn to the level of ordeals at the North Pole. On another level, his grandiose comparisons, of the mind's progression through presumed universals such as Q and R to explorers' progress through the wilderness, call into question a whole society. For his dreams show that the acquisition of "pure" knowledge often shades into the acquisition of colonies, just as Rayley's planting a stick relates taking a wife to taking a territory. Mr. Ramsay's explorers may claim to be exerting themselves merely in order to amass the "neutral" information contained in an encyclopedia: geographical, botanical, ethnographic, mineralogical. However, the expeditions to the Poles, to the source of the Nile, to find a Northwest Passage, did, as a matter of fact, lead to the acquisition of land. In *Empire and Commerce in Africa*, Leonard Woolf reports that, according to French historians, Britain in the 1880s encouraged Italy "to send 'scientific' and 'commercial' expeditions into the Harrar," in North Africa, when all the time Britain was scheming to use Italy against the Sudan and to let Abyssinia defeat Italy, leaving the spoils to Britain (159; cf. 187). Although Leonard at first labels such a "Machiavellian" British plan "singularly un-English," he has to admit that "many facts fit with a strange neatness into the French picture" (160). In other words, the great scientific expeditions which Mr. Ramsay admires are likely to precede colonization. After all, Mr. Ramsay casts himself not only as the leader of a "desolate expedition across the icy solitudes of the Polar region," but also as the captain of a ship's company, suggesting commerce, and as a soldier, implying war (54). Woolf spoofs Mr. Ramsay's neediness as well as his favorite word *expedition* and all it implies about explorers' laying the groundwork for the creation of colonies. The planned trip to the lighthouse is described from the first page as "the expedition," reducing Mr. Ramsay's idea of a heroic endeavor to a ride in a sailboat. When Charles Tansley and Mrs. Ramsay are "making the great expedition," it turns out to be only a walk to the village (19).

To the Lighthouse continues to connect the artificial relations between men and women in the private house with power relations in
the public world. This walk undertaken by Mrs. Ramsay and Tansley
(18–25), for example, comically undercuts typical male-female relations, at the same time that it interrogates both the class system and
the Empire. This carefully crafted, farcical scene exposes the common
thread of prideful ownership that chokes romance, class relations, and
foreign affairs. First, Tansley's ridiculously lyrical language, tiresomely
repeated, twits his romantic attraction to Mrs. Ramsay; he sees "stars
in her eyes and veils in her hair . . . stars in her eyes and the wind in
her hair" (25). Nevertheless, the passage does not just affectionately
tease one young man for an impossible infatuation. It also seriously indicts this form of chivalric sexuality—all too possible in Tansley's
world—because its conventions reveal possessiveness: "[Mrs. Ramsay]
made him feel better pleased with himself than he had done yet, and
he would have liked, had they taken a cab, for example, to have paid
for it. As for her little bag, might he not carry that?" (20). Just as
Tansley covets the power that money would give him to direct and
dispose of others, he wants to display a beautiful woman as a status
object.

Tansley's desire for control is expressed tacitly but clearly in the
debate about carrying her bag. At first Mrs. Ramsay asserts that she
always carries it herself, and he claims to admire her for doing so. However, by the end of the scene, in a line repeated heavily like gates clang-
ing shut after ardent paragraphs about violets and lambs, "He took her
bag. . . . He had hold of her bag" (25). Moreover, Mrs. Ramsay acquiesces—to Tansley and to the whole social system. When a woman of
her generation marries, she relinquishes control of her bag: uterus, re-
production, autonomy, income.

That Tansley's desire to carry Mrs. Ramsay's bag in part signals a
wish for economic control appears from the fact that this desire is
voiced right after his fantasy about paying for the cab. Woolf notes
angrily in *Three Guineas* that the Married Women's Property Acts did
not begin to be enacted until 1870 (*Guineas* 156; Vicinus 3–28; Perkin
305). Yet even after the passage of these acts and the admission of

women to the professions in 1919, English women still were unlikely, as Woolf points out, to have much of an income to put in a bag. In the first place, obtaining the education to get a lucrative job remained difficult for a woman. Even if, with luck, she acquired the qualifying education, "aroma" might deny her employment: discrimination stemming from fear that she will be sexually distracting. If she should win a job despite these continuing obstacles, she might earn less than a man doing the same work. If she married and stayed at home with the children, no one would think of paying her a salary, as Woolf suggests the state ought to do (*Guineas* 110–11). And without an independent income, Woolf asks, how can one maintain an independent opinion? Tansley indeed does have hold of Mrs. Ramsay's opinion. Despite "unconscious anger" (Lilienfeld 154), she flatters him, by suggesting and even largely believing in "the greatness of man's intellect, even in its decay, the subjection of all wives . . . to their husband's labours" (20). Woolf epitomizes Tansley's prideful possessiveness toward women in the image of carrying a bag, just as she represents the engagement of Paul and Minta as the placing of a gold watch in a bag.

Not only would Tansley like to possess Mrs. Ramsay as an object symbolizing status, but also he desires that she reflect and praise him. During their walk, he imagines that she can "see him, gowned and hooded, walking in a procession" (20). Instead of looking at him, however, she is eyeing a circus poster. Whereas Tansley thinks he ought to be the center of attention, Mrs. Ramsay studies "fresh legs, hoops, horses" (21). To her, Tansley himself is a circus animal. More important, Mrs. Ramsay's distraction, in addition to making Tansley's private dreams appear ridiculous, hilariously and devastatingly reduces the entire public procession, all the intellectual and heroic deeds that the society values, to the level of "twenty performing seals" (21).

Tansley's "procession" in *To the Lighthouse* anticipates, in fact, a key word in *Three Guineas*, the procession in which professors, lawyers, generals, bankers, and government officials swagger together: the whole male file of professionals. In the first part of *Three Guineas*, Woolf argues that women must have access to the professions and the colleges, in order to gain the independent opinion that goes with the independent income. The second part of her argument, however, poses a serious question. What if the women pass through the colleges and the professions to emerge with the same dangerous traits these institutions foster in men: materialism, competitiveness, and pride at being a member of the "right" school, the "right" religion, the "right" country? Because Woolf condemns the greed, combativeness, and complacency that thrive in the professions, she finally has to ask these women whom she has been advising to work, "do we wish to join that procession, or don't we?" (*Guineas* 62).

Although Alex Zwerdling insists that *Three Guineas* cannot be read into Woolf's earlier work (33), the word "procession" appears throughout her career in connection with similar doubts. In *Jacob's Room*, the lawyer Jacob arrogantly expects the drum and trumpets of a great "procession" to sound especially for him (112–13). In *The Waves,* the shipping magnate Louis, with his love of force and conformity, wants to become "a figure in the procession, a spoke in the huge wheel that turning, at last erects me" (35). In both the latter books, however, as in *Three Guineas,* these bourgeois professionals are marching toward war. In *Jacob's Room,* a "procession with its banners" is still passing, all oblivious, as World War I is declared (172). In *The Waves*, when Jinny endorses the "triumphant procession" of middle-class occupations, the financiers and lawyers and mothers themselves become an "army of victory . . . crowned with laurel-leaves won in battle" (*Waves* 194). The procession of middle-class life inevitably turns out soldiers or backers of soldiers.

Although Mrs. Ramsay might recognize that Tansley is as silly as a performing seal, she does not notice twenty performing seals: the whole corrupting procession. She does not realize, as Woolf will say in "A Sketch of the Past" (1939–40), that all men who are trained in "the great patriarchal machine" must always be "jumping through hoops" like an "acrobat" (*Moments of Being* 152–53). Not really questioning, Mrs. Ramsay "let it uphold her and sustain her, this admirable fabric of the masculine intelligence . . . upholding the world, so that she could trust herself to it utterly, even shut her eyes . . . as a child staring up from its pillow winks at the myriad layers of the leaves of a tree. Then

she woke up. It was still being fabricated. William Bankes was praising the Waverley novels" (159). In a 1924 article, Woolf describes the
author of those Waverley novels, Sir Walter Scott, as an appealing, even
seductive writer; nevertheless, he is "a man who, if he had lived today,
would have been the upholder of all the most detestable institutions of
his country" ("Indiscretions" 76). Mrs. Ramsay wakes up only to the
limitations of individuals, not to flaws in the fabric, at which she remains winking.

However clearly or even "maliciously" Mrs. Ramsay senses the limitations of individual men such as Tansley ("Odious little man"), she
does not, then, question the whole social system (77, 26). In fact, when
she imagines her six-year-old son "all red and ermine on the Bench,"
she perpetuates it (10). She wants James to be a great man, pursuing
the goals she knows in her heart to be so much garden havoc (108).
Mrs. Ramsay might plan a law career for James, but the phrase "all red
and ermine on the Bench" undermines the career, by leaving ambiguous just what is red: the robes, the face flushed with pride, or even a
few trails of blood, which, as Woolf could have heard from her complacent relatives, had to be let to maintain the machinery of state. Jane
Marcus reports that Woolf's uncle, James Fitzjames Stephen, "made it
very clear that physical force was necessary to control the working class.
In *Liberty, Equality, Fraternity,* he declares that women and the working class must be kept down forcibly in order to show the colonies how
rebellion will be treated" (*Patriarchy* 90). When Mrs. Ramsay projects
a six-year-old James "all red and ermine," Woolf further diminishes
the judges by making them childlike.

Another sign that Mrs. Ramsay does not question the conduct of
the professions, the Empire, or gender relations occurs in an incident
with a pig's skull (171–73). The hired help know that the Ramsays
"had friends in eastern countries" who might have sent the skull, implying that it is the product of a safari in one of the colonies (211).
Cam cannot go to sleep because she is afraid of the shadows from the
"horns" (boar's tusks), whereas James screams if the servant covers up
the skull. Appropriately, James likes the trophy, because he is the one
who will be called on to ride off and be a hero: rule India, march in

wars, sit on a judicial bench, or even translate "Hindustanee" (20). Cam, on the other hand, could never become an administrator, soldier, judge, or scholar. Even if she could join such a profession—based, as many of them seem to be, on the hunt, with its violence and need for a "subject race or sex"—would she really want to (*Guineas* 167 and 62)? Because Cam has been thwarted in so many directions, she might well feel excluded and threatened when "there was always a shadow some-where . . . branching at her all over the room" (172). Mrs. Ramsay per-forms a feat of diplomacy by hiding the *memento mori* with her shawl, to convince Cam that the "horrid" skull has disappeared, while reassuring James that it is still there.[3] Nevertheless, at the same time that Woolf compliments this mother on skillfully satisfying the conflicting de-mands of her children, she shows Mrs. Ramsay maintaining the links between Angel in the House and queen in her colony—a colony that strews skulls and wasted lives in the first place: "for see, she said, the boar's skull was still there; they had not touched it; they had done just what he wanted; it was there quite unhurt. He made sure that the skull was still there under the shawl" (173). Mrs. Ramsay provides tempo-rary comfort but promises no real changes in the social system.

Mrs. Ramsay approves not only Empire and its judges, but also the class system that favors her. She reveals her aristocratic pretensions when she invokes her "very noble, if slightly mythical" Italian ancestry (17). She accepts praise for the "triumph" of her famous Boeuf en Daube, although the reader already knows that the dish is "Mildred's master-piece" (121). One servant, Mildred, spends three days preparing it, and another, Marthe, takes the cover off; all Mrs. Ramsay does is serve and "manage" to find skillful employees even on an island. Her self-satis-faction, basking in the tribute for work she has not done, makes Mrs. Ramsay less likable.

To the Lighthouse also pays attention to class conflicts in the pres-ence of Charles Tansley at the Ramsays' summer house. Sympathy goes to lower-class Tansley because he "had paid his own way since he was thirteen," "went without a greatcoat in winter," and "was educating his little sister" (21–22, 293). Yet the ways in which he wants to "im-prove" himself perhaps reveal why Woolf both chose to belong to the

Labour Party and called it "'that timid old sheep' because its politics were not radical enough for her" (Marcus, *Art and Anger* 163). Tansley, with a grandfather who was a fisherman and a father who became a somewhat more prosperous shopkeeping chemist, resents his lot and is full of ambition to continue his upwardly mobile progress. Although he boasts of economizing with the cheapest tobacco, he feels more class shame than class solidarity. What he really longs for is to "return hospitality" and pay for the cab (22, 20). In other words, he wants to become the *seigneur* displaying *largesse* to inferiors, rather than to abolish the ways of the *grand seigneur* altogether.

Indeed, Tansley and Mr. Bankes leave Mrs. Ramsay's dinner table "as if, Lily thought, seeing them go, and hearing a word or two about the policy of the Labour Party, they had gone up on to the bridge of the ship and were taking their bearings" (168–69). As soon as Tansley and Bankes imagine more power, they simply join the fleet that, at that time, was policing and bringing raw materials from the colonies. This is the same mercantile and military image that taints Mr. Ramsay's quest for "pure" knowledge (54). Tansley talks about "helping our own class" and eventually harangues people in a political speech (22, 292). Nevertheless, the same person who is "preaching brotherly love" has also been "making it his business to tell her women can't write, women can't paint" (292). As Beverly Ann Schlack observes, "The more patriarchal Charles changes, the more he remains the same" (71). Not only does the "timid old sheep," the Labour Party, fail to include more women and more programs for women; it also teaches the upwardly mobile classes the same qualities that Woolf warns against in *Three Guineas* (70): greed, disdain, and competitiveness, as well as a frantic pace of life that leaves no time for children, sunsets, and art.

Just as *To the Lighthouse* questions Empire, marriage, and the competitive class system, it also mocks the military ideal. All references to the Great War in "Time Passes" are indirect but grim:

. . . there came later in the summer ominous sounds like the measured blows of hammers dulled on felt, which, with their repeated shocks still further loosened the shawl and cracked the tea-cups. . . . [A shell exploded. Twenty or thirty young men were blown up in France, among them Andrew Ramsay, whose death, mercifully, was instantaneous.] . . . There was the silent appearance of an ashen-coloured ship . . . there was a purplish stain upon the bland surface of the sea as if something had boiled and bled, invisibly, beneath. (200–201)

Although the tone is impersonal, Woolf does not hush up pain. The sense of boiling, bleeding, and falling indicate anguish throughout the passage. Yet the text resolutely returns to focus on the "bland surface" of the sea and the cupboards. To say that a war cracked the teacups brilliantly punctures the pretensions of strong warriors, even while the author bitterly mourns their deaths and the loss of faith in harmony between humanity and nature (201). Moreover, the resemblance of this "purplish stain" (beside the "ashen-coloured ship" of war) to the "triangular purple shape" of the Madonna tradition reveals how dangerous traditional gender dichotomies have been all along (81). To be "masculine," men must "drown," as Mr. Ramsay says, or give their blood in the war (245). To be "feminine," women must bring new victims into the world, mourn, and deaden their own impulses (to reform the dairy industry, for example). When Mrs. Ramsay lets herself be framed and limited by an "authenticated masterpiece by Michael Angelo," the scene chillingly recalls that Michaelangelo's most famous Madonna is, after all, the *Pietà*: devastated mother and dead son (48).[4]

Teacups, as the only enemy visible to be cracked, imply that World War I accomplished nothing great. Similarly, the yard of the Ramsay house obliquely reflects imperial battles: "The autumn trees, ravaged as they are, take on the flash of tattered flags kindling in the gloom of cool cathedral caves where gold letters on marble pages describe death in battle and how bones bleach and burn far away in Indian sands" (192). Instead of parading the "heroes" who fought on the Indian sands, the passage points to the bleak trace of humans in bones. The bones themselves have been obscured by marble pages and cathedral flags commemorating them. The flags in turn recede behind the autumn leaves said to resemble them. This elaborate distancing refuses to glorify the scene of battle. Nevertheless, despite the distance, the bones appear starkly, along with the protest against the waste of life for imperial ends.

In the word *caves,* the passage further suggests that the churches are primitive rather than civilized. The flags tatter not only on the battlefield but also in the cathedral, much as the ideals for which the men fought are fraying. Both World War I and these imperial battles dominate "Time Passes" and give it its keen sense of loss. Here individual deaths, such as those of Mrs. Ramsay, Prue, and Andrew, fit as instances of a larger design. Nevertheless, the larger purposes for which they are supposed to have died—patriotism, honor, motherhood, or imperial mission—do not deserve this sacrifice. These fraying ideals belong to the old order that stunts lives in the drawing room and insures mass death on the field.

In addition to deflating war through the somber distancing of "Time Passes," Woolf also mocks it through hilarious satire. As Mr. Ramsay declaims war poetry, his son James cuts a picture from the catalogue of the Army and Navy stores. John MacKenzie reports that this chain store, founded in 1871, "inevitably used patriotic images of the two services and their flags as its trade mark" (26). When the little boy cuts out a picture of a refrigerator for "heavenly bliss," the incongruity may seem just mild humor about children (9). Yet some of the adults—Mr. Ramsay and Tennyson, whom Ramsay quotes—think that the real Army and Navy convey a kind of "bliss." Mr. Ramsay, for example, experiences a "delicious emotion" as he recites lines from "The Charge of the Light Brigade" (41), in which Tennyson claims that "All the world wonder'd" at the deaths during the Crimean War (*Poems of Tennyson* 275). An observer might well have wondered if the loss of half a million men was worth it, since the Crimean War (1853–56) "arose from the conflict of great powers in the Middle East and was more directly caused by Russian demands to exercise protection over the Orthodox subjects of the Ottoman sultan. Another major factor was the dispute between Russia and France over the privileges of the Russian Orthodox and Roman Catholic churches in the holy places in Palestine" ("Crimean"). Tennyson, however, does not mean *wonder* in the sense of doubt as to whether the war was worth fighting, but rather in the sense of admiration and the bliss of the patriotic spirit.

To the Lighthouse punctures that patriotic spirit in several ways. Mr.

Ramsay, on his lawn before the house guests, lugubriously quotes lines about soldiers "stormed at with shot and shell." Simultaneously, Mrs. Ramsay directs James's attention in the Army and Navy catalogue to the "picture of a pocket knife with six blades" (29). The juxtaposition reduces the technical weaponry of "shot and shell" to childish gadgetry. Similarly, when Mr. Ramsay refuses to be "routed"—not from any battle, really, but from his declamations about battles—Jasper has just "routed" a flock of starlings with his gun (41–42). Juxtaposing soldiers' maneuvers to James's and Jasper's games pokes fun at lines not quoted by Mr. Ramsay but part of the poem he loves—"Theirs not to reason why, / Theirs but to do and die"—reducing them to childishness (*Poems of Tennyson* 275). And at one point the narrator catches Mrs. Ramsay fervently honoring the past—"Never should she forget"—but then finishes her sentence, "forget Herbert killing a wasp with a teaspoon on the bank!" (132) The paltriness of the deed parodies the kind of remembering that Tennyson had enjoined for the "Noble six hundred": "When can their glory fade? . . . Honor the Light Brigade" (276). The passage does not jeer at Herbert for failing to graduate from teaspoons to shot and shell. Instead, it mocks the need for "glory" and refuses to bestow it.

The line from Tennyson's poem that Mr. Ramsay quotes most frequently—"Some one had blundered"—targets several satiric objects (31, 41, 48, 52). The words boomerang upon Mr. Ramsay himself, as he blunders into his guests and ridiculously compares his intellectual struggles to leading men in battle (29). For Tennyson, who got the wording about a "blunder" from *The Times*, the label accuses the officers: "He had been greatly depressed by the course of the Crimean campaign. 'My heart almost burst,' he wrote, 'with indignation at the accursed mismanagement of our noble little Army, the flower of our men'" (Charles Tennyson 288). Later historians agreed with that judgment: "The Crimean War was managed and commanded very poorly on both sides" ("Crimean"). Yet Tennyson is questioning only local mistakes, not the imperial impulses of all the great powers behind the war. His grandson reports that a chaplain in the Crimea requested and was sent two thousand copies of the poem, which inspired the soldiers to go back into battle; the chaplain wrote, "The poet can now make heroes, just as in the days of yore" (Charles Tennyson 288). Woolf, on the other hand, does not want to invite heroics and implies that the whole wish to dominate—whether one's wife, one's guests to be married off, starlings, or colonized people—is itself a gigantic blunder.

Although it may seem that "nothing happens" in *To the Lighthouse,* actually quite a lot is happening, as the book dismantles marriage, the class system based on private property, and the Empire supported by the military. Woolf satirizes these institutions through incongruous juxtapositions. She reduces "sacred" marriage to clutching a gold watch or appropriating Mrs. Ramsay's shopping bag. She depicts the "grand" procession of the professions as twenty performing seals. She parodies "heroic" war as shooting starlings, displaying fancy pocket-knives, or cracking teacups. Moreover, she consistently registers her doubts about the "eternal necessity" of a "slave class" (67), submissive wives, and cowed colonies. Thus Rayley's planting a stick, which signifies both taking a wife and staking claim to a colony, brings into question the possessiveness of both acts. Carmichael's mummery to "Luriana, Lurilee" undermines both the Angel flattering men in her house and Victoria inspiring her knights to conquer the earth.

In keeping with this method of deconstructing conventions through non sequiturs, Woolf expresses her desire for radical change only by having Lily displace—a salt cellar (128). Lifting a salt shaker over a pattern in the tablecloth reminds Lily that she should "move the tree rather more to the middle" in her painting (154). Woolf's extensive satire in *To the Lighthouse* similarly uproots social assumptions that had come to seem natural, but nevertheless unbalanced in favor of one group over another. Momentous and courageous as Lily's "vision" of altering life-styles might be (310), Woolf pictures a deliberately unheroic salt cellar, so attuned is she to the dangers of heroics and hierarchies: to the false superiority of men over women, upper class over lower, and race over race.

Freshwater

Often critics dismiss Woolf's play *Freshwater* (versions from 1923 and 1935) as mere fluff. Alex Zwerdling brushes it off, along with *Orlando*, as representative of "the shallower aspects of Bloomsbury 'sophistication' . . . it is a mistake to think of such books as typical of Woolf's achievement" (28). The combination of humor and seriousness in *Freshwater*, however, does exemplify Woolf's method, and the satirical subject matter of this shrewd and hilarious play targets two of the institutions that she questioned throughout her career, the British Empire and marriage. As in *The Voyage Out, Night and Day,* and *To the Lighthouse,* Woolf links these institutions, showing that some of the requirements of Victorian marriage served as ideological supports for the Empire. Although the play mocks the notion that art must provide moral uplift, "The Utmost for the Highest," it is itself mildly didactic, to the extent that it satirizes society (75).

Freshwater conveys its criticism through two plots, loosely based on the lives of real people of the same names: Mr. and Mrs. Cameron wait for their coffins so that they can go from Great Britain to India, and Ellen Terry leaves her husband, the painter G. F. Watts. The real-life Camerons, Woolf's great-aunt Julia and her uncle Charles, did ship coffins with them when they left for Ceylon in 1875. By transferring the Camerons' destination to the more archetypally imperial India and by making the wait for the coffins its central dramatic element, *Freshwater* announces blatantly enough that, as *Mrs. Dalloway* and *The Years* showed, the main baggage that the colonizers have to take with them to the colonies is death. One deathly quality at the heart of the Camerons' society is hypocrisy about why they are traveling. Although the Camerons claim spiritual and aesthetic motives, materialism underlies their trip, along with an attendant militarism. As further deathly ingredients in the Camerons' civilization, repression of sexuality and limiting gender roles stifle both men and women; ironically, these limitations accompany the Camerons as Britishers abroad, though they as individuals try to escape the molds.

Freshwater mocks Mr. Cameron's purported spirituality by contrasting his abstract goals with his dependence on a servant for small, concrete services like washing his hair. In the 1923 version of the play, Mr. Cameron laments that, because of the delay of the undertaker, "I shall never learn the true nature of virtue from the fasting philosophers of Baluchistan. I shall never solve the great problem, or answer the Eternal Question. I am a captive in the hands of Circumstance—[MARY *now tugs his beard.*] Ah! Oh! Oh!" (65–66). Like her husband who dreams of Eastern religions, Mrs. Cameron considers ethereal subjects to be the most appropriate for her photography: Galahad's quest for the Holy Grail, for example. Observing the hair-washing session, she exclaims comically, "What a composition! Truth supping at the fount of inspiration! The soul taking flight from the body! Upward, girl, look upward!" (66). She dismisses any practical matters as unwarranted interruptions: "At the last moment up comes word that Galahad [her servant dressed for the part] has to take the sheep to Yarmouth. It's market day. Sheep! Market day" (66).

Although both Camerons deny any crass interests, their prototypes did depend on markets for Ceylonese coffee, as Woolf reports in her introduction to a book of Julia Margaret Cameron's photographs. Business people as well as jurist and photographer, the Camerons went to Ceylon to check on their coffee plantation: "'Julia is slicing up Ceylon,' he would say, when she embarked on another adventure or extravagance" (Woolf, "Julia" 18). *Freshwater* sets the action at their home on the Isle of Wight, Dimbola, named after their estate in Ceylon—a reminder of the material basis of their existence. Thus, when the Camerons scorn all markets, their claims to highmindedness are quietly undermined by the fact, evident in their surroundings, that the entire Cameron life-style depends on markets.

One reason why ordinary business may mean taking death to the colonies is that military action becomes necessary to maintain the Empire. In the play, Tennyson foolishly praises the warrior's life, in and of itself, without considering causes for which a soldier might die. As *To the Lighthouse* undercuts Tennyson's enthusiasm for the Crimean War through Mr. Ramsay's recitation of "The Charge of the Light Brigade," *Freshwater* exposes the superficiality of the character named for Tennyson. Hearing of the Siege of Sevastopol distresses him only because his poetic ear cannot tolerate so many *s* sounds together, not because of the deaths involved (78). *Freshwater* further undermines Tennyson's praise for the navy by spoofing the soldiers, so eager to fight any "'em" on any pretext: "Hearts of oak are our ships. Hearts of oak are our men. We'll fight 'em and beat 'em again and again! No ant can eat through that" (45–46). Just as British plantations need the armed forces to install or preserve them, the Camerons need strong coffins to fend off ants from their bodies—and particularly from the copy of Tennyson's *Maud* with which Mrs. Cameron intends to be buried. Whereas Mrs. Cameron identifies the source of threat as the jungle, *Freshwater* conspicuously defines the enemy as a "White Ant" (68, 8). In the same way that the Camerons fail to notice the role of whites in a deadly imperial enterprise, this Tennyson misses the irony of his own contribution to destruction. To prove the stoutness of the oak coffins in keeping out ants, he himself bores a hole—all the better to let in ants (45). His glorification of heroism, without questioning causes, similarly multiplies death.

Maud (1856) forms a particularly appropriate backdrop for *Freshwater* because its narrator, if not Tennyson himself, voices opinions about war and conservative rule that Woolf regarded as dangerous. When the narrator in *Maud* thinks that war comfortingly "mixt my breath" with that of other patriots and longs for "one still strong man," whether "aristocrat, democrat, [or] autocrat" (288, 313), Woolf could have learned a prototype for Louis in *The Waves* or Evan in *Jacob's Room.* In each of these cases, Woolf shows up as fascist the male character's desire for unanimity, his nostalgia for "great men" past, and his invitation to autocrats in the present. Similarly, when *Maud*'s narrator declares that, by fighting the Crimean War, Britain will forget a "lust of gold" and devotion to "commerce" (312–13), Woolf would have noted the contradictions. Britain may have wanted to push back Russia's imperial advance in the Crimea, but only to further its own imperial aims, not to pursue notably "higher aims," as Maud's suitor believes (313). Throughout the nineteenth century, Britain was afraid—even paranoid—that Russia would move too far south and interfere with the British route to India—where "commerce" and the "lust of gold" certainly played some role. Woolf knew from Leonard Woolf's *The Future of Constantinople* that British material and imperial ambitions as much as Russian ones fueled wars, including both the Crimean War and World War I, so she had the benefit of hindsight to make Tennyson appear ridiculous declaiming *Maud* throughout *Freshwater*.

In addition to the glorification of war, the Camerons' society is characterized by two other deathly aspects unworthy of exportation abroad: the sexual repression that affects both men and women and the denial of fulfilling work that stifles women. Mr. Cameron and Tennyson imagine love without shame in the raspberry canes—a dream remote from the realities of their own households (73). When Ellen's husband Watts gives her white roses instead of kisses, she leaves to seek both passion and a career (70). Mrs. Cameron, at last spying someone handsome enough to pose as the quester Galahad, cannot believe that this person in trousers is Ellen, in the arms of a lover (79–80). No longer the object of Watts' quest, Ellen now quests on her own behalf. Making a similar point, the 1935 version of *Freshwater* has Ellen throw away her wedding ring, said to have been inherited from Beatrice and Laura (31). Ellen thus rejects the role played by Dante's and Petrarch's ideal women, confined to heaven, relegated to the task of inspiring men's art from afar, and denied work of their own. Indeed, when Woolf, in an essay, again considers Ellen Terry's life (1941), she transforms the leap of a horseman over a wall, which in *Freshwater* had signified the call of love, into the call of "her genius," some need in Ellen that urges her toward a career as actress, writer, and critic (*Collected Essays* 4: 70).

In addition to questioning marriage for its role in repressing both sexuality and women's work, Woolf further criticizes that institution for its economic function in supporting patriarchy and Empire. When Watts paints his wife as "Modesty crouching at the feet of Mammon," his allegory inadvertently exposes the economic basis of middle-class marriage (69). This economic basis is revealed in *To the Lighthouse* by Rayley's display of a gold watch at his engagement and in *The Voyage Out* by Rachel's uncomfortable financial dependence. Watts is further horrified to find that his trusty guidebook defines the Milky Way, which he has painted as a starry veil for Ellen, as a more earthy symbol of fertility. Here Woolf burlesques Watts's prudery, as well as his need for pat symbols. Denying any sexuality for Ellen, he repaints Modesty as Maternity, without any intervening intercourse. In his revised, still exploitative framing of women's lives, he enlists his wife in the cause of Empire. He now calls his picture "Mammon trampling upon Maternity, or the Prosperity of the British Empire being endangered" (77). Marriage not only ensures legitimate heirs to Mammon but also provides more boys to grow up and maintain the fleet; in Watts's relentless allegory, Maternity typifies "two million horse marines" (77).

Freshwater ends with a visit by Queen Victoria, just at the moment when the coffins finally arrive. In the play's 1935 version, Victoria means to refer to Albert's death but gets mixed up and labels the wedding an "ever to be lamented day," making matrimony itself lamentable (53). She thus pronounces a fitting conclusion to *The Voyage Out, Night and Day,* and *To the Lighthouse,* all of which castigate middle-class marriage for requiring the restriction of women's sexual expression and varied work (Rachel's music, Katharine's mathematics, Mrs. Ramsay's dairy reform, and Ellen's acting). Marriage in the era under consideration also lamentably either limits women's property or transforms wives into property, crouched at the feet of Mammon or staked out with Rayley's staff as mute territory.

In her role as Empress of India, Queen Victoria ushers in the coffins, providing an apt finale to Woolf's criticism of Empire as literally deadly, just as marriage is figuratively so. The river of imperial trade in *The Voyage Out* dominates the view, as well as the views of the characters who, in all four books, adopt the values of economic imperialism: competitiveness, acquisitiveness, need for inferiors (the Brazilian peasants of *The Voyage Out* and the "monster" women and "black dwarves" of *Night and Day*), and glorification of force. Thus, when Tennyson "grimly" pronounces beside Victoria that "the comedy is over" (84), Woolf punctures an imperialism that spreads only the "purplish stain" of blood (*Lighthouse* 201) and lets in a destructive White Ant (*Freshwater* 68).

3.
Securing the Circle:
The Education of
an Empire-Builder

Jacob's Room

Chapter 2 showed how Woolf criticizes as a tool of the British Empire
the institution of marriage in the nineteenth and early twentieth centuries. In *Jacob's Room* (1922) and *The Waves* (1931), she explores a
whole range of social institutions and life-styles which foster imperialism and, in turn, militarism. *Jacob's Room* traces these attitudes to the
Christian church, the stifling parochialism of a small town, the universities, and the class system, as well as gender relations. The novel also
exposes an ancient paradigm for modern heroics, the Ulysses quest (already scorned in *Night and Day* and *Mrs. Dalloway*), as a selfish drive
for profit. Investigating a similar range of institutions, *The Waves* examines the dangerous training given the characters in public schools,
universities, and middle-class work and leisure: Louis's international
finance, Susan's landowning, Bernard's business, and all the friends'
idealizations of lovers. In *Three Guineas,* Woolf labels the socially sanctioned traits that further war: competitiveness, materialism, and pride
in *my* school, *my* children, and *my* country, which are, *a priori,* better
than *your* school, *your* children, and *your* country. Although she does
not directly name these traits until *Three Guineas,* she thoroughly satirizes them and their connections with Empire and violence in *Jacob's
Room* and *The Waves.*

Both novels portray characters who are not so much autonomous individuals as products of a culture. *Jacob's Room* introduces dozens of names, each of which at first seems to be well provisioned with the details of a nineteenth-century realistic novel: physical description, brief background, and a few internal thoughts. However, the novel, after a vignette of only a paragraph or two each, summarily drops most of these personae, who together represent a cross-section of socioeconomic classes. A few names, such as Jacob Flanders, Betty Flanders, or Clara Durrant, do recur, yet even these familiar figures develop as types. Although Judy Little perceptively recognizes that in *Jacob's Room* Woolf "teases" the classic *bildungsroman* genre, she believes that Woolf satirizes Jacob's socialization because it "seems in his case—like a faulty vaccination—not to have 'taken'" (*Comedy* 39, 49). On the contrary, he unquestioningly accepts his society's values. Like Little, Carol Ohmann correctly sees *Jacob's Room* as a "critique of Western culture" and especially "an anachronistic and irrelevant heroic ideal" (171). Yet she adds that Woolf is advising an intense "individual sensibility" as adequate resistance against "the tyranny of what *Mrs. Dalloway* was immediately to term Conversion and Proportion" (171). Jacob, however, manages no intense individual sensibility but only a muddled acquiescence to the norm. He represents any similar young man who might attend a university, tour Italy and Greece, and work in a law office. As the title indicates, the book illuminates Jacob's *room*, the social space that allows him the only scope he will ever attain, rather than some supposed "soul" of Jacob.

Instead of sketching a multitude of contingent personalities such as those who impinge on Jacob, *The Waves* focuses on six characters, seen from the inside through their stylized "I." In her diary for October 1931, Woolf muses over a baffling review of *The Waves* from *The Times*: "Odd, that they should praise my characters when I meant to have none" (*Diary* 4: 47). Despite the sympathy which the first-person point of view draws to the six speakers, their typicality again predominates over both individuality and verisimilitude. While it might be possible that the child of a banker in Australia and the sons of gentlemen attend the same English public school, it is not realistic to imagine all six children in the same nursery. Yet they join together from a young age in a sort of nursery of England, the middle-class social conditions that are the real topic of the book, as they are in *Jacob's Room.*

These social conditions unfortunately may encourage force and repression: the hostilities of World War I in *Jacob's Room* or the iron fist of a shadowy, impending police state in *The Waves.* When the reader of the earlier book has to infer on the last page that Jacob has died, no doubt in the war, the rather offhand notice is shocking. Nevertheless, in retrospect his death is no surprise, having already been announced in the discreet references to troop movements (76, 86, 125, 129, 135, 173) and, even more importantly, in his general social conditioning. Alex Zwerdling shrewdly explains why Woolf might avoid a grand announcement of Jacob's demise. He argues that most World War I literature, whether "patriotic or bitterly disillusioned," presented "the war dead with absolute seriousness, in a style that is characteristically intense and even reverent . . . such attitudes indirectly glorified war, even if the writer was, like Wilfred Owen, consciously working against the martial myth" (73). *Jacob's Room,* by contrast, "small-scaled, mischievous, and ironic," can invoke the war deaths without exalting them (Zwerdling 73).

Woolf's guarded, unheroic manner does not just prefigure war as an external threat. Instead, the style suggests that early death, as an internal English problem, is an appropriate denouement for the particular plot of Jacob's life. That is, *Jacob's Room* explores why this society has been stultifying all along, and why it may unconsciously solicit the cataclysm of war. Although the book sympathizes with Jacob in a general sense, as a victim of war, he is not an innocent scapegoat. Rather, he is a full participant in his society, with all its dangerous failings. Similarly, while *The Waves* elicits pity for Percival, who dies young in India, and for his friends, who long for him, the novel also unflinchingly diagnoses their corruption by their culture.

As *Jacob's Room* probes the conditions in England that invited World War I, *The Waves* condemns an English flirtation with imperial attitudes very much like fascism. Woolf had already warned in *A Room of One's Own* against the symptoms of fascism in Italy: militarism and claims of superiority by one group over other whole groups, such as Jews or women (30, 36, 107). In *The Waves,* she warns against similar symptoms at home. In the first volume of *After the Deluge,* published the same year as *The Waves,* Leonard Woolf, like his wife, refuses to put England and Germany into completely different camps: "This psychology of mechanical authoritarianism amalgamated with patriotism to form imperialism is not confined to Germany. It has been an important ingredient in the psychology which has produced the British Empire" (331).

Jacob's Room and *The Waves* examine this English contribution to World War I and to the authoritarian imperialism leading to World War II, not discursively but through concrete language, resonating into images. In the former novel, meaning is carried in two ways: by incongruous juxtapositions of apparently dissimilar details, which turn out after all to be related; and by echoes of similar vocabulary in different settings, spaced over a few pages or far apart in the book. Such unexpected juxtapositions and haunting echoes frequently create a kind of non-sequitur poetry, in the style of T. S. Eliot's *The Waste Land,* published the same year. Just as Woolf, in *Jacob's Room,* creates images that satirize society, she also described *The Waves* as "poetry": dense, concrete, and suggestive. Such poetry must, she insisted, "include nonsense, fact, sordidity: but made transparent" (*Diary* 3: 210).

Most critics of *The Waves* have emphasized its supposedly delicate lyricism. For example, Rachel Duplessis, representing a common approach, calls *The Waves* an "asocial utopia of the word," in which "the trappings of social division (class, gender, sexuality, ethnicity) are not relevant" ("WOOLFENSTEIN" 104). On the contrary, divisions into colonizer and colonized; male and female; and upper, middle, and lower classes strictly determine the experience of the characters, as Jane Marcus insists (Colloquium). Even Zwerdling, usually an astute observer of Woolf's dissatisfaction with society, omits *The Waves* from his study *Virginia Woolf and the Real World.* Yet along with "poetry," social "nonsense, fact, sordidity" do inhabit *The Waves* as much as *Jacob's Room.* For example, when Louis compares himself to the Pharaohs and shuts his "bony hands . . . like the sides of a dock closing" (275), very particular facts—about the Suez Canal and the acquisition by force of European imperial protectorates in North Africa—inform the image. According to Leonard Woolf's scathing report in *Empire and Commerce in Africa,* the facts of the English and French dealings in Egypt and Abyssinia, such as a threat to blow up rocks in the highlands and cause the Nile to flood (155), might well be classed as "nonsense" and "sordidity." Virginia Woolf obliquely works such details into the fabric of *The Waves.*

Louis consolidating the Empire and Jacob marching to war are not aberrant cases but predictable products of a training that affects everyone. Jacob's predisposition toward death is already set in childhood, a training epitomized in two scenes: picking up a sheep's skull and collecting butterflies. The opening scene with the sheep's skull encapsulates the key themes of the book. Jacob is climbing a rock on a beach at Cornwall. The feat is paltry enough, but to Jacob the rock looks huge: "A small boy has . . . to feel rather heroic" (9). When he reaches the top, he plunges his hand into a pool and captures a crab. As he is about to jump down with his prize stowed in his bucket, he sees a man and a woman stretched out in the sand, faces red. Jacob feels frightened and looks around for comfort. A distant, dark shape which he takes to be "Nanny" turns out to be only a rock. He feels "lost" and is about to "roar," when he is distracted by a sheep's skull. He runs, "sobbing, but absent-mindedly . . . until he held the skull in his arms" (10).

Jacob's childhood sheep's skull is echoed by a ram's skull on the last page. After Jacob's death, his mother and his friend Bonamy go through his belongings in his room, where, over the doorway, "a rose or a ram's skull is carved in the wood" (176; cf. 70). The two death's heads thus frame the book and suggest a connection between the social values that Jacob absorbs as a child and his death as a soldier. Rather than simply prefiguring Jacob's fate, the early scene with the skull intimates how his society deadens people all along, and how it prepares Jacob to be harmful toward others. The opening scene shows that the boy has already learned three dangerous lessons: aggression, greed, and a fear of sexuality.

Jacob does not just observe the crab but aggressively captures it, appropriating a treasure for his private store. Conquest and hoarding might come naturally, but his society reinforces such instincts by marking them as "heroic" (9). By assigning the label to a small boy, however, Woolf undermines the concept of heroism. The glorification of conquest is taught especially to men, who are thus groomed for the military. Nevertheless, women do not entirely escape the push toward competitive acquisitiveness. When Betty rocks Jacob's brother to sleep by conjuring visions of "lovely birds settling down on their nests," she focuses, unfortunately, on a ruthless "old mother bird with a worm in her beak" (12). We see later how Betty's own unconscious resentments at the restrictions placed on a woman actually fuel the violence of her world, making her into a voracious creature exclusively concerned with her own young, ignoring the larger community. This image of birds' attacking worms or snails becomes even more important in *The Waves,* where it implies the motherly Susan's urge to amass more land and supplies than she needs, for the benefit of her children alone and not other people's children (191).

The third characteristic taught in this beach scene, besides aggression and personal appropriation, is a skewed view of gender relations that pervades Jacob's whole society, repressing sexuality and emotion for both sexes and preventing full development of women's talents. Although Jacob knows nothing about the amorous couple in the sand, his expectations for another female, his Nanny, already predict why gender relations depicted later might be so smothering: those between Betty and the Captain, or between Jacob and Florinda, Laurette, Clara, and Sandra. Not comprehending the excitement of the lovers, Jacob reacts with fear and feels that someone should comfort him:

> [Jacob] trotted away very nonchalantly at first, but faster and faster as the waves came creaming up to him. . . . A large black woman was sitting on the sand. He ran towards her.
>
> "Nanny! Nanny!" he cried, sobbing the words out on the crest of each gasping breath.
>
> The waves came round her. She was a rock. She was covered with the seaweed which pops when it is pressed. He was lost. (10)

When he concludes that his nurse has rebuffed him (although she is not even on the scene and should not be blamed), he embraces death instead, holding the skull "in his arms" (10). The skull's deathliness becomes a substitute for missing love, a solicitation of any intensity—even the negative intensity of war and annihilation—if a tender response is not forthcoming.

Not only does Jacob feel "lost," but also Nanny herself suffers a loss when she undergoes an Ovidian metamorphosis in his shifting interpretation: "The waves came round her. She was a rock" (10). This line evokes other references in the book to women changed into, or chained to, rocks. Clara Durrant, for instance, is "a virgin chained to a rock (somewhere off Lowndes Square) eternally pouring out tea for old men in white waistcoats" (123). This allusion to Ovid's Andromeda is repeated, even more explicitly, when characters at a dinner party gaze through a telescope and dutifully listen to a recital of constellations; the name of the star-group Andromeda echoes from spinster to ingenue (59). In fact, an Andromeda syndrome, in which women wait for a Perseus to rescue them, afflicts both middle-class Clara, pouring out tea and waiting for a husband to take her away, and the governess Nanny, circumscribed by her low station and by Jacob's assurance that she exists only for him. The inability of both women to move from the home and act in the public world makes them resemble inanimate, inarticulate stones.

Nanny seems subject not only to metamorphosis into a rock but also to drowning: "The waves came round her. . . . She was covered with the seaweed" (10). Because Jacob sobs out his call to her "on the crest of each gasping breath," the vocabulary makes it seem as if his call is a wave, perhaps the very wave which kills her (10). His patriarchal word eclipses her. Yet if Jacob Flanders seems ready to take on the powerful role of the fathers, here on the beach he is weak and frightened; soon he will be "trott[ing] away very nonchalantly" to another land of skulls, where young men feed "crows in Flanders" (97). As Zwerdling points out, "nearly a third of the million British soldiers killed in World War I lost their lives in the Flanders mud," so that Jacob's patronymic announces his future lack of power (64). Nanny and the governesses are not the only ones drowning, figuratively, for young men will drown, literally, in the war: "With equal nonchalance a dozen young men in the prime of life descend with composed faces into the depths of the sea; and there impassively (though with perfect mastery of machinery) suffocate uncomplainingly together" (155). As a Perseus hero, Jacob will not forever outwit his Medusa, his own distorted image of women. He, too, will be turned to stone, to dust, or to fish food, as much as Nanny is wasted in her constricted role. Already the opening scene hints that class assignments, gender roles, repression of sexuality, and aggressive acquisition of goods all consign people to deadened existence or literal premature deaths.

Another suggestive childhood scene, which announces not only Jacob's future death but his lifelong unconscious implication in oppression, shows Jacob and his brother collecting insect specimens: "The stag-beetle dies slowly. . . . Even on the second day its legs were supple. But the butterflies were dead. A whiff of rotten eggs had vanquished the pale clouded yellows which came pelting across the orchard. . . . A fritillary basked on a white stone in the Roman camp" (23). The next paragraph consists only of the line, "Rebecca had caught the death's-head moth in the kitchen" (23). Jacob and his brother do not merely suffer the evanescence of beauty but actively kill the creatures they claim to admire.

Jacob's hunt for a rare specimen prefigures his later life, especially his role in the war: "The tree had fallen the night he caught it. There had been a volley of pistol-shots suddenly in the depths of the wood. And his mother had taken him for a burglar when he came home late. The only one of her sons who never obeyed her, she said" (23). When Betty mistakes Jacob for a burglar, she correctly identifies her son as someone who will come to participate in the crimes of his society. That society, gilded as a butterfly, already feeds on victims: "The blues settled on little bones lying on the turf with the sun beating on them, and the painted ladies and the peacocks feasted upon bloody entrails dropped by a hawk" (24). The phrase "painted ladies" looks forward to Jacob's series of lovely girlfriends—Florinda, Laurette—who flit from man to man, as the "peacocks" evoke Jacob's own cocksure strutting, when he grows "satisfied," "masterly," and certain of "himself the inheritor"

(45). Moreover, the vocabulary of the butterfly hunt again announces World War I: "admiral," "camp," "bones lying on the turf," "pistol-shots," and perhaps "whiff of rotten eggs" for mustard gas. Even the pathetic movements of John's slow-dying beetles resemble the later spasms of anonymous soldiers: "the army covers the cornfield, moves up the hillside, stops, reels slightly this way and that, and falls flat, save that, through field-glasses, it can be seen that one or two pieces still agitate up and down like fragments of broken match-stick" (155–56). Nevertheless, the threat in the passage about the butterflies does not derive from some outside force which invades a realm of fragile innocence. Instead, the training that Jacob and his brothers undergo, to capture and kill, implies that the society itself is already unsound. The "death's-head" moth, after all, inhabits the "kitchen," and Jacob has clasped a death's head in his arms on the beach. When he himself becomes a kind of "stag-beetle" dying—the male of the species, regarded by governments as expendable—he is no more guilty than anyone else, but no purer either.

As Jacob grows up, the institutions of English life reveal their complicity in death-dealing. In church, for example, Jacob watches "how airily the gowns blow out, as though nothing dense and corporeal were within. What sculptured faces, what certainty, authority controlled by piety, although great boots march under the gowns" (32). The deadly force of a tramping battalion hides beneath a doctrine which denies corporeality to life forces such as sexuality. One source of that hostility which sets ominous boots marching, immediately becomes apparent from Jacob's scorn: "But this service in King's College Chapel—why allow women to take part in it? Surely, if the mind wanders . . . it is because several hat shops and cupboards upon cupboards of coloured dresses are displayed upon rush-bottomed chairs" (32–33). Although he admits that the women distract him because he thinks that they are lovely, he projects his guilt at ignoring the sermon onto the women themselves: "They're as ugly as sin" (33). Echoing Samuel Johnson's comparison of women preachers to dogs prancing on their hind legs (quoted in *Room of Own* 56), Jacob rants: "No one would think of bringing a dog into church. For though a dog is all very well on a gravel path, and shows no disrespect to flowers, the way he wanders down an aisle, looking, lifting a paw, and approaching a pillar with a purpose that makes the blood run cold with horror . . . a dog destroys the service completely. So do these women" (33). Whereas Jacob resents the women's intrusion into his church, his wording allows the reader a certain retaliatory pleasure in imagining the dog urinating on the august pillar, which props up a creed of misogyny and exclusion.

As Woolf argues in *A Room of One's Own*, arrogance, possessiveness, and hostility, sanctioned toward one group of people, women, primes a society to displace such feelings toward other groups as well. Harking back to the same equation of women and dogs that occurs to Jacob in church, Woolf in *A Room of One's Own* castigates the reflex reaction ingrained in any European male, "Alf, Bert or Chas.," that "murmurs if it sees a fine woman go by, or even a dog, Ce chien est à moi. And, of course, it may not be a dog, I thought, remembering Parliament Square, the Sieges Allee [*sic*] and other avenues; it may be a piece of land or a man with curly black hair" (52). Leonard Woolf also quotes this French phrase from Pascal as an epigraph to *Empire and Commerce in Africa*: "*Ce chien est à moi . . . voilà le commencement et l'image de l'usurpation de toute la terre.*" When Jacob's church drills its worshipers to a military tread, it opens the way to the usurpations of Empire-building and the waging of war (Handley 120).

Jacob's Room further connects the heavily booted churchmen with the scene of Jacob's hunt for butterflies. The stained glass is supposed to enlighten and comfort the congregation: "As the sides of a lantern protect the flame so that it burns steady even in the wildest night—burns steady and gravely illumines the tree-trunks—so inside the Chapel all was orderly" (32). The order turns out to be an illusion, however, as the comparison of the stained glass to a lantern for luring butterflies to their death immediately calls up a vision of aggression: "Ah, but what's that? A terrifying volley of pistol-shots rings out—cracks sharply; ripples spread—silence laps smooth over sound. A tree—a tree has fallen, a sort of death in the forest" (32). The "pistol-shots" directly echo Jacob's experience during the butterfly hunt, when he confuses the sound of a tree falling with "a volley of pistol-shots" (23). In both cases the sound ominously previews the Great War. Something "senseless" inspires the parishioners, insectlike, to crowd to their "great white book," led by their "toad," who can only be the priest (32). The satirical tone of the passage implies that the church not only ignores the pistol-shots of the world but actually makes them possible. It does so because the institutionalized church teaches Christians to be complacent and helps them accept unjustified hierarchies. Churchgoers' practice in believing that men are better than women prepares them to accept other hierarchies, such as "England is better than Germany" or "our navy is better than your navy." For Woolf, the "great white book" further shabbily tries to justify the rule of toadlike authorities in church or government, such as the "White Queen Victoria" of *Between the Acts*, who maintains her position not by right but by might, her policeman's truncheon (162).

In addition to the church, another aspect of British society that breeds death is the stultifying atmosphere of small towns. Seaside Scarborough at first may appear innocent enough, even idyllic. Nevertheless, residents and visitors alike betray a chilling lifelessness; they "all wore the same blurred, drugged expression" (18). At the museum, the idler finds "Cannon-balls; arrow-heads; Roman glass and a forceps green with verdigris. . . . And now, what's the next thing to see in Scarborough?" (19). The causes that people once fought over, now forgotten, are reduced to an afternoon's entertainment, one not very thrilling at that. Still, the military items that predominate at this museum signal a constant preoccupation with war, from distant past to disturbing future: "Archer and Jacob ran in front or lagged behind; but they were in the Roman fortress when she came there, and shouting out what ships were to be seen in the bay" (17). Old men have left the town only once in their lives, to fight in the Crimea (117), the war which Woolf mocks in *Freshwater* and *To the Lighthouse*. In *Jacob's Room*, she implies that, if the dullness of small town life is not alleviated, the restless men will welcome war and imperial conquests merely for the chance to escape. As David Thomson similarly explains, Rudyard Kipling's adventure stories appealed to lower-middle-class bank clerks and shop assistants in towns and suburbs because of these workers' longing to get away, vicariously or in person, from conventionality and monotony to the "spiciness of the East" (205). A "raucous patriotism and a cult of brutal impatience with all resistance to British rule overseas" arose as "over-compensation for the utterly unromantic conditions in which his civilization forced him to live" (Thomson 207).

Although the two landmarks in Jacob's conventional town, the museum and the aquarium, preserve the traces of past adventure, those accomplishments seem simultaneously paltry and monstrous. The impressions of an aquarium tour "remained in the mind as part of the monster shark, he himself being only a shabby yellow receptacle, like an empty Gladstone bag in a tank" (18). This image may satirize the nineteenth-century prime minister Gladstone, who claimed to dislike the British Empire but nevertheless expanded it (Graham 164, 182). When the war breaks out at the end of *Jacob's Room,* Gladstone appears again in a list with other Empire-builders—Pitt, Chatham, Burke—as they "looked from side to side with fixed marble eyes and an air of immortal quiescence" (172). As vapid yet shark-toothed as the "empty Gladstone bag in a tank," these eighteenth- and nineteenth-century leaders join the heads of 1914, "bald, red-veined, hollow-looking," who "decreed that the course of history should shape itself this way or that way, being manfully determined, as their faces showed, to impose some coherency upon Rajahs and Kaisers and the muttering in bazaars" (172). The repressed citizens of small-town Scarborough find their vicarious outlet in the coercive imposition of "coherency" by the imperialists, whose overseas adventures in places such as India and Africa in turn contribute to war. As Leonard Woolf argued in 1920, economic imperialism was "a very material cause" pushing the world "over the brink in 1914. . . . European policy in Africa may not have been the immediate cause of the Great War, but you cannot have a policy such as Europe pursued in Africa between 1880 and 1914 without great wars" (*Empire and Commerce* 321).

Besides the church and the town, another aspect of British society that might be expected to stand as a bulwark against war but instead actually encourages it is the university, represented by Jacob's Cambridge. In their smugness and proprietary pride, his professors echo the snobbish chapel and the shopkeeping town: "How priestly they look! How like a suburb where you go to see a view and eat a special cake!

'We are the sole purveyors of this cake'" (40). Because the university grounds its students in arrogance, competitiveness, and exclusivity, it prepares them for the power-mongering and belligerence of war, as Woolf will make explicit in *Three Guineas* (21, 29). Already in *Jacob's Room,* the imagery associated with the self-satisfied Professor Huxtable renders his thought patterns ominously martial: "Now, as his eye goes down the print, what a procession tramps through the corridors of his brain, orderly, quick-stepping, and reinforced, as the march goes on, by fresh runnels, till the whole hall, dome, whatever one calls it, is populous with ideas. Such a muster takes place in no other brain" (40). The bald "domes" in 1914 register similar converging runnels, "remarking that Prime Ministers and Viceroys spoke in the Reichstag; entered Lahore; said that the Emperor travelled; in Milan they rioted; said there were rumours in Vienna; said that the Ambassador at Constantinople had audience with the Sultan; the fleet was at Gibraltar" (171). Unfortunately these leaders will call up musters not only in their heads, as Professor Huxtable does, but on the field and the oceans.

Jacob may arrive at Cambridge University inclined to scoff at ceremony, but soon he succumbs to the temptations of power: "Insolent he was and inexperienced, but sure enough the cities which the elderly of the race have built upon the skyline showed like brick suburbs, barracks, and places of discipline against a red and yellow flame. . . . Every time he lunches out on Sunday . . . there will be this same shock—horror—discomfort—then pleasure" (36). Cambridge itself appears to be "burning" with a great light (42), yet the buildings stand out against a red and yellow flame—perhaps of factories, perhaps of impending war—much more scorching than the elusive light of wisdom. The elders have built campuses or barracks indiscriminately, imposing discipline and sameness everywhere. In this passage, even the rigid classrooms seem to give the blueprint for the barracks. The school imbues its students with conformity and with the desire to maintain privilege, even by force.

Jacob does indeed accept the lessons in complacency that his university grafts in him. He and his friends discover that intellectual debate is "damnably difficult. But, after all, not so difficult if on the next staircase, in the large room, there are two, three, five young men all convinced of . . . the clear division between right and wrong" (44). As Jacob learns simplistic solutions that put him in the privileged camp of "right," he reinforces his earlier churchly practice in excluding others. Together he and his friends "rolled up the map, having got the whole thing settled" (42). They can imagine "the bare hills of Turkey . . . [and] women, standing naked-legged in the stream to beat linen on the stones. . . . But none of that could show clearly through the swaddlings and blanketings of the Cambridge night" (44–45). The school allows few women's bodies on campus, naked-legged or otherwise, and it allows very few women's minds either. The one professor mentioned from Newnham, the newly founded women's college at Cambridge, soon learns to mask her responses (42). As Woolf sarcastically records in *Three Guineas*, Cambridge did not permit its female students to be voting members, and it imposed a strict limit on the number of women admitted: one-tenth the male population (30, 154). Jacob, however, unquestioningly swallows the prevailing views of women. When he completes a foreign tour, the final stage of his typically male education, he assumes that female tourists cannot appreciate Greece as he can: "Damn these women. . . . How they spoil things" (151).

Meanwhile, as Jacob's classmates are rolling up their figurative map of right and wrong, the real European empires were rolling up countries on the globe. The students, educated in past literature and history but not in current developments, can imagine only an exotic, rustic Turkey. By contrast, during Jacob's time at Cambridge, 1911 or so, urban Constantinople and the Turkish straits were fueling nationalist and imperial rivalries. As Leonard Woolf argued in 1917:

Constantinople and the narrow straits upon which it stands have occasioned the world more trouble, have cost humanity more in blood and suffering during the last five hundred years, than any other single spot upon the earth. . . . It was the direct origin and cause of a large number of the wars fought in the nineteenth century. It is not improbable that when Europe in her last ditch has fought the last battle of the Great War, we shall find that what we have again been fighting about is really Constantinople. (*Future* 11–12)

In contrast to Leonard Woolf, who envisioned the internationalization of Constantinople as a means of thwarting all imperialist aims, including those of Great Britain, Jacob and his family uncritically grow into an easy acceptance of the British Empire and the need to defend it militarily. His brother Archer, whose very name predicts that his main purpose in life is to be a warrior, joins the navy and periodically is reported at Gibraltar or Singapore, defending British possessions and policing the world (125, 173). The same discussion talks "about the King's Navy (to which Archer was going); and about Rugby (to which Jacob was going)" (22). The parallel of navy and Rugby, a school whose name epitomizes the playing field, reveals that war is accepted as just another game, a misapprehension that the book constantly attempts to correct. Other commentators besides Woolf have pointed out the role of the public schools in preparing boys to die in war: "If life itself was a fight, so too could fight—battles—be what counted and what was meaningful in life. If the boy was prepared for life by playing games . . . then necessarily he was also prepared for war" (MacDonald 18).[1]

The boys' Uncle Morty, much less respectable than Archer, also adventures as far as the colonies, where he mysteriously disappears. He provides a topic of exotic speculation: "'I expect he's feeding the sharks, if the truth were known,' said Jacob. 'I say, Durrant, there's none left!' he exclaimed, crumpling the bag which had held the cherries, and throwing it into the river" (38). To be killed by sharks is more or less the same in the minds of the gossip-mongers as being killed by natives; derogatorily, Morty's death and his possible conversion to Islam are also conflated (15, 91). Nevertheless, Woolf's imagery has already implied that it is prime ministers like Gladstone and not "natives" who most resemble the sharks and the empty bags (18), as the European nations gobble up all the countries of the world until, almost literally, "There's none left!" As Leonard Woolf reported, by 1914 England, France, and Germany alone had taken more than eight million square miles and almost a hundred million non-European subjects (*Empire and Commerce* 24). Jacob, however, remains unconcerned about either these people or his uncle, regretting only the end of his snack.

Part of Jacob's education in Empire making consists of nothing more strenuous than visiting elderly aristocratic women, whose militarism he imbibes along with their wine. Anticipating the brutish Lady Bruton of *Mrs. Dalloway,* who wants to ride down "barbarian hordes" (274), an aggressive Lady Rocksbier "used her knife with authority, tore her chicken bones," and, one might say, approves employing force in the colonies, since she "talked of Joseph Chamberlain, whom she had known" (100). A few years before *Jacob's Room,* Leonard Woolf had lambasted Chamberlain, secretary of state for the colonies, for insisting in 1895 that the state exists "to further commerce" and that it should exert its power in the world to promote trade (*Empire and Commerce* 8, 10). Leonard charged that policies like Chamberlain's have "caused more bloodshed than ever religion or dynasties" and were "the chief cause of the war which we have just been fighting [World War I]" (10). In light of Leonard's accusations, Lady Rocksbier's parting gift to Jacob of a "good cigar" sounds like a bad joke, accompanying her bad doctrines, which may well blow up in his face (100). The Countess Rocksbier's very name presages a coffin, as her servant's name, Boxall, announces world war.

As *Jacob's Room* is deriding church, small towns, university, and Empire, it also mocks the heroism of Odysseus, a paradigm which still may underlie these modern aspects of British life. *Night and Day* already questioned this cultural icon, when Mary Datchet associated a statue of Ulysses in the British Museum with a man who could have "commanded a whole tribe of natives" (83). One of Jacob's women, neglected at home while he tours Greece, uses this same "battered Ulysses" at the museum to revive her fading memory of Jacob (170). In a parodic version of the Odysseus quest, Jacob and a friend navigate a boat to an island off Cornwall during their college years. The ideal of young men braving the elements turns out to be overrated. On the way to the Scilly Isles, whose name suggests Odysseus's encounter with Scilla and perhaps also the silliness of the young men, Jacob and Timmy Durrant grow bored, quarrel over the right way to open a tin, and engage in giddy and pompous speculation as to whether the Duke of Wellington, Keats, Lord Salisbury, and God are all gentlemen (51). The glory of athletic prowess means only that Jacob "gulped in water, spat it out, struck with his right arm, struck with his left, was towed by a rope, gasped, splashed, and was hauled on board" (48).

Moreover, the real motive of the Odysseus quest proves to be not healthy exercise and disinterested knowledge of the world, but power and profit. The young men's fledgling boat faces its adult counterparts in the nearby ships, whose shipping line Timmy can name "and even guess what dividends it paid its shareholders. Yet that was no reason for Jacob to turn sulky" (47). Remaining as "profoundly unconscious" as he was in childhood (14) and seldom questioning his society's values, Jacob fails to grasp that the need to pay dividends to shareholders might well be a reason for malaise. He cannot see the cause-and-effect relationship between Odysseus's reckless curiosity and profit seeking—his desire to see what a Cyclops is and also to take his cheese—and the outcome of those drives, a violent confrontation and the unnecessary loss of a number of his men (Homer 145).

Although Jacob cannot interpret the signs, a threat of death already hangs over this seemingly innocent expedition to Cornwall and its islands. For example, the cottage smoke on shore droops "a flag floating its caress over a grave" (49). The sunlight also makes tombs seem delusively attractive: "The Scilly Isles now appeared as if directly pointed at by a golden finger issuing from a cloud; and everybody knows how portentous that sight is, and how these broad rays, whether they light upon the Scilly Isles or upon the tombs of crusaders in cathedrals, always shake the very foundations of skepticism" (51). Boyishly inclined as Jacob and Timmy are to joke about God, their own sense of youthful power to storm the island nevertheless gilds their adventure into a divine mission, obscuring any healthy skepticism. The "golden finger issuing from a cloud" prepares them to project as their representatives such "Fingers of Destiny" as Napoleon and Mussolini, whom Woolf mocks in A Room of One's Own (36). A divinely sanctioned adventurer—whether he be an Odysseus, sure of his right to cheese and wool, or a crusader certain of proprietorship in the Holy Land—cannot perceive the tombstones ahead, those of his victims or his own premature grave. As modern descendants of the Homeric or medieval profit-seekers, the ships of Empire similarly will pay their shareholders by shedding blood, including Jacob's.

Whatever tinge of outdoor health the boat offers fades soon enough, despite Jacob's satisfied "paean, for having grasped the argument, for being master of the situation, sunburnt, unshaven, capable into the bargain of sailing round the world in a ten-ton yacht, which, very likely, he would do one of these days instead of settling down in a lawyer's office, and wearing spats" (50). Actually, he joins a law firm only four chapters later. Yet the offices of law, finance, and government in the business district do reach out ominously to envelop the globe, continuing the Ulysses quest on more prosaic terms. Immediately after Fanny Elmer looks at "the battered Ulysses," she complains of Jacob's indifference: "'One's godmothers ought to have told one,' said Fanny, looking in at the window of Bacon, the mapseller, in the Strand—told one that it is no use making a fuss; this is life, they should have said, as Fanny said it now, looking at the large yellow globe marked with steamship lines" (170). While Jacob tours the countries of his classical training, the European powers are consolidating their Empires, indicated by this globe with steamship lines:

> "A very hard face," thought Miss Barrett, on the other side of the glass, buying maps of the Syrian desert and waiting impatiently to be served. "Girls look old so soon nowadays."
>
> The equator swam behind tears.
>
> "Piccadilly?" Fanny asked the conductor of the omnibus, and climbed to the top. After all, he would, he must, come back to her. (171)

Even a bystander, Miss Barrett, can put her British fingers on Syria, which, by 1922, had passed from the decaying Turkish Empire to France and Britain. France held a mandate in a smaller area still called "Syria," while Britain governed "Iraq," made up of Mesopotamia and part of Kurdistan, and "Palestine," part of the old province of Syria (Lloyd 289). In Jacob's youth, Europe was acquiring such territories in part through war, until, as Woolf says, "The equator swam behind tears" (171). Fanny's private and rather ridiculous infatuation with

Jacob reverberates into the much greater grief of all those who make sacrifices for Empire, including Syrians, European soldiers like Jacob, and the lovers of soldiers, like Fanny.

Once Jacob returns from his Greek jaunt to take up his law career, Woolf even more clearly skewers the commercialism which she began exposing with the net of shipping lines expanding like a noose beyond the Scilly Isles. Profits do not flow equally to all. Moreover, the class system separates people who otherwise might find interests in common. Betty and her maid, for instance, mind the children companionably, in a way that should draw them together, yet "Rebecca called her ma'm, though they were conspirators plotting the eternal conspiracy of hush and clean bottles" (13). Jacob's training at home to assume that people like Rebecca stand beneath him in a fixed scale of worthies is reinforced by attitudes of the church. When the young lawyer steps out of the cathedral, "Nothing could appear more certain from the steps of St. Paul's than that each person is miraculously provided with coat, skirt, and boots; an income; an object. Only Jacob, carrying in his hand Finlay's *Byzantine Empire* . . . looked a little different" (66). He uses his recondite reading to distinguish himself from pedestrians whom he thinks of as philistines, but who actually include despairing street peddlers: "A woman stares at nothing, boot-laces extended, which she does not ask you to buy" (66). Unconsciously, Jacob uses the church and the contemporary British Empire called up by his book's title to back his claim to a "miraculously provided" income, though the income and the ownership of whole boots obviously do not devolve on all equally.

Meanwhile, at that very moment, inside the church class divisions are clearly evident:

> For ever requiem—repose. Tired with scrubbing the steps of the Prudential
> Society's office, which she did year in year out, Mrs. Lidgett took her seat be-
> neath the great Duke's tomb . . . and out steal on tiptoe thoughts of rest, sweet
> melodies. . . . Old Spicer, jute merchant, thought nothing of the kind though.
> Strangely enough he'd never been in St. Paul's these fifty years, though his
> office windows looked on the churchyard. "So that's all? Well, a gloomy old
> place. . . . Where's Nelson's tomb?" (65–66)

Old Spicer, whose name epitomizes the lure of the East, directly participates in the Empire through his commodity, jute. One historian reports that the British jute industry in India in the late nineteenth and early twentieth centuries operated under "much fouler conditions, though rather less cruel," than those that existed on tea and indigo plantations, where unsanitary space, failure to pay workers in full, and flogging were common (Moorhouse 155). If Woolf includes no specific details of working conditions in India, she nevertheless effectively blasts the merchant's pretensions to piety by showing that he worships the tomb of a military man more than the crucifix. Meanwhile, the jute workers were putting in ten- to twelve-hour shifts around the clock, making sandbags for war (Moorhouse 156). Ironically, Jacob, who worships near a merchant glad to sell jute, will soon die in a setting which is likely to include just such sandbags.

Although the Christian church supposedly welcomes all souls equally, St. Paul's in fact sanctions the class divisions between jute seller and jute weaver, duke and cleaning lady (who will not receive a lavish crypt), and men and women. By 1938 Woolf was openly criticizing the biblical St. Paul: "He was of the virile or dominant type, so familiar at present in Germany, for whose gratification a subject race or class is essential" (*Three Guineas* 167). Already, however, *Jacob's Room* warns against the dangers of hypocritical churchly hierarchies, when a perpetual "requiem" sounds behind the jute merchant: a prayer for the dead in a morally deadened England.

The church and the university together breed in Jacob an inability even to perceive the ranks shut out from these institutions by class, gender, or race. Oblivious, he sits "regal" and "pompous" in the library (107) and does not notice the cries of those excluded from upper-class and middle-class society:

> Stone lies solid over the British Museum, as bone lies cool over the visions and heat of the brain. Only here the brain is Plato's brain and Shakespeare's; the brain has made pots and statues, great bulls and little jewels, and crossed the river of death this way and that incessantly, seeking some landing, now wrapping the body well for its long sleep; now laying a penny piece on the eyes;

now turning the toes scrupulously to the East. Meanwhile, Plato continues his dialogue; in spite of the rain; in spite of the cab whistles; in spite of the woman in the mews behind Great Ormond Street who has come home drunk and cries all night long, "Let me in! Let me in!" (109)

By cataloguing together the books and the mummies of the British Museum, the passage reduces the whole Western tradition to so many coins paid to take the populace into a living hell. When Jacob arrives home from the library, he continues "reading the *Phaedrus,* heard people vociferating round the lamp-post, and the woman battering at the door and crying, 'Let me in!' as if a coal had dropped from the fire, or a fly, falling from the ceiling, had lain on its back, too weak to turn over" (109–10). His learning enables him to ignore the clamor of people who have been marginalized, a number which expands from the drunken woman to include all the poor, as well as "the Jews and the foreign woman" further down the street, who mean no more to Jacob than a dying fly (110).

Although Woolf does not specify which lines from *Phaedrus* most impress Jacob, his insensitivity to women and foreigners might well be reinforced by this Socratic dialogue. Most obviously, women are absent from the pursuit of "the just and the good and beautiful" (Plato, *Phaedrus* 569). Moreover, Socrates's famous image of the two horses in the soul appears to carry a racist tinge. When a man sees a beautiful boy whom he loves, the part of his soul which is constrained by modesty, so as not to "leap upon the beloved," is compared to a horse which has "an aquiline nose" and is "white in colour," yoked on the right-hand side (495). The more forward, left-side horse in the soul is described with "his nose flat, his colour dark" (495). Just wanting to "approach the beloved and propose the joys of love" seems to slur this latter creature as rapacious (495). Lust, then, is viewed as a trait belonging more "naturally" to flat-nosed, dark-skinned horses/races, although Socrates himself seems to want to propose just such physical sharing to Phaedrus several times during the dialogue. After the younger man rebuffs his teacher's hints, however, preferring the pleasures of discourse to "nearly all bodily pleasures" (dismissed by Phaedrus as "slavish" [511]), then Socrates is forced to distance himself from his own sexual longings by blaming them on dark creatures. Although Socrates keeps the possibility of "left-handed" or physical love alive as a secondary route to the "light," he makes the "right-handed," less physical love more virtuous, apparently in deference to Phaedrus's aloofness (503, 535). The pleasures of the body must be postponed and displaced into heaven, where the philosophers, having restrained themselves on earth, finally will feel the phallic "quills of the feathers swell and begin to grow from the roots over all the form of the soul" (487).

Jacob's Cambridge, in fact, replicates the contradictory ethereal-erotic atmosphere of Plato's groves. Professor Sopwith admires "a Greek boy's head" and goes on "talking; twining stiff fibres of awkward speech—things young men blurted out—plaiting them round his own smooth garland" (41). Sopwith's reliance on conversation resembles that of Socrates, who is led in *Phaedrus* to praise the spoken word over the written word precisely because speech at least ensures the physical presence of his beloved. Oral discourse allows the speaker to create "his own legitimate offspring, first the word within himself, if it be found there, and secondly its descendants or brothers which may have sprung up in worthy manner in the souls of others, and who pays no attention to the other words" (*Phaedrus* 575). The speaking philosopher breeds more words in the receptively "female" mind of his male student, jealously guarded from the seminal language of other teachers. The student's descendant words, unfortunately, must exactly mirror the image of the father. Although *Phaedrus* creates a strong sympathy for Socrates as a struggling and only partially requited lover, the philosopher, like Sopwith, unattractively limits "dialogue" to a monologue and its assenting murmur, which will affirm a patriarchal legitimacy. Both teachers, Socrates and Sopwith, also unattractively exclude from the discussion students of different gender and, implicitly, race.

Woolf's Jacob becomes so absorbed by Socrates's arguments in the *Phaedrus* that "it is impossible to see to the fire" (110). Neglecting his grate, he also ignores the spark of sexual longing which Bonamy, "who couldn't love a woman," perhaps feels for him when they tussle together at the university, "like two bulls of Bashan driving each other up and down" (140, 102). The kind of half-encouraged, half-denied homosexuality at Cambridge makes Jacob regard women as only a "flaw" in the landscape (37), while still thwarting Bonamy's erotic desires. Although Bonamy's name makes him the "good friend" incarnate, Jacob prefers to forget him and instead dally with a married woman in Greece. If Jacob's little heap of coals is also his home hearth, England, then to become distracted by *Phaedrus* to the point that it is "impossible to see to the fire" may also imply that the country could become a rebellious conflagration someday, if it continues to exclude women, servants such as the cleaning lady at St. Paul's, homosexuals, and the Jews and foreigners on the corner (110).

Of all the interactions of classes and groups investigated in *Jacob's Room*, gender relations receive particular attention. The contemporary structure of such relations, stultifying people at church and university, in some ways also facilitates wars. When Jacob listens to Wagner at the Opera House, for example, the opera indoctrinates him in the bizarre trope of the "love-death." As Denis de Rougemont has argued in *Love in the Western World*, Tristan and Iseult "do not love one another"; they love "being in love" and they want to intensify longing through obstacles, especially the supreme obstacle, death (41). Woolf's comic depiction of the Wagnerian opera based on the medieval story shows that the invitation to death engulfs not only the immediate couple: "Tristan was twitching his rug up under his armpits twice a week; Isolde waved her scarf in miraculous sympathy with the conductor's baton. In all parts of the house were to be found pink faces and glittering breasts. When a Royal hand attached to an invisible body slipped out and withdrew the red and white bouquet reposing on the scarlet ledge, the Queen of England seemed a name worth dying for" (68). The silliness of this fussy Tristan debunks the iconic European romance plot. One flaw that weakens this paradigmatic male-female relationship is that only male sexuality seems to count. Isolde has to wave her scarf in homage to a kind of phallic baton. On the same page, an excessive number of masculine wands and gold-headed canes stroll down "crimson avenues" and engage in "intercourse with the boxes," displaying themselves as if in a bedroom. Moreover, the strutting extends onto crimson fields of battle, where the queen only "seemed" worth dying for. The romantic conventions idealize a delicate and threatened womanhood, needing strong defense by chivalric warriors, who simultaneously neglect the real needs of their idols. Even as late as 1990, London published a book for children on the British Empire with the obscurantist title *Queen Victoria's Enemies,* as if a sweet and innocent lady were just sitting sewing, when out stormed barbaric enemies to attack her (Knight).

Further mixing military and sexual images in *Jacob's Room,* Woolf describes the physical environment: "The lamps of London uphold the dark as upon the points of burning bayonets. The yellow canopy sinks and swells over the great four-poster" (97). The four posters of the bed, which might witness nuptials, ominously resemble weapons. Elsewhere, non-sequiturs in a conversation at a party similarly juxtapose love and war. A passing reference to a brother in the "Twentieth Hussars" precedes a stray question, "But what proof was there that the marriage service was actually performed?" A half-stated political opinion follows: "'There is no reason to doubt that Charles James Fox [. . . ,]' Mr. Burley began; but here Mrs. Stretton told him that she knew his sister well; had stayed with her not six weeks ago; and thought the house charming, but bleak in winter" (86–87). In one of Woolf's most characteristic juxtapositions, the military (hussars), gender relations (marriage service), and the Empire (the eighteenth-century politician Fox) again cluster together. Although Fox may have reproved the East India Company for abuses, he recommended solving the problem by giving the powers of the company not to Indians but to the British government. However, as the hussars in this passage remind the reader, once a government insists on annexing territory, military force becomes necessary in order to hold onto it. Woolf pursues such analysis not in essays or abstractions, but evocatively, in concrete language. Thus a "charming, but bleak" house lends its foreboding to the flattering but "bleak" gender expectations, which eventually send men, defined as defenders of women, to war and to colonies.

The constant juxtaposition of scenes of war and sex carries several implications in this novel. The first is that the assigned relations between men and women deaden their minds and bodies. There is no "proof" that a true "marriage service" took place (87), or, as Woolf judges the whole nineteenth century in her important 1931 speech before the London/National Society for Women's Service, "a real relationship" between men and women "was then unattainable" (*Pargiters* xxx). A second implication is that when men are trained to dominate—to assume that their sexual pleasure, their learning at the university, and their fulfilling work all take precedence over women's pleasure or work—this upbringing prepares countries to dominate other countries. Third, *Jacob's Room* speculates that a resort to force abroad may serve as a compensation for failures in sexual relations.

Thus, men who approach women in this book, both Captain Barfoot and Jacob, assume a depressingly martial bearing. When the captain visits Betty Flanders, there is "something military in his approach" (26). Most obviously, he brings with him the recollection of his past military service. The book does not specify where he served, although the fact that he has lost two fingers in battle (25) prefigures Abel Pargiter in *The Years*, who has lost two fingers in the Indian Mutiny of 1857. Whether this younger captain actually fought in the colonies or not, he strongly supports the British Empire. Jacob learns, in humorously but ominously jumbled letters from his mother, that "the Captain was enquiring for her about Garfit's acre; advised chickens; could promise profit; or had the sciatica . . . or the Captain says things look bad, politics that is, for as Jacob knew, the Captain would sometimes talk, as the evening waned, about Ireland or India" (91). The topics range from *me* to *mine;* and it becomes clear that profit is the main motive—whether on the part of the captain and Betty, in dealing with agricultural investments, or on the part of the nation, in dealing with Empire.

The captain's "military" approach to Betty Flanders implies not only his past service as a soldier of Empire but also his present attitude toward her. Lame as a result of his war wounds, the captain supports himself on his way to his date with a rubber-tipped stick, referred to as a "flagstaff" (25). Just as Paul Rayley in *To the Lighthouse* plants his staff in the in-coming tide at the moment of his engagement to Minta (117), so Captain Barfoot comes to Betty staking *her* out as his territory. If he does not directly buy her, he secures an orchard for her, ensuring her gratitude. He claims her as a sign of his attractiveness, as he believes in laying claim to India and Ireland as England's signs of power. The analogy between territories and women works in both directions, to taint the relations of men and women with possessiveness, and to indict the relation of England to colonies as substitute sexual thrills, an inference which we have seen developed most thoroughly in *The Years*.

Captain Barfoot's proprietary interest in Betty does not reside in a personal idiosyncrasy but in a widespread social attitude, illustrated when his stance is immediately duplicated by his employee's relation to Ellen Barfoot. Mr. Dickens wheels out Mrs. Barfoot in her bathchair, giving her husband a chance to slip off to his lady friend, Betty. As the underling surveys his charge, "The feelings of a man had not altogether deserted him . . . he leant forward unsteadily, like an old horse who finds himself suddenly out of the shafts drawing no cart. . . . He was thinking how Captain Barfoot was now on his way to Mount Pleasant; Captain Barfoot, his master" (25–26). The employee accepts the feudal hierarchies of man and master as long as he can take vicarious pleasure in his lord's conquests, and as long as he can dominate someone even lower than himself: "He liked to think that while he chatted with Mrs. Barfoot on the front, he helped the Captain on his way to Mrs. Flanders. He, a man, was in charge of Mrs. Barfoot, a woman" (26). The battleground language of the "front" parallels the captain's "military" approach to Betty. Moreover, Mr. Dickens's pride in a "great silver watch" reinforces the captain's treatment of Betty as property to be appropriated. The servant displays the watch and Ellen with equivalent pride, as if she, too, were a status object firmly within his control. He thus anticipates Rayley in *To the Lighthouse,* flashing his gold watch as he announces his engagement, his acquisition of Minta (175). Full of arrogance, Mr. Dickens might consult his watch as if "he knew a great deal more about the time and everything than she did," but the narrator immediately deflates his presumption: "But Mrs. Barfoot knew that Captain Barfoot was on his way to Mrs. Flanders" (26). Realizing more about her own betrayal than the men give her credit for, she also refutes the assumption that women, as inanimate objects of exchange, cannot think.

The narrator even more bluntly undermines this nineteenth-century assignment of rationality only to men by asking of the captain, "Did he think?" (28). The narrator can detect in the captain's mind only repetitive fantasies featuring himself as the central character: "Women would have felt, 'Here is law, here is order. Therefore we must cherish this man. He is on the Bridge at night,' and, handing him his cup, or whatever it might be, would run on to visions of shipwreck and disaster"(28). He imagines the same self-glorifying, self-pitying exploits as Mr. Ramsay in *To the Lighthouse* (54). Usually assuming victory, such dreamers allow just enough loss to require the succor of a good woman. No one dares contradict the captain aloud, but one doubtful voice interrupts at least the record of his reveries: "'Yet I have a soul,' Mrs. Jarvis would bethink her, as Captain Barfoot suddenly blew his nose in a great red bandanna handkerchief, 'and it's the man's stupidity that's the cause of this, and the storm's my storm as well as his'" (28). If nature inescapably threatens, a woman also must face it, and she, too, suffers the wars—stupid and avoidable—if she sends loved ones or endures privations.

Mrs. Jarvis's assertion that she has a soul further refutes the common Western postulate, derived from Aristotle and adopted by the captain and his helper, that women cannot think. Aristotle defines women as "mutilated males, devoid of the principle of soul" (quoted in Lerner 207). *Jacob's Room* takes an additional jab at this opinion by naming a waiter on Jacob's tour of modern Greece after the old philosopher: "Aristotle, a dirty man, carnivorously interested in the body of the only guest now occupying the only arm-chair, came into the room ostentatiously" (138). This line may also lament the Greeks' misuse of male homosexuality as a further excuse to exclude women from public life, reserving the "only arm-chair," the seat of power, for men. Yet if the narrator and Mrs. Jarvis burlesque Captain Barfoot's claims to rationality and power, Betty Flanders does not follow her neighbor in questioning the social prescriptions for "heroic" fighting men on the bridge and passive, unthinking women in the home: "But Betty Flanders thought nothing of the kind" (28).

Even so, if Betty does not consciously rebel as she quietly goes about making the system of gender relations work for her, she unconsciously resents her position. In fact, in her lack of awareness she, as much as the captain, may perpetuate the system and even fuel the world's violence. Mrs. Jarvis certainly sentimentalizes Betty by rhapsodizing that "marriage is a fortress and widows stray solitary in the open fields, picking up stones, gleaning a few golden straws, lonely, unprotected, poor creatures," yet she exposes a rude truth about her neighbor: as a widow with three children, Betty needs money (8). So the young mother gets busy and does grasp a few golden straws. Although her letters to Captain Barfoot, "many-paged, tear-stained," do express some real grief, they also serve as a hard-headed, practical genre (17). The tears add a little color to her life, a wider blue to the page, and, eventually, by displaying a supposedly sexy vulnerability, they attract a provider.

From the opening scene in which the sheep's skull "would disperse a little dust—No, but not in lodgings," it is clear that Betty resents being reduced by widowhood to living in a lodging house. Indeed, only a few pages later she commands a house and comfortable kitchen garden (10, 17). Apparently she can afford this property because the captain intervenes, just as Jacob can go to Cambridge because his mother's friend has connections (29). Does Betty sell herself to get what she wants? Yes and no. Although she reddens with genuine pleasure for the captain, economic ambition also motivates the relationship. Betty is an entrepreneur at heart, wanting Garfit's acre and chickens: land and capital. She does advance financially with his help, while still managing to make the village regard her as respectable, despite the captain's visits.

Betty cannot marry the captain, of course, because he already has a wife, but there are indications that she prefers the unmarried state. She refuses Mr. Floyd's proposal. His love letter arrives as her son Johnny is chasing geese with a stick (21). Betty is angry—at Johnny? at the letter? at the fact that Mr. Floyd is chasing her with a phallic stick that is offered only on the condition that she give up control? As Woolf points out in *Three Guineas*, it was not until 1870 that a half-hearted Married Woman's Property Act was passed, and the ostensible opening of the professions to women in 1919 had not, by 1937, provided women with a noticeable increase in income (16, 47, 156). The fury that Betty, this would-be businesswoman, feels at her economic dependence must be greater than anyone suspects, because soon we hear "how she had had [Mr. Floyd's cat] gelded, and how she did not like red hair in men," suggesting that she would just as soon have gelded Mr. Floyd (23).

This same frightening violence surfaces in Betty when she accepts a knife that her young son Archer offers for protecting herself from the roosters: "Sounding at the same time as the bell, her son's voice mixed life and death inextricably, exhilaratingly. 'What a big knife for a small boy!' she said. She took it to please him" (16). Because her legitimate resentment at exclusion from remunerative work never comes to consciousness, she dangerously finds violence "exhilarating." Glad that the captain struts on the bridge and proud that her son handles knives, she is preparing to be a good backer of empires and wars. In this failure to recognize and direct her anger, she resembles Evelyn Murgatroyd of *The Voyage Out*, who resists what she considers domestic incarceration only by imagining herself a Renaissance colonizer. Betty even seems to be building her own private Empire when she plans her chicken farm, "sketching on the cloudy future flocks of Leghorns, Cochin Chinas," in the process conjuring up the French colony of Cochin China (91). Her thwarted energies require at least a vicarious field of activity, as if her psyche were calling, "Let's have a little excitement and blow this mess up!" Similarly, Woolf warns in *Three Guineas* that, unless conditions change for the middle-class woman confined to the home, she regrettably might be lost to the cause of peace. After noting that World War I gave such a woman her first real chance to work in field or factory, Woolf explains, "So profound was her unconscious loathing for the education of the private house with its cruelty, its poverty, its hypocrisy, its immorality . . . [that] consciously she desired 'our splendid Empire'; unconsciously she desired our splendid war" (*Three Guineas* 39).

Growing up with this outwardly placid but inwardly war-mongering mother and her attentive veteran, Jacob absorbs both their easy acceptance of the inevitability of military service and their attitude toward gender relations, which makes woman an object of conquest—at least in rhetoric, if not in fact. When Jacob first sleeps with Florinda, after persuading himself that her dubious claim to virginity must be true, he acquires an "authoritative" though simultaneously babyish air. The scene is presented from the unusual point of view of his mother's letter, which remains neglected on the hall table throughout the couple's copulation. Thoroughly indoctrinated in the double standard, Betty Flanders would blame only Florinda for the affair, although both partners consent equally: "Indeed, when the door opened and the couple came out, Mrs. Flanders would have flounced upon her—only it was Jacob who came first, in his dressing-gown, amiable, authoritative, beautifully healthy, like a baby after an airing, with an eye clear as running water" (92). Jacob is now convinced that he deserves all the power to direct others which his society bestows on him.

He also feels in command when he has an affair with a married woman, Sandra Wentworth Williams. Just as Captain Barfoot looks most obviously like a military man when he swaggers off to Betty's house, to his neglected friend Bonamy Jacob looks like a "British Admiral," "fixed, monolithic," when Jacob ignores Bonamy to dream of Sandra (165). Actually, Sandra has conquered Jacob. She adds the book which he presses on her as a memento to a shelf where "there were ten or twelve little volumes already," presumably from former young lovers (161). When it does dawn on Jacob that his women have had other affairs, he fails to draw the parallel between their behavior and his own. Instead, he gets over his shock at seeing Florinda "turning up Greek Street on another man's arm" by turning, himself, to the solaces of Empire. He reads about a new Home Rule bill and puts off the possibility of an independent Ireland as "a very difficult matter. A very cold night" (98). For his lost authority over Florinda, Jacob substitutes his country's dominion over colonies. Similarly, when Evan Williams gives his grudging consent to his wife Sandra's affair with Jacob, he shifts his thoughts to the need for "great men" like "Chatham, Pitt, Burke, and Charles James Fox" (143). Unable to take action himself, he admires Empire-builders. Appropriating other people's countries becomes a way of striking back when other men have appropriated his wife.

Another clear indication that relations between men and women pave the way for habits of thought that allow one country to control another occurs when Jacob visits the prostitute Laurette: "The fire burnt clear between two pillars of greenish marble, and on the mantelpiece there was a green clock guarded by Britannia leaning on her spear. As for pictures—a maiden in a large hat offered roses over the garden gate to a gentleman in eighteenth-century costume. . . . As she shut the door he put so many shillings on the mantelpiece" (104–5). The painting of a maiden is, on the one hand, ironic, as Laurette is no innocent girl but a knowing woman selling the rose of her sex. On the other hand, idealized maidens like Clara and less respectable women like Laurette constitute two sides of the same coin—perhaps the coins to which Jacob has greater access through his law office, whereas Laurette gets only shillings, and Clara, as a tea-pourer in a middle-class house, receives no income at all. Through all his experiences with women, Jacob is learning that he has the right to give orders, or to pretend to do so. When he is recovering from Florinda's "treachery," he still waffles a bit on the question of Irish independence, calling the problem "difficult" (98); but shortly after his visit to Laurette, he distracts himself from a gloomy mood by carrying his political convictions a step further: "Nor was he altogether in favour of giving Home Rule to Ireland" (139). Britannia leaning on her spear thus presides appropriately as a beneficiary of the lessons of the brothel.

A further example of the way Jacob learns from the available relationships with women to become an Empire-builder occurs when he sits in Greece dreaming of Sandra. He muses, "Why not rule countries in the way they should be ruled? . . . Greece was over; the Parthenon in ruins; yet there he was" (150). Out of a need to bolster an enormous yet insecure ego, an emphatically displayed "he" derives his self-worth by identifying with the new British Empire, much as his counterparts in other European countries also learn to project themselves abroad. Indeed, after the reminder that "Greece was over," the very next line mentions "French ladies on their way to join their husbands in Constantinople," the city, as we have already seen, that became a focus of rivalry among empires (150).

Jacob's endorsement of English rule over other countries will concern him more than he imagines, when he must fight in a war occasioned, at least in part, by the need to protect that dominance. *Jacob's*

Room shows the main character playing an imperial role that slowly becomes less fantasized and more real. As he looks like an admiral when he dreams of Sandra, he dresses like an emperor (Roman) to please yet another lover, Fanny Elmer: "He looked terrible and magnificent and would chuck the Forest, he said, and come to the Slade, and be a Turkish knight or a Roman emperor (and he let her blacken his lips and clenched his teeth and scowled in the glass)" (124). Fanny might appear to be getting her way, flattering him into accompanying her to a costume party. Nevertheless, world events, not women, will most effectively manipulate Jacob. Although he may feel like an admiral or an emperor, real admirals will direct him to maintain the Empire, at his expense.

Jacob, in fact, is being co-opted into a game, a play, a sacrificial ritual, which he does not understand. At a bohemian gathering, "they were binding his eyes for some game" (111). At the Durrants' party, his hostess commiserates, "Poor Jacob. . . . They're going to make you act in their play" (62). When he meets Florinda on Guy Fawkes Day, "They wreathed his head with paper flowers. Then somebody brought out a white and gilt chair and made him sit on it. As they passed, people hung glass grapes on his shoulders, until he looked like the figure-head of a wrecked ship. Then Florinda got upon his knee and hid her face in his waistcoat" (75). Reinforcing the ominous tone of the image of a wrecked ship, morbid celebrations on Guy Fawkes Day included the burning of "guys," effigies of a sixteenth-century conspirator. Fawkes had wanted to blow up Parliament "in reprisal for increasing oppression of Roman Catholics in England" ("Fawkes"). Because men like Jacob and Evan Williams are also being trained in revenge, as a means of compensating for lost loves, it is appropriate but horrifying that Jacob will become a new "guy" burned in the war.

Jacob may think that he is only playing when he dresses as the emperor, but, just one page earlier, the narrator reports: "The chestnuts have flirted their fans. And the butterflies are flaunting across the rides in the Forest. Perhaps the Purple Emperor is feasting, as Morris says, upon a mass of putrid carrion at the base of an oak tree" (123). Not just sketching scenery, the passage suggests that the "splendid" Empire, as Woolf ironically calls it in *Three Guineas* (39), actually is sustaining itself by means of corpses. The oak tree might resemble the aristocratic oak of *Orlando,* the foundation of old England. Yet England, in this picture, seems rotten to its roots. The corruption lies in the exclusions of church and university, the dullness and repression of small-town life and conventional gender roles (which cause thwarted women and bored men to welcome even dangerous excitements), and the aggressive acquisitiveness which allows a boy to appropriate crabs or shipping companies to lace up the globe. The Empire, purpled with blood, feeds on others in the system who make sacrifices—women, servants, the colonized—and, eventually, on its own soldiers. Jacob, for instance, soon will be carrion.

The Waves

The Waves differs from Woolf's other novels criticizing the Empire in that it focuses on a psychological cause for dominating others: the desire on the part of a person who has been made to feel inferior to find even lowlier victims. Nevertheless, if Woolf blames a psychological, perhaps innate need, she even more powerfully indicts the social arrangements that reinforce and develop such urges. Like *Jacob's Room, The Waves* exposes aspects of English life that groom ordinary citizens to take their place in a threatening community. The public (i.e., private) schools, the universities, and the common middle-class occupations all teach two dangerous traits: conformity and resort to force. Beginning by segregating the sexes, this education goes on to instill possessiveness and an arrogance actually grounded in insecurity. Social attitudes encourage ignorance and isolate an *I* which is, for all its bravado, not powerful but self-doubting, bolstered by a small, exclusive, and intolerant *we.*

Such training inevitably throws up a colonizer like Percival: "The boat has floated through the arch of the willows and is now under the bridge. Percival, Tony, Archie, or another, will go to India" (*Waves* 90). Jane Marcus shrewdly locates the mainspring of the book when she calls Percival—idolized, distant, never heard from—"the last shabby chivalric imperialist" (Colloquium). The relentless waves of this education also abrade and shape the six speaking characters. The uniformity of diction and rhythm in their monologues has puzzled many critics: "The speeches often seem like one pervasive voice with six personalities; and, as . . . [Jean Guiguet] has remarked, 'to define that voice is to solve the whole problem of *The Waves*'" (quoted in Naremore 152). Marcus assumes, unnecessarily, I think, that Bernard has presumed to speak for all his friends in his own invariable style, foisting his fictions off as their own talk ("Eyes" 64). Instead, the telltale cadence could simply mean that the voice of "culture," not of any one person, "speaks" the characters into being. Although the book creates much sympathy for them in their poignant longing for other human beings and their occasional, admirable self-awareness, it also questions pervasive social expectations.

This determining cultural voice naïvely praises a single hero, like Percival, whom Bernard only fleetingly recognizes as "conventional" (123). Hero-worship was an integral part of imperialism between 1870 and World War II in Great Britain (MacKenzie 2). After Percival's death, what his friends imagine he would have accomplished in India becomes increasingly grandiose. Neville imagines that Percival would have "sat in Court and ridden alone at the head of troops" (152). Bernard asserts that the young administrator would have protected people "dying of famine and disease"; he would have "done justice" and "shocked the authorities" (243). Nevertheless, when Bernard tries to specify something more concrete than "justice," all he can picture is an Englishman spurring on a stalled cart with curses (136). Marcus suggests that this scene alludes to Rudyard Kipling's *Kim*, exposing what Bernard assumes is British justice as really bullying. She points out several elements undercutting Percival's status: the pompous word "behold" introducing the scene, the ironic claim that "the Oriental problem is solved" by a few expletives, and the inflated label "God" for Percival (136; Colloquium). Like the merchant Willoughby Vinrace in *The Voyage Out,* who breaks up a strike of "wretched little natives" by shouting "English oaths" at them (196), Percival adopts the tactics of the schoolyard. Yet, if Willoughby and Percival personally look childish, they are institutionally powerful, as they ensure that workers remain "beggars."

Whereas Neville thinks that Percival would have "denounced some monstrous tyranny," the young man in India just plays quoits with a colonel (152). He dies not at the head of troops but in a race, when his "horse tripped" (151). Riding with troops, however, would have been just another version of races or quoits. If the name Percival conjures up medieval quests, that ideal is already tainted as militaristic. Like Woolf, her husband demythologized chivalry when he condemned British companies abroad at the end of the nineteenth century for "the profitable business of financial knight-errantry and exploitation, in the undeveloped regions of the world" (*Empire and Commerce* 206). Woolf also satirizes her "mediaeval commander" Percival, who has hardly matured beyond the level of games at school (37). As an adult he puts into practice his earlier training to pit the "blue boy" against the "red boy," mindlessly, by asserting English superiority over Indians (31).

In contrast to his friends' idealization of Percival, his behavior in school already casts doubt on the grand claims. Instead of "protecting" people, Percival disdains others and looks as if he might even enjoy hurting them: "He would make an admirable churchwarden. He should have a birch and beat little boys for misdemeanours. He is allied with the Latin phrases on the memorial brasses" (36). Instead of leaving at his death "whipped dogs and crying children . . . bereft" (243), he is likely to have been the one flogging them in the first place. Instead of shocking the authorities, Percival reveres tradition, power, and the status quo. He assumes a monumental, autocratic style, which is immobile until it darts out in animalistic blows: "That is Percival, lounging on the cushions, monolithic, in giant repose. No, it is only one of his satellites, imitating his monolithic, his giant repose. He alone is unconscious of their tricks, and when he catches them at it he buffets them good-humouredly with a blow of his paw" (82). That paw still belongs to a cuddly cub, but, as Rhoda suspects, the tiger may leap more powerfully one day (130).

Percival epitomizes, in fact, two of the most dangerous qualities inculcated by the schools—regimentation and militarism (cf. Eby 247). College as well as elementary school fosters the abdication of individual will to a leader like Percival: "They [the students] are now smashing china—that also is the convention. . . . On they roll; on they gallop; after hounds, after footballs; they pump up and down attached to oars like sacks of flour. All divisions are merged—they act like one man" (91). In this comic catalogue of undergraduate antics, the erosion of dissent and difference is the most ominous result. The six speaking characters conform from childhood to adulthood, all in military imagery: "We who yelped like jackals biting at each other's heels now assume the sober and confident air of soldiers in the presence of their captain" (123). Although Bernard mocks the little boys, actually he is caught up in the same emulation. Even at his last meeting with the friends, he is still envying the boys "all turning their heads the same way as the brake rounded the corner; and I wished to be with them" (234). Elevating Percival as "commander" or "captain" leads to the frightening prediction that the followers may be "shot like sheep" (37).

Not only is Percival an imperialist, as Marcus observes (Colloquium), but Percival's unhealthy training affects all six of his friends. Moreover, Woolf connects the "totalizing" impulse of the child, who just wants to be taken into the group, with much more ominous totalitarian politics. Registering through Louis the signs of growing repressiveness in Europe, she proceeds to link the goals and methods of the continental autocratic governments with those of the British Empire. As Leonard Woolf warned in the first volume of *After the Deluge,* "The authoritarian elements in the psychology of socialism, communism, and fascism spring from the same recesses of the human mind and heart as do those in patriotism, nationalism, and imperialism" (334). *The Waves* demonstrates that Empire making may stem from a psychological need for unity, misdirected into dangerous substitutes for love. Characters who, like Louis, feel left out of the social circle long to secure a bigger circle—by force, if necessary.

Even a helpless character like Rhoda displays this alarming urge to incise a world order. As she sits alone after school over insoluble math problems, Rhoda focuses on the clock and the numbers on her page: "The two hands are convoys marching through a desert. The black bars on the clock face are green oases. . . . Look, the loop of the figure is beginning to fill with time; it holds the world in it. I begin to draw a figure and the world is looped in it, and I myself am outside the loop; which I now join—so—and seal up, and make entire" (21). Although Rhoda loses confidence that she herself could really join any community, others with as little inner peace but more outward power pursue her dream of sealing herself into a protective, worldwide loop. Active colonizers like Percival and multinational businessmen like Louis try to patch up the fragmentation in their thoughts and in the splintered classes of their society by imposing a single identity. As Percival inspires the schoolboys to turn in exactly the same direction, Louis too will attempt to lose his awkward difference in artificial sameness. Empire becomes a corrupted facsimile of the homogenous, accepting community which they think they need in order to consolidate their fractured identities. Whereas Rhoda only dreams her oases, the administrators of Empire, like Percival, and its financial moguls, like Louis, send real convoys through real deserts. Louis, in fact, is laying the groundwork of an international financial network to perpetuate British control even after the restive colonies of his time officially achieve independence.

All six characters project onto Percival their need for union, as with a mother or sexual partner; at their dinner before his departure for India, they find comfort in "this globe whose walls are made of Percival" (145). However, this "moment [made] out of one man" encloses not only ordinary tables and chairs but also "forests and far countries . . . seas and jungles; the howlings of jackals," scenes reminiscent of the Empire (145). If the glow from Percival seems to enhance mundane objects, it also unpleasantly lights up knives which can "cut again" when he arrives, implying the foundation of Empire in force (122, 145). Immediately after Percival conjures up this enclosing and only apparently innocuous global bubble, Bernard betrays a bit of bad conscience about that Empire: "We are not slaves bound to suffer incessantly unrecorded petty blows on our bent backs. We are not sheep either, following a master" (146). Louis, however, has already admitted that English children, including himself, follow Percival as "sheep" (37). By denying that they are "slaves," Bernard reveals that the seas and jungles which Percival will command have made him think, guiltily, of the bent backs of the Empire's colonized people. Indeed, Leonard Woolf slammed British policies in East Africa as "a demand for slavery pure and simple" (*Empire and Commerce* 347). He himself became disillusioned with his years as a colonial administrator in Ceylon after presiding at "barbarous" British hangings and floggings and after personally beating the bent backs of Arab oyster divers, who "will do anything if you hit them hard enough with a walking stick, an occupation in which I have been engaged for the most part of the last three days and nights" (*Growing* 91, 166). Whereas Leonard eventually regretted his sheeplike acquiescence in brutality and undertook to document the stupidities of Empire, Bernard denies the complicity which he nevertheless glimpses.

The character who demonstrates this totalizing impulse most frighteningly is Louis. He also is the one most actively involved in creating and maintaining the Empire. Coveting "a house in Surrey, two cars, a conservatory and some rare species of melon," he does want material goods (200). Nevertheless, his main motive is not money—he continues to live in an "attic" (198)—but rather a desire to be included. Louis first feels like an outsider because of his Australian accent, a small difference which nevertheless determines his whole life. Although Louis invites sympathy as a lonely child and an unfunded scholar (67, 92), he responds to adversity by inflicting a worse oppression on others. Ironically, his resentment at being a product of England's imperial expansion into Australia causes him to extend that Empire even further.

One scene which epitomizes Louis's alienation and his retaliatory response to it is an incident at school:

> I like the orderly progress. We file in. . . . Dr. Crane mounts the pulpit and reads the lesson from a Bible spread on the back of the brass eagle. I rejoice; my heart expands in his bulk, in his authority. He lays the whirling dust clouds in my tremulous, my ignominiously agitated mind—how we danced round the Christmas tree and handing parcels they forgot me, and the fat woman said, "This little boy has no present," and gave me a shiny Union Jack from the top of the tree, and I cried with fury—to be remembered with pity. Now all is laid by his authority, his crucifix. . . . (34–35)

Whereas Neville already understands the narrow-mindedness of a headmaster and a church that would condemn his homosexuality as something different—"The brute menaces my liberty"—Louis requires such coercive sameness (35). He identifies with an "orderly progress" that gains its "authority" through "bulk," not through integrity or compassion. Sheltering under a Christianity represented as a crusading bird of prey rather than as a lamb, Louis assures himself that he, too, will dominate: "I become a figure in the procession, a spoke in the huge wheel that turning, at last erects me" (35). The Union Jack of Empire has conspicuously replaced any Christian symbol at the top of the tree. Although Louis recalls that he was furious at being offered the flag in lieu of a package, he does, in fact, accept it. Later in life, through his worldwide business network, he will treat the Empire as his own private gift.

At first Louis announces that he will find "orderly progress" only through poetry, an apparently innocent pursuit. He has already admitted that he envies the common folk, but when he does not fit in with the crowd in the streets, he scorns them as the embodiment of "disorder" (94). He counteracts the supposed "aimlessness" of the working class by reading a book, containing "some forged rings, some perfect statements" (94). Woolf, of course, also prized "order" in art, for the "synthesis" which it gave to her life, appreciating "how only writing composes it: how nothing makes a whole unless I am writing. . . . Odd how the creative power at once brings the whole universe to order. I can see the day whole, proportioned" (*Diary* 4: 161, 232). Nevertheless, she recognizes in *The Waves* a real danger when that need for synthesis expands beyond patterns in a fiction to tracings on a map. For it soon becomes clear that Louis's "perfect statements" command "a binding power [that] ropes you in" (95). His desire to exert control taints Louis's love of words. When he declares, "I oppose to what is passing this ramrod of beaten steel" and adds despotically, "I will reduce you to order," one wonders how long he will be content with steely words (95).

Louis would impose his order both at home and abroad. Bernard sometimes resents that Louis is "adding us up like insignificant items in some grand total which he is for ever pursuing, in his office. And one day taking a fine pen and dipping it in red ink, the addition will be complete; our total will be known; but it will not be enough" (92). In Louis's totalizing scheme, individual people do not matter. Although he still masks his plans behind poetry, his ruminations become more politically authoritarian: "I have read my poet in an eating-house, and . . . listened to the clerks. . . . I said their journeys should have an end in view; they should earn their two pound ten a week at the command of an august master; some hand, some robe, should fold us about" (168–69). Once Louis has invoked an "august master," his "few words" and hammered "ring of beaten steel" reverberate beyond poems to commands carried out by weapons. For him order means control in society and not just rhythm on a page. Among his safe pillars and brasses, memorializing other people's deaths in battle, he seeks a preemptive control: "There is no crudity here, no sudden kisses" (35). As Louis's chilling dismissal of "crudity" implies, a totally predictable world precludes love as well as threat.

Just as Louis would rein in spontaneous life to create something terrifyingly close to a police state at home, abroad he is furthering Empire. The image of "red ink," which Bernard mentions when he pictures Louis adding insignificant people into never-sufficient sums (92), alludes to the red in which British possessions were depicted on maps (Moorhouse 11). The red of the pitchers in Louis's daydreams also may acquire their tint from the Empire—and from blood (95). He claims, "I have fused my many lives into one; I have helped by my assiduity and decision to score those lines on the map there by which the different parts of the world are laced together" (168). Approaching Empire through finance, Louis "tore the date from the calendar, and announced to the world of ship-brokers, corn-chandlers and actuaries that Friday the tenth, or Tuesday the eighteenth, had dawned on the city of London" (126). His grand announcement only informs his colleagues of the obvious, undercutting his contribution. Moreover, it is perhaps appropriate that actuaries totting up risks cap his list, since tables of death might accompany the days he "tore." He forges the world into rows where all eyes are trained on him: "The globe is strung with our lines [of shipping]. I am immensely respectable. All the young ladies in the office acknowledge my entrance" (200). Fanning his own ego through Empire, he is an equivalent of Abel Pargiter and his son Martin in *The Years*. As he props up his manhood in a power play that tries to make the whole world his compliant mistress, Louis croons eerily, "I love the telephone with its lips stretched to my whisper" (168). As he dehumanizes people, he transfers his affection to the inanimate props of his power.

Woolf thus exposes the totalizing impulse of Empire as totalitarian, and, in fact, Louis resembles the fascists coming to power in Europe in the decade before *The Waves*.[2] His calls for an "august master" (169) reveal him as the citizen who would abdicate decisions to a Führer or Duce. Such tyrants may even enlist literature and art, as Louis does, in the cause of an imposed unity. As Woolf reports in *A Room of One's Own*, Italy was developing prescriptions for artists: "The Fascist poem, one may fear, will be a horrid little abortion such as one sees in a glass jar in the museum of some country town" (107). Behind his aestheticizing, however, Louis traces the musculature of force, displaying first the inferiority complex and then the hostility characteristic of fascism. Woolf's Bloomsbury friend John Maynard Keynes had warned in *The Economic Consequences of the Peace* (1919) that if Germany's reparations from World War I were too great and Germans felt left out of Europe, the country would try to get revenge (Taylor 136); in her diary she praises Keynes's book (2: 33). When Louis feels left out of his community, he fuels his ambition with a similar desire for revenge, willing himself to be "born entire, out of hatred" (39).

Louis seems willing to express this resentment in sadistic ways. He watches "with envy" the students who "leave butterflies trembling with their wings pinched off" or "make little boys sob in dark passages" (47). These cruel older students are "always forming into fours and marching in troops with badges on their caps; they salute simultaneously passing the figure of their general. How majestic is their order, how beautiful is their obedience! If I could follow, if I could be with them I would sacrifice all I know" (47). Even Louis's childhood belt with a brass snake seems to be an attempt to flash special insignia, like the badges on the caps of the "troops," to set himself above most people, while still safely supported in his eminence by a corps of elite companions.

With such an apprenticeship in childhood, Louis in his adult life also threatens a sadomasochistic force: "I must drop heavy as a hatchet and cut the oak with my sheer weight, for if I deviate, glancing this way, or that way, I shall fall like snow and be wasted" (167). Because he has imagined, just a few lines before, "dark men and yellow men migrating east, west, north and south," he intimates that his megalomania may require cutting down colonized people with that hatchet (167). Despite his demurral that he issues only "courteous commands on the telephone," his velvet glove covers an iron fist (167). His violence drives an apocalyptic excess that would destroy the very "oak" he worships, if the village green will not accept him. Like Woolf's Orlando, whose oak tree symbolizes rootedness in a noble family, Louis, too, according to Neville, pretends, "I am a Duke—the last of an ancient race" (119). Louis then repeats an image of knocking on a "grained oak door" to be admitted to the common halls (201). If the door does not open to suit him, however, "The hatchet must fall on the block; the oak must be cleft to the center" (171).

Just as Louis's conformity and resort to force suggest fascism, so does this need for a past and a tradition. When he feels excluded from the "safe traditional ways under the shade of old yew trees," the university paths where Bernard and Neville can walk because they are the "sons of gentlemen" (67, 20), Louis fabricates an even older tradition for himself, not unlike the Italian revival of old Rome or the Nazi appropriation of an "Aryan" history in Germanic myth. Louis inserts himself into an ancient "history that began in Egypt, in the time of the Pharaohs, when women carried red pitchers to the Nile. I seem already to have lived many thousand years" (66).

Sidling up to Pharaohs, Louis is not merely fashioning poetic phrases, nor does he remain in the past. He helps to recreate the Egyptian kingdom in the present, to support his financial dealings. Bernard describes his friend: "Louis, whose bony hands shut like the sides of a dock closing themselves with a slow anguish of effort upon an enormous tumult of waters, who knew what has been said by the Egyptian, the Indian, by men with high cheek-bones and solitaries in hair shirts" (275). As a shipper, Louis would know about modern Egypt and its appropriation by Britain to facilitate trade with India. Leonard Woolf recorded in *Empire and Commerce in Africa* that "in 1879 England, Germany, and France deposed the Khedive Ismail; in 1881 came the mutiny of Arabi; in 1882 the bombardment of Alexandria and the landing of a British army in Egypt . . . within about a decade of the opening of the Canal, Egypt was under the military occupation of that European State which ruled India" (139). Egypt was formally annexed in 1914, then granted a nominal independence in 1922; even then, the British still controlled the country through a High Commissioner "whose advice on a number of military and diplomatic subjects had to be taken very seriously" (Lloyd 291).

Because Louis imagines that he must drop "heavy as a hatchet" while "dark men" migrate "east, west, north and south" (167), he conjures up the means by which Great Britain acquired control of Egypt. Lytton Strachey sarcastically notes in his essay on General Gordon that, after British forces crushed the nationalist revolt of Arabi in Egypt, the British command sent out the relics of Arabi's army—ten thousand men in chains—in a forced migration, to fight another nationalist uprising in the Sudan (*Eminent Victorians* 272). All but three hundred of Arabi's men were slaughtered. Woolf, who read this essay in 1917, seems to have borrowed some of its details for Louis's cryptic mutterings about populations shifting and hatchets falling (*Letters* 2: 205).

Inflating himself into a new pharaoh under the aegis of the British Empire, Louis wants to regulate the confluence of all waters; he projects his own skeletal hands onto the Suez Canal (275). Here Virginia Woolf implicitly compares the British ideal of Empire to a totalitarian drive for conquest. Just as she will warn in 1938, the focus on a tyrant abroad prevents Britons from noticing a similar menace at home: "He is called in German and Italian Führer or Duce; . . . we cannot dissociate ourselves from that figure but are ourselves that figure" (*Three Guineas* 142). Louis, then, betrays a broad kinship with fascism in his love for conformity, aestheticism without compassion, praise for an "august master," resort to simple symbols, appropriation of a validating past, sadism, and militarism.

Even more frightening than Louis's personal susceptibility, however, is the fact that, in *The Waves,* the English school system fosters these same traits. Woolf condemned the private schools many times throughout her career. In *A Room of One's Own,* she charges the schools with conferring only "a Master in Lunacy. All this pitting of sex against sex, of quality against quality; all this claiming of superiority and imputing of inferiority, belong to the private-school stage of human existence where there are 'sides,' and it is necessary for one side to beat another side, and of the utmost importance to walk up to a platform and receive from the hands of the Headmaster himself a highly ornamental pot" (110). In *The Pargiters,* Woolf similarly criticizes the complacent and exclusive spirit of both the schools and the universities, where the pillars and marble tablets go on recording "the names of the old boys who had fought in war after war . . . for five hundred years; . . . [with] Marlborough, with . . . Nelson, with Wellington; whose bones lay unburied in India" (61). These pillars, like the ones so comforting to Percival and Louis (35–36), advertise dangerous values of "the Jew, the Greek & the Roman"—revered authorities from the Old Testament, which influenced Judaism, Christianity, and Islam, and from the classics (*Pargiters* 61). Like *Jacob's Room,* which mocked a whole literary tradition by cataloguing Plato and Shakespeare along with the mummies (109), *The Pargiters* and *The Waves* broadly take aim at the Western tradition. Woolf indicts this tradition so sweepingly because it teaches "intrepidity" and "self-sacrifice," abstract ideals that may lead the chosen or the elect to fight out of pride, whether any specific cause exists or not (*Pargiters* 61). Woolf blames the educational system for encouraging "simultaneity" of movements, arrogance, and brutal intolerance toward outsiders—all habits of mind that make wars possible.

Louis, like Jacob, is the complacent "inheritor" of this Western tradition (*Jacob* 45). Despite his real motive in a need to belong, and despite his real means in force, Louis offers more and more idealistic justifications: "My shoulder is to the wheel; I roll the dark before me, spreading commerce where there was chaos in the far parts of the world" (168). Exalting himself into a god drawing order out of chaos and light out of darkness, he sits at his typewriter, as Bernard perceives, "for our instruction, for our regeneration, and the reform of an unborn world" (198).

Bernard tolerates Louis's unctuousness with bemusement, but he would do well to worry. Although Louis may claim to civilize, his love for command *is* barbarity. Soon he is congratulating himself:

> The weight of the world is on our shoulders; its vision is through our eyes; if we blink or look aside, or turn back to finger what Plato said or remember Napoleon and his conquests, we inflict on the world the injury of some obliquity. This is life; Mr. Prentice at four; Mr. Eyres at four-thirty. I like to hear . . . the heavy male tread of responsible feet down the corridors. So by dint of our united exertions we send ships to the remotest parts of the globe; replete with lavatories and gymnasiums. (169)

The transportation of lavatories undermines the grandness of Louis's enterprise. He does not seem to notice the waste that he is producing, as he tries to recreate even the smallest signs of English life around the world. He turns aside from the history of Napoleon and the writings of Plato not to reject them but only to put their precepts into practice, the better to hear the tread of male feet dominating the globe. He obviously admires the Empire making of Napoleon, and, although Louis, like Jacob, does not specify what attracted him to Plato, he might approve the Greek philosopher's emphasis on a martial stoicism as the only lesson in poetry and his willingness to censor literature and lie to the citizenry. Poets, according to Plato, must not depict men or women weeping for companions slain in battle, because listeners might get the idea that war is bad. Poets must hush up "whining," and rulers of the state may lie outright "for the public good" (Plato, *Republic* 24–25).

Louis's other idols corroborate these inferences that he might admire Plato's military ethic and Napoleon's Empire building: "If I press on, from chaos making order, I shall find myself where Chatham stood, and Pitt, Burke, and Sir Robert Peel" (168). Peel, founder of the Conservative party, set up the London police force, the "Bobbies." The elder William Pitt, Earl of Chatham, in the eighteenth century engineered "a fundamental shift in British imperial strategy," acquiring enormous inland territory in North America and India for a new goal of national prestige, instead of maintaining coastal areas for the usual goal of trade (Graham 71–73). William Pitt the Younger introduced a bill in 1784 to set up a government-appointed Board of Control over the East India Company. Edmund Burke had supported the younger Pitt by criticizing the grasping employees of the company to the House of Commons: "animated with all the avarice of age and all the impetuosity of youth, they roll in one after another; wave after wave; and there is nothing before the eyes of the native but an endless hopeless prospect of new birds of prey and passage, with appetites continually renewing for a food that is continually wasting" (quoted in Moorhouse 53). Nevertheless, if Burke wanted to curb the excesses of company employees, his solution was to transfer power to the British government, not to Indians. Louis approves the emphasis on law and order and worldwide domains, advocated by all his role models, as he sends his ships out "wave after wave." Burke, Chatham, and Pitt are, as we have seen, the same figures Evan Williams invokes in *Jacob's Room* to bolster him when he feels weak because his wife has an affair with Jacob (143). Louis too requires imperial backers, because he feels left out.

Among Louis's high-flown ideals that mask dangerous oppressions is a version of Kipling's "white man's burden," which Leonard Woolf decried as "the white man's burden of lucrative imperialism" (*Empire and Commerce* 356). Louis boasts in self-pity, "My task, my burden, has always been greater than other people's. A pyramid has been set on my shoulders. . . . I have driven a violent, an unruly, a vicious team. With my Australian accent I have sat in eating shops and tried to make the clerks accept me, yet never forgotten my solemn and severe convictions and the discrepancies and incoherences that must be resolved" (201). Claiming a "destiny," he puffs himself up to hide a fear that in reality he still grovels before clerks. Like Jacob, Louis must have read *Phaedrus*, to borrow Socrates's image of the soul as a charioteer and two horses (*Phaedrus* 495). Yet Louis's desire to resolve "discrepancies" only highlights his willingness to rein in his own softer emotions and drive a "vicious team"; he identifies his own rejected emotions with the "disorder[ly]" working class or unruly colonized peoples who dare to be different from himself (94).

The other characters only occasionally betray an uneasy awareness of Louis's despotism. Rhoda muses, "He says, looking at the people passing, he will shepherd us if we will follow. If we submit he will reduce us to order" (161). She seems uncertain if she will masochistically "submit" to a powerful guide and be "reduced" after all. Eventually she follows so far as to become Louis's lover (170), but Louis's initial attraction to her, when they were still children, bodes ill for their adult relationship: "She has no answer for them. She has no body as the others have. And I . . . do not fear her as I fear the others" (22). Although it might seem natural that two outsiders draw together for comfort, Louis wants not an equal but someone even more cowed than he, who will not talk back. Like Napoleon and Mussolini, whose habit of using women as looking glasses Woolf criticizes in *A Room of One's Own* (35–36), Louis requires Rhoda as his mirror, which cannot have a body of its own. One of the self-proclaimed "Supermen and Fingers of Destiny," Louis craves an assurance of his own grandeur; otherwise, Woolf asks sarcastically, "How is he to go on giving judgement, civilising natives, making laws, writing books, dressing up and speechifying at banquets, unless he can see himself at breakfast and at dinner at least twice the size he really is?" (*Room of Own* 36). When Louis calls Rhoda's eyes the "colour of snail's flesh," he uncomfortably echoes the preferences of the birds which peck at snail shells until they break, implying that he would lean on Rhoda even if his demands harmed her (200, 109).

Rhoda spends a long time deluding herself about Louis's destructiveness, which injures both friends at home and strangers around the globe. When she finally leaves him, she explains, "I feared embraces. With fleeces, with vestments I have tried to cover the blue-black blade" (205). The word *vestments* suggests that missionary claims may have helped her to justify his imperialism. *Fleeces* conjures up propagandistic myths of conquest, such as Jason and the Golden Fleece, as well as schemes for "fleecing" the indigenous inhabitants of colonies and for using Medea-women like Rhoda. Leonard Woolf censures companies like Louis's and the British government for fleecing victims: "By fraud or by force the native chiefs and rulers were swindled or robbed of their dominions" (*Empire and Commerce* 353). Louis's *blade,* mentioned after *embraces,* sounds phallic, but its sexuality is displaced onto weaponry,

as in the case of Peter Walsh's knife in *Mrs. Dalloway. Blue-black* perhaps announces the color of bruises. Thus, when Rhoda shudders, "I
feared embraces," she is far from confessing a frigidity that would shun
all touch. Instead, she finally admits the steely coldness in Louis's will
to power.

Like Rhoda when she hesitates to submit to Louis's domination,
Bernard sometimes questions Louis's sway over the friends and over the
colonies: "How then, I asked, would Louis roof us all in? How would
he confine us, make us one, with his red ink, with his very fine nib? . . .
So into the street again, swinging my stick, looking at wire trays in
stationers' shop-windows, at baskets of fruit grown in the colonies,
murmuring Pillicock sat on Pillicock's hill, or Hark, hark, the dogs do
bark, or The World's great age begins anew, or Come away, come away,
death—mingling nonsense and poetry, floating in the stream" (282).
Bernard's nonsense rhymes mock Louis, but they also allow Bernard to
evade the very issues of colonies (source of the fruit), swagger (the cock
on the hill), and poverty ("Hark, hark . . . Beggars are coming to town")
which briefly he has raised (Baring-Gould 28, 84). He hints that Louis's
tight control and his propensity for grandiose phrases like "the world's
great age" may lead to destruction; such poetry may only invite, "Come
away, death" (Shakespeare, *Twelfth Night* 2.4). Yet Bernard does not
pursue these intuitions. Despite his skepticism, he has not, after all,
distanced himself from Louis. Internalizing the magnate's vocabulary of red
pitchers and nightingales, Bernard regrets that he has not achieved "coherency": "It had been impossible for me, taking snuff as I do from any
bagman met in a train, to keep coherency—that sense of the generations, of women carrying red pitchers to the Nile, of the nightingale
who sings among conquests and migrations" (283). Bernard's desired
"coherency" resembles all too closely Louis's code word "order," denot-
ing solidarity under his thumb. The conquerors continue treading on
people while Bernard tries, less successfully than Louis, to forget contemporary Egypt behind picturesque women and nightingales.

In fact, all of Percival's friends, like Bernard, display this combined
awareness and evasiveness about Louis's destructive imperialism. Although Rhoda seems to differ radically from Louis (her helplessness

contrasting with his outward vigor), she salves inner hurts by similar stratagems. They lament in identical terms how naked and defenseless they are (96, 106). If Rhoda had been a man, with Louis's opportunities to advance in business, she might have tyrannized as readily. Her characteristic gesture of setting white petals sailing in a brown basin may look like innocence itself, yet she immediately inflates her ships into a "fleet" and an "Armada," emphasizing their capacity for war (18–19, 27–28). She takes revenge on her more assured companions by imagining that all their ships "have foundered, all except my ship which mounts the wave and sweeps before the gale and reaches the islands where the parrots chatter" (19). In her longing to escape from discomfort at school to an exotic paradise, she glosses over the question of whether someone might already inhabit the island which she wishes to appropriate for herself. *The Waves,* however, airs this problem immediately after Rhoda sails her petals, when Neville wants his knife back to make boats: "The big blade is an emperor; the broken blade a Negro" (19). When Louis then arrives, bemoaning his isolating accent, his presence completes the chilling prediction that to pocket private islands of refuge is to break black men, perhaps with Louis's "blue-black blade," and create more refugees, Louis's "dark men and yellow men migrating" (205, 167).

Although Rhoda sometimes wishes to climb over others as ruthlessly as Louis, she lacks the social standing of a man and the associated confidence to maintain her dream of dominance. Thus, even as a child, she glimpses her armada sinking, a vision that prefigures her suicide by drowning (28). As an adult, she still imagines escaping her squalid London surroundings to reach a "mountain, from the top of which I shall see Africa." In seeing Africa, however, she admits that she is "corrupted" (203). She could never escape without taking her destructive London values with her and so corrupting Africa in turn. Although she does perceptively analyze and condemn herself and her whole crowd, she cannot conceive any real alternative to their social training: "All were dressed in indeterminate shades of grey and brown, never even a blue feather pinned to a hat. None had the courage to be one thing rather than another. What dissolution of the soul you demanded in order to get through one day, what lies, bowings, scrapings, fluency and servility!" (204). Despite her insight, she has no power to reform: "But I yielded . . . I did not go out into the street and break a bottle in the gutter as a sign of rage. . . . What you did, I did" (204). As she follows her peers, she cannot even picture any form of protest against Louis's totalitarian leanings except to smash glass, a tactic which would only bring about more destruction.

The character who at first sight seems to contrast most starkly with both the uncertain Rhoda and the "opulent" Louis (198) is Susan, sure of her love for the earth and content with simple onions and sweet babies: "Yet more will come, more children; more cradles, more baskets in the kitchen and hams ripening; and onions glistening; and more beds of lettuce and potatoes" (173). Unfortunately, it is the need for *more* onions and everything else that predominates. Susan, a conservative landowner, is as concerned with getting and keeping as Louis in his counting house: "Now I measure, I preserve" (192). Something possessive and even bloodthirsty taints her child-rearing also:

> My children will carry me on; their teething, their crying, their going to school
> and coming back will be like the waves of the sea under me. . . . I shall possess
> more than Jinny, more than Rhoda, by the time I die. . . . I shall be debased
> and hide-bound by the bestial and beautiful passion of maternity. I shall push
> the fortunes of my children unscrupulously. I shall hate those who see their
> faults. I shall lie basely to help them. . . . I love with such ferocity that it kills
> me when the object of my love shows by a phrase that he can escape. (132)

She displays, in fact, the same ruthlessness that a character in *The Years* detects even in the best of his "deformed" relatives: "If it were a question . . . of 'my' children, of 'my' possessions, it would be one rip down the belly; or teeth in the soft fur of the throat" (380). As Leonard Woolf argued in a 1928 pamphlet "The Way of Peace," a "competitive psychology" and the institutions that encourage it, based on the needs of the individual manufacturer, middleman, unionist—or parent, one might add—"makes for international hostility and war" (26). By contrast, the Co-operative Movement which he advocates represents consumers' interests and fosters peace (6, 29). Susan's individual concern for her own storehouse and her own relatives blocks her view of the needs of the whole community and makes her ferocious, even when her children are already reasonably safe and prosperous.

Indeed, fortifying the private household seems to require greater and greater public domains, so that the "waves" that buoy Susan signify Empire for her as much as for Louis (132). She imagines herself surviving through a colonizing son: "I . . . shall see India. He will come home, bringing me trophies to be laid at my feet. He will increase my possessions" (172). In 1928 Leonard Woolf punctured the common boast of Empire, "Britannia rules the waves," along with other competitive creeds:

> The hand of every nation was assumed to be by a law of nature armed against every other nation. . . . Hence the savage nationalism, the crude patriotism, the fierce imperialism of 19th century Europe; the *machtpolitik* of one nation and the jingoism of another; the policy of the "mailed fist" on one side or of "Britannia rules the waves" on the other; and finally, the struggle to balance power in the vicious circle of the competition in arms. ("Way of Peace" 5)

Occasionally a similar awareness begins to dawn on Susan, when she realizes that her emphasis on goods and private security might be dangerous to others: "Yet sometimes I am sick of natural happiness, and fruit growing, and children scattering the house with oars, guns, skulls, books won for prizes and other trophies. I am sick of the body, I am sick of my own craft, industry and cunning, of the unscrupulous ways of the mother who protects, who collects under her jealous eye at one long table her own children, always her own" (191). Nevertheless, despite her suspicion that the shiny trophies depend on guns which scatter skulls, she is too deeply enmeshed in her life-style to change.

Images of domesticity become as morbid for Bernard as they do for Susan. As he is riding in a train and thinking of getting married, his image of the train as a missile exploding "in the side of some ponderous, maternal, majestic animal" corrupts both the relation of husband to wife and of men to their natural environment (111). A coached ability to attack and to appropriate drives the accepted forms of sexuality, as much as it characterizes the push to colonize. When Bernard hints at an affair, he juxtaposes mistress with colonies in the same way that Martin in *The Years* courts a "purely virginal" girl with chatter about Ireland (250–51). Similarly, Jacob in *Jacob's Room* bolsters his doubts about his love affairs by hardening his opposition to Irish Home Rule (139). Bernard confesses, "Then says some lady with an impressive gesture, 'Come with me.' She leads one into a private alcove and admits one to the honour of her intimacy. Surnames change to Christian names; Christian names to nicknames. What is to be done about India, Ireland or Morocco? Old gentlemen answer the question standing decorated under chandeliers" (254–55). In their own eyes, Bernard, Jacob, and Martin stand "decorated" equally by women and by indirect military honors from the colonies.

Capable of some self-mockery, Bernard, like Susan, does become conscious from time to time of possible harm done by the gender relations with which he grew up. When he gets older he realizes, "For many years I crooned complacently, 'My children [. . .] my wife [. . .] my house [. . .] my dog.'. . . I do not want possessions now" (186). He can criticize not only domestic arrangements but also the grand array of state: "I know for a fact . . . that a King, riding, fell over a molehill here. But how strange it seems to set against the whirling abysses of infinite space a little figure with a golden teapot on his head" (227). Nevertheless, if Bernard sometimes pokes fun at himself and his society, at other moments he accepts the acquisitiveness of the monarchs, amassing kingdoms in their gaudy crowns, and fussy businessmen, competing for profits:

Toast and butter, coffee and bacon, the *Times* and letters—suddenly the telephone rang with urgency and I rose deliberately and went to the telephone . . . it might be (one has these fancies) to assume command of the British Empire . . . [I] had created, by the time I put back the receiver, a richer, a stronger, a more complicated world in which I was called upon to act my part and had no doubt whatever that I could do it. Clapping my hat on my head, I strode into a world inhabited by vast numbers of men who had also clapped their hats on their heads, and as we jostled and encountered in trains and tubes we exchanged the knowing wink of competitors and comrades braced with a thousand snares and dodges to achieve the same end—to earn our livings. (261)

The paltry and emphatic gesture of clapping hats on heads, along with the shoddiness of "snares" and "dodges," undercuts the pretensions of building both portfolios and empires.

Bernard inadvertently condemns this society when he admits, "We have destroyed something by our presence . . . a world perhaps" (232). Although he refers most immediately to the way the companions disturb the privacy of Rhoda and Louis, he reveals the larger impact abroad of the group's attitudes. Rhoda, in fact, has just compared the returning group of friends to "the relics of an army, our representatives, going every night (here or in Greece) to battle, and coming back every night with their wounds, their ravaged faces" (231–32). This scene alludes to the ravaging of Greeks and the hunger of Turks (230–32), recalling that in 1922, as the British were incorporating sections of the decaying Turkish Empire into their own Empire, they were also recklessly encouraging Greece to attack Turkish coastal cities (Lloyd 291). The Turks routed the Greeks and negotiated with British forces at the Dardanelles to withdraw (Taylor 191). Rhoda's version of this conflict mythologizes and universalizes hardship, glossing over what Woolf knew to be a British contribution to a very particular pain. Woolf records in 1922, "Here I am sitting in my garden room, with Morgan Forster beside me writing an article for the Nation upon the East—upon this new war" (*Letters* 2: 559). In "Our Graves in Gallipoli" (1922), Forster sarcastically criticizes Lloyd George for trying to enter Asia by means of the Greeks. Although the prime minister in Forster's sketch claims that the new "heap of stones for ever England" will provide honor, Forster suspects that the graves will only provide rich men with more gold and oil (*Abinger Harvest* 32). Rhoda, Bernard, and their crowd, oblivious to the role of gold and oil, view these armies of the British Empire as their "representatives," because they want to dominate, hoard, and conform as much as their compatriots overseas do. Thus, when Bernard addresses his long recapitulation at the end of the book to an acquaintance met "on board a ship going to Africa," he must appropriately try to explain "the meaning of my life" in the face of colonization (238).

Along with Rhoda, Susan, and Bernard, other attractive, likable characters such as Jinny and Neville also participate in the general guilt about Empire. The text admires these two hedonists for a number of reasons. The heterosexual Jinny and the homosexual Neville, each with a long series of affairs, at least celebrate sexuality. Unlike so many stifled characters in *Mrs. Dalloway* and *The Years,* they do not repress their feelings. They try to defy death by living intensely. With affecting poignancy, they long for another human being. Because they have retreated from the world into private bodies, Jinny and Neville apparently contrast with Louis, who is publicly engaged in spreading the "red ink" of Empire. Nevertheless, their ruminations reveal that private sanctuary is an illusion. To ignore Louis and Percival's coercive totalizing is to let the process go on. Even if Jinny and Neville could not, by coming out of their cocoons, personally reform Louis with his "hatchet" (167) and Percival with his "birch" to beat little boys (36), they benefit indirectly from the wealth generated by the Empire and so have an unconscious stake in its continuation. Most depressingly, their private oases do not so much shut out the desert as reflect many of its characteristics. They, too, solicit the hurtful antlers of beasts and endorse a voracious private enterprise in precisely Louis's terms.

Jinny, for example, claims that they "who live in the body" can detach themselves from all the pursuits of her society which she at first appears to scorn, "as a monkey drops nuts from its naked paws." She disdains her peers trudging through mundane lives, "some by going to the Law Courts; others to the city; others to the nursery; others by marching and forming fours. . . . Some take train for France; others ship for India" (176). Her acquaintances are bringing up "scores of children," mainly "to inherit our houses," and along the way to "build cathedrals, dictate policies, condemn men to death" (175–76). Both lists of occupations end in draconian law and order: "marching and forming fours," "condemn men to death." Although Jinny assumes that she can slip out of the nooselike network of commerce, law, family, church, and military service whenever she wants, actually she remains implicated.

For one thing, she loves finery and powerful cars. Her source of income is unclear (her grandmother? her lovers?), but her guest list testifies to both wealth and colonial connections. Her crowd includes a millionaire; a judge; a man who "shot his governess through the heart with an arrow when he was ten years old" and later rode "through deserts with dispatches"; and a woman with "pearl pagodas hanging from her ears" and "a coffee-coloured youth whom she calls the Messiah" under her wing (175).[3] The pagodas, which Bernard has already, rather sloppily, pictured in India (136), now dangle as personal possessions. Although Jinny's acquaintances may occasion pleasure for the reader by their wonderfully bizarre detail, they also repulse by their violence, hostility toward women ("shot his governess"), excessive wealth, and a patronizing adulation of Asians.

Even when Jinny believes that she is escaping the stolidity of raising inheritors, as Susan does, and the tedium of personally totting up sums, in the style of Louis, her imagery for the excitement of accepting trysts is imbued with her knowledge of the flora and fauna of Louis's outposts: "I am pursued through the forest. All is rapt, all is nocturnal and the parrots go screaming through the branches" (177). Jinny has borrowed the parrots with their raucous behavior and the monkeys with their "naked" paws to stand for an imagined paradise, a place of sexual freedom to contrast with British society's staid decorum. Almost a parody of D. H. Lawrence, she idealizes the forests as teachers of a saving primitivism, forgetting their use as raw materials shipped out of a colony. Yet she does not even allow to the forests the freedom that first attracted her to them. When she appropriates a few parrots, she resembles the woman with pagoda-earrings who adopts a "Messiah" without wondering why a savior would need a paternalistic sponsor other than a god, or his own self-sustaining society.

In trying to recreate an unspoiled land in England, Jinny further forgets that she has portrayed the jungle not only as a refuge of beautiful license but also as a place of death. Deadened emotions and death-dealing attitudes reside in Jinny herself and in the whole social system of which she is a part: "Jug, jug, jug, I sing like the nightingale. . . . Now I hear crash and rending of boughs and the crack of antlers as if the beasts of the forest were all hunting, all rearing high and plunging down among the thorns. One has pierced me. One is driven deep within me. And velvet flowers and leaves whose coolness has been stood in water wash me round, and sheathe me, embalming me" (177). Jinny's imitation of the sound of a nightingale recalls T. S. Eliot's line in *The Waste Land*, "'Jug Jug' to dirty ears" (l. 103), which in turn alludes to Ovid's story of how Tereus's raped and mutilated victim, Philomela, turned into a bird (Ovid 175–83). "Jug jug" in Elizabethan poetry was "a conventional way of representing bird-song; it was also, in contrast, a crude joking reference to sexual intercourse" (Southam 78–79). Jinny seems to accept a certain amount of violence, which she reinterprets as the good intensity of intercourse as well as the pain of eventually losing people. Nevertheless, by alluding to *The Waste Land* (published by the Hogarth Press in 1922), Woolf adds to Jinny's evocation of abundant sexual feeling the lack of tenderness depicted in that poem. The last words in the paragraph, "embalming me," also introduce a morbid note incongruous in someone who has supposedly been opposing death with the energies of life. Despite the wonderful excess of her senses, she hints at numbed emotions. The words "jug," "nightingale," and "embalming" further recall Louis's dream paraphernalia of pitchers, nightingales, and Egypt. Because the nightingales are, in Ovid's terms, raped women, or in Eliot's poem, indifferent lovers, Louis stands condemned as a kind of Tereus, and Jinny, as one of Eliot's women who "fiddled whisper music" on their hair, only to distract themselves from a death knell (Eliot, l. 379).

Jinny catches a brief glimpse of herself, her friends, and their whole society as benumbed when she watches people going down into the subway as into Eliot's Dantesque underworld: "I admit, for one moment the soundless flight of upright bodies down the moving stairs like the pinioned and terrible descent of some army of the dead downwards and the churning of the great engines remorselessly forwarding us, all of us, onwards made me cower and run for shelter" (194). In part, Jinny perceives a terrible descent because she is now aging and realizes her mortality. The "great engines," however, suggest death not only as a biological fact but also as a social result, a death-in-life caused by all the scrambling and getting she summarized earlier: raising inheritors and squaring off in military ranks.

When Jinny brushes aside her sobering vision of an underworld, she does so by justifying precisely those activities—the drudgery in law courts and nurseries—that she had earlier rejected in favor of the more exciting life of naked monkeys. Now she sanctions that same bourgeois enterprise: "Think how they organise, roll out, smooth, dip in dyes, and drive tunnels blasting the rock. Lifts rise and fall; trains stop, trains start as regularly as the waves of the sea. This is what has my adhesion. I am a native of this world, I follow its banners. How could I run for shelter when they are so magnificently adventurous . . ." (195). When Jinny praises the adventurers who "dip in dyes," one would not expect her to know, for example, that indigo plantations run by Britons in Bengal during the nineteenth century "were notorious for awful working conditions and cruelty to the labourers" (Moorhouse 149). Yet Jinny is, indeed, well aware of workers in the colonies, whose low state she is suddenly anxious to excuse by asserting their inferiority and her grandeur: "This is the triumphant procession; this is the army of victory with banners and brass eagles and heads crowned with laurel-leaves won in battle. They are better than savages in loin-cloths, and women whose hair is dank, whose long breasts sag, with children tugging at their long breasts. . . . I too, with my . . . reddened lips and my finely pencilled eyebrows march to victory with the band" (194). Despite Jinny's personal exclusion, as a woman, from the ranks of lawyers, bankers, and generals (a prohibition that never comes into her consciousness), she now feels herself fully a member of that "procession" which Woolf spurns so thoroughly in *Three Guineas* (62). Jinny earlier had pictured the forests as containing only animals, a state that gave rise to the images of her lover as antlered beast and herself as a "little animal . . . sucking my flanks in and out with fear" (177, 193). The indigenous people were then conveniently absent from the landscape. Now, however, she openly dismisses those people as inferior. Yet the childish brightness of the victory bands reveals her paean to commerce as a desperate and specious attempt to blot out the darkness of her Dantesque underworld, where, as the passage about the "army of the dead" announces, her fellow citizens already dwell (194).

Ruthless enterprise, whether carried out under a churchly brass eagle or the banners of state, is supported by the old tooth and claw of "laurel-leaves won in battle" (194). This laurel, like the "darts shot through laurel groves by shameless, laughing boys" in one of the italicized sections (207), perhaps alludes to Ovid's Apollo, who appropriates Daphne's laurel for his conquering Roman legions (Ovid 46). Daphne is an important allusion in *Mrs. Dalloway* (85), and her picture floats, forebodingly, on Orlando's tapestry (111). The winning of glory requires the confinement and coercion of many Daphnes in their tree trunks: the women with children tugging at their long breasts and the "savages" in loin cloths. In 1920 Leonard Woolf sarcastically transferred the terms "savage" and "uncivilized" from Africans to Europeans, a concept lost on Jinny (*Empire and Commerce* 155). Whereas she has imagined her exciting love affairs as the antithesis of trudging off to dull law court and nursery and shipping dock, her own exclusivity, in fact, transforms her into an apotheosis of "business as usual," a ship: "I am going to be buffeted; to be flung up, and flung down, among men, like a ship on the sea" (176). At the time, such a ship was likely headed to the colonies, for trade or naval threat.

Resembling Jinny in attractive sensuality and apparent independence, Neville also follows her in not, after all, completely escaping the coercion and conformity of his fellows. Because Neville always focuses on "one person," while Jinny refuses "to attach [her]self to one person in particular," he seems emotionally richer than she does (174). Yet he approaches his series of monogamous partners using imagery that shows how caught up he is in the general willingness to sanction force, best seen in Louis and Percival: "Alas! I could not ride about in India in a sun-helmet. . . . I cannot tumble, as you do, like half-naked boys on the deck of a ship, squirting each other with hose-pipes. I want this fire, I want this chair. . . . After quarreling and reconciliation I need privacy—to be alone with you, to set this hubbub in order" (180). Neville's domestic fireside seems to contrast with Percival's exertions on the field. Yet Neville avoids the military life not because he condemns it but because he feels too frail to undertake it. Although he says he could not literally adventure to the exotic ports of the world, his continuing identification with cabin boys keeps him tied to the enterprising "ship" as closely as Jinny. Neville appears to be a peaceful man, reading a book or caressing a friend, yet he identifies his lovers with "heroic" warriors: "And the poem, I think, is only your voice speaking. Alcibiades, Ajax, Hector and Percival [both the medieval spear-bearer and his friend in India] are also you. They loved riding, they risked their lives wantonly, they were not great readers either" (181). To risk lives "wantonly," however, one's own and another's, undermines Neville's ideal.

Like Louis in his need "to set this hubbub in order," to compensate for feeling "ugly" and "weak" (180–81), Neville admires a regimen that shades, unintentionally, into the same coercive totalizing. When he is old, after dreaming again about boys aboard ship, he suddenly protests: "After all, we are not responsible. We are not judges. We are not called upon to torture our fellows with thumbscrews and irons; we are not called upon to mount pulpits and lecture them on pale Sunday afternoons. It is better to look at a rose, or to read Shakespeare" (196). His need to dissociate his private aestheticism and sensuality so explicitly from the judges and the security police betrays a guilty conscience, a worry that perhaps thumbscrews and irons do attend his own attitudes—for example, his admiration for military heroes. He approves overmastering force, perhaps as a defensive strategy. He may imagine, masochistically, the punishment prescribed by his uncomprehending society, whose strictures against homosexuality he cannot entirely forget; meanwhile, the fantasy of being forced defiantly allows him the intensity he craves. Yet the effort of deflecting his society's incomprehension into images of warring heroes makes even the peaceable Neville complicit in his society's militarism.

Because the six speaking characters and the silent Percival all endorse conformity and force, Percival's death in India seems less the catastrophe of an innocent young man and more the predictable death by violence of one who lives by violence. One image in *The Waves* that lends a sense of foreboding and then of inevitability to Percival's accident is the motif of the "chained beast" stamping on the shore (58, 67). Perhaps related to W. B. Yeats's "rough beast" in "The Second

Coming," Woolf's "chained beast" appears in a simile immediately preceding the announcement that Percival's "horse tripped" (151): "The waves . . . rippled as the backs of great horses ripple with muscles as they move. The waves fell; withdrew and fell again, like the thud of a great beast stamping" (150). Although this image might seem to suggest a natural death, the biological end that comes to all, its chaining makes it sound imprisoned, perhaps ready to rebel. The beast imagined by Louis and Bernard is sometimes an elephant, with its foot chained or its eye shot; Rhoda's bogey is always a tiger (10, 22, 126, 130). Rhoda is the only one who displays much fear of these animals native to the colonies, either because she is the most timid or because she admits to a guilty conscience about Empire and pictures the territories fighting back, devouring the devourers. Woolf, however, does not let the friends dismiss the colonized as "beasts." One of her most frightening variations has Louis identifying himself with the caged tiger (128); and, as we saw, Percival swings a "paw" (82). Louis and Percival, as imperial tigers, should not be surprised if their quarry leaps back at them.

Woolf creates another threatening image, like that of the beast stamping, when she describes turbaned men with "assegais." In *Empire and Commerce in Africa,* Leonard Woolf condemns the way that "irresponsible [European] traders armed with rifles believe it's their right and duty to exploit Africans armed with assegais" (353). If these slender spears in *The Waves* conjure up a scene in Africa, the turbans suggest India. Such a composite warrior introduces social issues concerning the colonies into the italicized sections that otherwise focus on nature in an English seaside. At first the fighters attack animals: "The waves drummed on the shore, like turbaned warriors, like turbaned men with poisoned assegais who, whirling their arms on high, advance upon the feeding flocks, the white sheep" (75). Since Louis has described Britons as sheep, this passage is not entirely comforting (37). Soon, however, the men leave off hunting to become more soldierly, as the "spray rose like the tossing of lances and assegais over the riders' heads. . . . the sea . . . beat like a drum that raises a regiment of plumed and turbaned soldiers" (108–9). Who are these warriors? On the one hand, they could be local men serving with the British Army throughout the Empire. Such soldiers in full-dress uniform did wear turbans and sometimes retained their traditional weapons, like "the famed kukri or Gurkha knife" (Moorhouse 13–15). Woolf's shadowy warriors could, then, be local soldiers maintaining the Empire, doing the "dirty work" that Louis can hush up with his "courteous commands on the telephone" (167). Indeed, the image of the warriors leaks from the italics into the chapters, to characterize Louis and his whole group as "naked men with assegais" (140). The friends generate similes for hurtfulness most obviously because their egotism, jealousies, and lack of confidence result in sparring and slights at the dinner table. Nevertheless, as seen especially through Louis, such emotions also motivate Empire making.

On the other hand, if the turbaned warriors further Empire, they may also threaten rebellion, as in the Sepoy Mutiny of 1857. As we saw in *The Years,* this mutiny becomes the founding event in the Pargiters' guilty past. Leonard Woolf warned in *Empire and Commerce* that, if the League of Nations did not create truly international mandates in the colonies after World War I and prepare them rapidly for independence, the mandate system would just add "new, fine names" onto "ancient evils . . . we shall call exploitation trusteeship, slavery labour, and profit-making patriotism" (367). If such evils continue, "destruction may come, sooner than some people expect, by a tremendous catastrophe, perhaps a revolt of the 'beneficiaries' against their guardians and benefactors" (*Empire and Commerce* 367). *The Waves* also hints at impending revolt by the restless, turbaned warriors.

In the same way that the assegais in the italicized sections pass alarmingly to the friends in their dining room, thus implicating them in the Empire, so, too, do the ruthless birds, attacking snails or worms in the introductions, come to stand for the characters (74–75, 108–9). The sound of the birds, in chorus or in discordant stridency, announces the experiences of the characters in regimentation or selfish individualism. Bernard unpleasantly compares even his wedding engagement to the cracking of a snail shell (123). Woolf already has used the image of cracking snail shells in other books to suggest colonization. In *Mrs. Dalloway,* for example, one of the observers of the sky-writing airplane longs for adventures in "foreign parts" and thinks of her nephew, a missionary; a few lines later, the plane flies over "woods where adventurous thrushes hopping boldly, glancing quickly, snatched the snail and tapped him on a stone, once, twice, thrice" (40–41). The juxtaposition reduces the colonizing missionary with his rituals to an officious and destructive thrush. Similarly, Shelmerdine in *Orlando* illustrates his exploits in South Africa by moving twigs and snail shells, unwittingly mocking his own grandeur as broken scraps of nature (257). The image of the snails makes colonization seem paltry, unglorious, and violent.

Because *The Waves* compares the friends in particular and colonizers in general to birds attacking snails, private lives and public policy are linked. The attitudes that determine the pecking order at home also fix the hierarchical oppressions of the Empire. Louis's iron rings of international shipping, Bernard's business "snares and dodges" (261), Susan's "bestial" child-rearing and hoarding (132), Rhoda's and Jinny's desire to appropriate exotic islands, or Percival's, Louis's, and Neville's glorification of military heroes—all allow the conformity, force, intolerance, and possessiveness which make colonization possible and oppressive.

Thus, when the time of day in the italicized sections changes from sunrise to sunset, the timetable may sardonically announce that an end must come to that "Empire on which the Sun never Sets" (MacKenzie 27). More immediately, the chronicling of light corresponds to the aging of the characters, from early childhood to the "sunset" of their lives. Yet the fact that the light at least once plays over mosques and mules from the East and not just the English coast forces the reader to think of Empire and predicts that the sun indeed will set on it (148–49). *Jacob's Room* similarly climaxes in a sunset seen from many angles (168–75). As the day begins to fade, the events insistently form into Woolf's most characteristic constellation of gender, Empire, and military. Jacob's former girlfriend admits an unwanted pregnancy, the Cabinet imposes "coherency" on the "mutterings in bazaars," and a riderless horse gallops by, as if in a military funeral (172). As the sun further reddens, another girlfriend passes lamps with "repressed primrose lights," Mrs. Flanders writes to a son in Singapore, and a voice from Whitehall announces soothingly that "The Kaiser . . . received me in audience" (173–74). The passage thus repeats a sequence including unhappy gender relations (pregnancy, "repressed" lights), coercive Empire (Indian bazaars, Singapore), and impending war (riderless horse, Kaiser). In both *Jacob's Room* and *The Waves,* then, the sun must set on the makers of the British Empire, whose society is not worth exporting; if it is exported, the effort inevitably leads to violence.

4.
Playing Out History: Becoming a Woman

Orlando

Whereas *Jacob's Room* and *The Waves* give a cross-section of contemporary training that may prepare for oppression and war, *Orlando: A Biography* (1928) and *Between the Acts* (1941) provide a historical overview of past events and attitudes that have contributed to these present problems. *Orlando* allows the main character to live through centuries, from the Renaissance to 1928. Similarly large in scope, *Between the Acts* presents villagers in June, 1939, acting out parts in a pageant of English history, offering brief glances at Anglo-Saxon, medieval, and Elizabethan times and longer excursions into the eighteenth-century Age of "Reason," the Victorian era, and the twentieth century.

Several readers have assumed that through this pageant Woolf expresses "nostalgia" and "acute longing" for a lost rural, feudal, and unified community, "an earlier, more civilized phase of English culture" (Zwerdling 308–9).[1] Although a villager at La Trobe's pageant also suspects "glamour" thrown over the "ancient" times, La Trobe fumes that he has missed the point (97). Howard Harper similarly mistakes the return to the past in *Orlando* as a glorification of "nationality and chivalry" (179). Instead, in both novels Woolf illuminates the past not as a sanctuary but as a source of modern problems of colonization, gender, and class. For a contemporary character in either novel, whether Orlando or a villager, to play out a role from the past implies not timeless truths but a recognition that history is still dictating parts. As a social construct, however, the script may be open to revision. Satirizing rather than glamorizing historical periods, Woolf sums them up by saying that Queen Bess from the Renaissance, Reason from the eighteenth century, and Budge the policeman from the Victorian age all "hobnobbed with the foreparts of the donkey" (*Between* 195). In other words, the scrutiny of British history in the pageant reveals the past to be in many respects asinine, for all Woolf's heartfelt love of the English "haystack in the fields" (*Diary 5*: 336).

Orlando reviews social attitudes and literature from the Renaissance to 1928 through the eyes of an undying character who spends half this long life as a man and half as a woman. Both the panoramic view and the male-female transformation make the novel in some ways an answer to James Joyce and T. S. Eliot, as Sandra Gilbert argues in her perceptive essay "Costumes of the Mind." Joyce, for example, in *Ulysses* (1922), creates a pastiche of styles from English literary history, and in the Circe chapter, he treats Bloom as a woman. Eliot, who alludes in *The Waste Land* (1922) to the legends of many cultures and times, draws on Ovid's story of the prophet who was changed into a woman for seven years, to create his own version of Tiresias, "Old man with wrinkled female breasts" (Ovid 95; Eliot 38). Woolf, however, does not merely allow a primary male character a few moments or years for spying out an essential "femaleness"; instead she dismantles the whole notion of gender as a social construct, forged, in part, for imperial, military, and economic purposes.

One definition of masculinity emerges shockingly in the opening line of *Orlando*: "He—for there could be no doubt of his sex, though the fashion of the time did something to disguise it—was in the act of slicing at the head of a Moor which swung from the rafters" (13). When the narrator-biographer assures us of Orlando's sex, the testimonial insinuates the very doubt which it purports to dispel. The ambiguity announces that expectations for gender are shifting, according to time period and culture, not fixed by nature. In the Renaissance, Orlando learns from his father that masculinity requires striking "many heads of many colours off many shoulders" (13). Yet the tiresome repetition of "many" mocks the father's enterprise, as Orlando's own zeal, in rhymed excess, to "lunge and plunge and slice the air with his blade" makes his swordplay silly (13). Whatever innate impulse toward rambunctiousness Orlando may possess, it takes long practice sessions in the attic to magnify his aggression into the capacity for murder, to select his enemies among the "heads of many colours," and to hide the details of violence in a romantic fantasy. His father might ride in romantic-sounding "fields of asphodel," but, as Woolf could have learned from the *Odyssey*, the "meadow of asphodel" is the underworld of disembodied wraiths "gibbering like bats," both foolish and powerless (Homer 351). To be a "man" as expected of Orlando means murderous racism or suicidal sacrifice.

Although Orlando's father wants to call Africans "pagan" and primitive, he himself carries out the head-hunting. Moreover, no matter how far he may have wandered, his trophies come home, to serve as warnings over his house. Just as Jacob acquired his death's-head moth in the kitchen (*Jacob's Room* 23), Orlando faces a skull in his attic (13). In both cases, the death's head advertises something deadly in the character's own society.

Besides militarism, another stifling aspect of these cultures, whether recent or remote, is their attitudes toward women. This topic is broached in *Orlando* by the arras which sways in the breeze as the young man practices swordsmanship (14). Later references to this arras clarify that it pictures Apollo pursuing Daphne (111, 171, 317). As we saw from Peter Walsh's dream woman, debilitated as if confined to a tree (*Mrs. Dalloway* 85), for Woolf Daphne epitomizes the woman whose society immobilizes her. Orlando's acquired definition of masculinity as aggression, enacted against both Moors and women, creates an uneasy equation of phallus with weaponry: "his manhood awoke; he grasped a sword in his hand" (40). If references to "sword" and "crevice" in this passage provide anatomical euphemisms, they also convey an expectation that courtship will be a battleground. Yet his lover's prosaic comment, "pass the salt," in the same sentence about Orlando's awakening manhood, undermines the equation of "love" with a hunt between Apollo-hound and Daphne-hare, even as the opening passage about the Moor's head ridicules the equation of masculinity with fighting.

Whereas the deflationary juxtapositions of the narration satirize such social expectations, Orlando himself participates fully in the spirit of the Elizabethan age. In addition to absorbing unconsciously the definition of maleness as conquest, he unquestioningly accepts, as a natural right, his upper-class access to riches. When he clasps his lower-class sweetheart Sukey among the sacks of treasure, they seem as important to him as she is, just objects that are not individualized (130). Orlando enjoys his opulence and titles well enough. Not until the gypsies reproach her (after the change of sex) does it even enter consciousness that any social assignments might exist besides born noblemen and born servants: "Looked at from the gipsy point of view, a Duke, Orlando understood, was nothing but a profiteer or robber who snatched land and money from people who rated these things of little worth, and could think of nothing better to do than to build three hundred and sixty-five bedrooms when one was enough, and none was even better than one" (148). Exaggerated as the gypsy view is, it contains a grain of truth, in its suspicion about the profiteering that procured some of the Elizabethan wealth. When Orlando's biographer describes the sailors "trolling their ditties, and telling their stories of Drake, Hawkins, and Grenville, till they toppled off the benches and rolled asleep on the sanded floor," the indignity of the tellers undercuts the supposed glory of their tale (59). As historian Gerald Graham admits, "Hawkins, Drake and their confreres may have been smugglers, slavers and perhaps pirates, but they were also popular idols" (19). T. O. Lloyd similarly reports that when Sir John Hawkins bought slaves in West Africa and resold them in the Caribbean in the mid-sixteenth century, Queen Elizabeth had invested in his slave-trading; less openly, she profited from Sir Francis Drake's piratical attacks on Spanish ships (9). The view from Orlando's oak thus might include pleasure boats, but if he keeps following the line of sight, he comes up against armadas and forts and cannon (18). The "lunging and plunging" which he is being taught to pursue ensure that one person's pleasure depends on somebody else's pain, in Africa or the Indies (29).

This reckless Renaissance quest for knowledge, power, and wealth affects every aspect of Orlando's world. The scene from the Great Frost, with the carnival built on the frozen Thames, portrays a cross-section of Elizabethan life. Stranded on separate floes but united by ideology, some revelers suicidally dive for gold goblets, an old man reads from a holy book, a couple lie in bed, and a nobleman curses "Irish rebels" as the cause of all his problems (63). These apparently incongruous activities are actually related, by the drives to amass gold and to dismiss inferiors. If women destined to be married off as property are considered unworthy of an education, as Woolf says in *A Room of One's Own* (48–49), then that willingness to rank people hierarchically by sex may prepare the ground for similar scapegoating of Irish or Indians. The need to "save" inferior souls with words from a holy book may justify a land grab. Whereas Orlando's cohorts during the Great Frost imagine that their customs and outlook are permanent, the cataclysmic thaw reveals that notions viewed as "natural" by the Elizabethans are only ideologies: a frozen shape which can melt or a carnival tent which can be struck after its day.

The Renaissance idea that "manly" men must dominate—Ireland, the Indies, women—does not disappear entirely when the attitudes of the Elizabethan age, like the frozen river, finally break up. This masculine sense of superiority over women, however, combines with other elements of the cultural shift, so that disdain for rough actresses as "poodles dancing," worthy to be kicked away (*Room of One's Own* 50), becomes reverence for delicate women as lap dogs, worthy to be petted. Thus a female Orlando in the age following the Renaissance is so coddled that she has to have her meat cut up for her (155). Nevertheless, if the notion of womanhood is modified slightly, the ideal of manly conquest survives unchanged, fueling the later imperialism that grew out of Renaissance expansionism.

In fact, the moment when Orlando turns from a man into a woman illuminates a crucial element in the ideology of Empire building. Just as the Turks in Constantinople rise up against the Sultan, Orlando falls into a trance from which he awakens transformed into a woman (133, 139). Susan Squier labels the simultaneity of Orlando's metamorphosis and the rebellion a "coincidence," explaining that Woolf is overturning the requirement of the realistic novel for cause and effect (170). Woolf, however, exposes a direct correlation between Orlando's sex change and the presence of the British in Constantinople. Orlando becomes a woman for the imperial age because the British Empire needs a woman. That is, the presence of ladies justifies British intervention in a local conflict. One of Woolf's characters, a British Lieutenant Brigge, exclaims gallantly, "English ladies in the company, [. . .] I own that my hand went to my cutlass" (127).

In the telescoped time of the novel, Orlando's transformation in Constantinople and escape to the gypsies take place in a matter of weeks—actually, the 1600s to the 1800s. Thus the scene of a Turkish rebellion in the 1600s can also reflect the nineteenth- and early twentieth-century British desire to take advantage of the power vacuum created with the decline of the Ottoman Empire. The weakening of that empire set the stage for the acquisitive designs of England and Russia during the Crimean War, whose follies Woolf mocked in *To the Lighthouse*. Instead of encouraging local groups who were attempting to break away from Ottoman overlords, the European powers continued to intrigue and fight to gain the spoils for themselves. Edward Said describes the British and French poised to take over the "now hopelessly ill Ottoman Empire. . . . Both before and during World War I secret diplomacy was bent on carving up the Near Orient first into spheres of influence, then into mandated (or occupied) territories" (220). Woolf would be familiar with this controversy from Leonard Woolf's *The Future of Constantinople* (1917), in which he argues that imperial rivalry for this city was one of the factors contributing to World War I; to prevent its future destabilizing role, he proposes the internationalization of the city (11–12). Having drawn on this argument about Constantinople in *Jacob's Room,* Virginia Woolf in *Orlando* again exposes the ideological window dressing of the struggle over the city.

Thus the sailors of the British navy, rather than admit that they would like to incorporate Constantinople into their own Empire, resort instead to a more glowing ideology; they say that they are protecting women. The Empire recruits Orlando to be a woman, so to speak, but it needs womanhood of a certain sort only. As she wakes up in her new state, three allegorical figures, Chastity, Purity, and Modesty, throw the naked Orlando a towel (138). The English soldiers require not just any woman but a chaste woman, who must be, moreover, under attack by "natives," in order to excuse the soldiers' display of arms. Brigge prefers to imagine Turks motivated by lust for English "ladies," rather than admit that the Turks might be motivated by a desire for independence from any overlord, whether Ottoman sultan or British queen.

After thirty years as a man, Orlando has no shame at nudity and is not alarmed when the towel falls short. The scene implies that both men and women start out frank, but women learn a greater inhibition.[2] The three allegorical figures, who seem so concerned for Orlando's welfare, betray their own hypocrisy and destructiveness. Purity, without herself needing to be pure, simply keeps up decorous appearances. She admits, "I cover vice and poverty" (135). Chastity spitefully acknowledges that she would "freeze" Orlando to the bone rather than let a woman awaken to her own sexual potential (135). The three guardians gain support among censorious advocates: "those who prohibit; those who deny; those who reverence without knowing why" (137). Furthermore, this ignorant "tribe of the respectable" really idolizes Purity, Chastity, and Modesty because such ideological constructs "have given them Wealth, Prosperity, Comfort, Ease" (137). As historical analysts after Woolf too have argued, the "respectable lady" did indeed serve prosperity in a lucrative Empire: "She stood for the civilizing mission which, in turn, justified the colonization of benighted peoples" (Enloe 48).

As suggested when Peter Walsh and Lady Bruton in *Mrs. Dalloway* define English "civilization" as guarding "girls in their security" against "barbarian hordes" (82, 274), this ideology requires the fabrication of three types: non-European men unable to control their sex drives, superior European men, and European women too weak to protect themselves. To bolster the myth that Turks or Indians are inherently lascivious, Lieutenant Brigge needs to regard them as inferior in all ways. When he catches himself admiring Turkish architecture, he stifles the acknowledgment of merit in a general deprecation of Eastern "ignorance": "I found myself alternately praising the Lord that he had permitted [. . .] and wishing that my poor, dear mother [. . . .] By the Ambassador's orders, the long windows, which are so imposing a feature of Eastern architecture, for though ignorant in many ways [. . .]

were thrown wide" (127). Brigge might claim divine sanction for the activities of the British navy abroad, but his fragmentary sentence about the Lord remains incomplete, implying that his holy, civilizing message is really a blank.

If intervention requires the fabrication of invariably uncivilized non-European men, it also posits European men who are always above reproach. Woolf constantly challenges this claim. In *Mrs. Dalloway*, she juxtaposes Peter Walsh's concern for "girls in their security" with his own behavior stalking a woman through the streets of London (79, 82). Similarly, in *Orlando,* just as Brigge is claiming to protect English ladies, he himself betrays the ideal. He can observe the Turkish rebellion in the first place only because he has perched in a Judas tree to ogle "the astonishing conduct of Lady—which was of a nature to fasten the eyes of all upon her, and to bring discredit upon her sex and country" (128). Pretending to be scandalized, he nevertheless drinks in all details, and when the tree branch breaks, one feels that Woolf unceremoniously dumps him for his hypocrisy.

Although the English bluejackets might wish to think of themselves as bearers of light, the luminous Apollo role suggested by that image is tainted by repeated references throughout the book to Apollo's planned rape of Daphne. Moreover, Brigge's light turns out to be merely the glitter of fireworks: "I came to the conclusion that this demonstration of our skill in the art of pyrotechny was valuable, [. . .] because it impressed upon them [. . .] superiority of the British" (127). "Superiority" turns out to mean not more kindness, better architecture, or less violence, but more effective gunpowder. Only the superior "Martini-Henry rifle and the Gatling gun," as Robert MacDonald sarcastically remarks, make the "best" team win during imperial battles (27).

To use Constantinople as the setting for Orlando's transformation, Woolf may have learned from Leonard Woolf's analysis of that city. She may also have been inspired by Harold Nicolson, husband of Vita Sackville-West, on whom Orlando is modeled (Knopp 33); Nicolson had served in the embassy at Constantinople in 1911 (Woolf, *Letters* 3: 83). On 4 July 1927, Woolf records a conversation with him in which she disputes his enthusiasm for the Empire. Because she conceived *Or-*

lando in March 1927 but did not write prolifically on it until October (*Diary* 3: 131, 161), this debate may have contributed to the formulation of the novel:

> After dinner last night we discussed the Empire . . . [Harold began,] "After all, it's our younger sons out there. I feel proud of it." . . . "The governed don't seem to enjoy it," said Raymond [Mortimer]. Silly ass, said Harold. "We do our job: disinterestedly; we don't think of ourselves, as the French do, as the Germans do. Take the British oil fields. There's a hospital there where they take any one, employee or not. The natives come from all over the place." (*Diary* 3: 145)

When Nicolson adds that the great age of England is the period of colonial expansion, Woolf objects: "'But why not grow, change?' I said. Also, I said, recalling the aeroplanes that had flown over us, while the portable wireless played dance music on the terrace, 'can't you see that nationality is over?'" (*Diary* 3: 145). Where Nicolson praises the British, Woolf blames them equally with the French and the Germans for the "patriotic" sentiments that mean violent appropriation of foreign land and inevitably lead to European rivalry over apportionment, culminating in one world war and, very likely, another. Woolf further undercuts Nicolson's position by recording his claim of British disinterest next to a reference to "British oil fields." Similarly, Lieutenant Brigge in *Orlando*, falling from his voyeuristic perch on a tree limb, is less than candid when he proposes a disinterested motive of protecting ladies, leaving unspoken his own interest both in ladies and in an equivalent of oil fields: control of a strategic site on the route to India.

After her metamorphosis, Orlando must learn to serve the Empire by taking on a whole range of attributes deemed "womanly" in the late eighteenth, nineteenth, and early twentieth centuries. In addition to acquiring an unwanted chastity, she becomes "obedient," "scented," and "apparelled" (156). Although Orlando used to be well muscled, her new voluminous skirts interfere with exercise, so that she does indeed grow weaker, as labeled. While she deteriorates into physical fragility, she more frequently displays emotion, because such volatility also is expected. She learns to give way to weeping and to be shocked if men weep, although Orlando knows very well from her days as a man that men are as readily inclined to cry as women (165, 180). The new Orlando further understands that she is supposed to defer to men, even if insincerely; in consequence, womanhood "meant slavery, meant deceit, meant denying her love, fettering her limbs, pursing her lips, and restraining her tongue" (163). She is indoctrinated to feel more "modesty as to her writing, [more] vanity as to her person," because, as a woman, she is not expected to formulate an intelligent opinion or to express it in a forceful, articulate way (187).

Although Orlando from time to time still suspects that she has a thinking mind and a desiring body, it becomes harder and harder to maintain her belief in herself. She manages a few minor rebellions, resenting the eighteenth-century view of middle-class women as children to the point that she rudely plops the sugar into the tea that she is eternally supposed to be serving (213–14). She resists the imposition of chastity by occasionally dressing as a man and adventuring through back streets. She visits prostitutes for conversation and physically loves both sexes (221). Nevertheless, if Orlando sometimes avoids her society's prescriptions for women, gradually she acquiesces. Her partial capitulation suggests that no one can entirely evade the ideology of the age. Moreover, Orlando not only succumbs against her will but also collaborates in her shackling. If confining clothes render her helpless in an emergency, rescue by a dashing sailor flatters her and silences any objections. Orlando, like Mrs. Dalloway and Mrs. Ramsay, is enticed by men's adoration into accepting patriarchy. By contrast, the narrator-biographer of *Orlando* caustically comments that "her arguments [in favor of dependency] would not commend themselves to mature women" (156).

Just as Orlando sporadically remembers that, for all her new, lowly status as a woman, she can still think, desire, or even manage property (168), she also recognizes a continuing impulse to settle disputes by the sword. Considered unable to defend herself, she is also thought unwilling to attack others. This notion of women as innately more spiritual than men (the Angel in the House) and perhaps more peaceable was accepted by some nineteenth-century advocates of women's rights in England and America; Margaret Fuller, for example, believed the "especial genius of Woman" was to be "intuitive in function, spiritual in tendency" (Chevigny 263). Indeed, women's innate concern for community is still claimed by some twentieth-century feminisms (Gubar 304, 311–13). Woolf, however, rejects this gender division into essentially quiescent, conciliatory women and aggressive men. Orlando detects in herself just as much violence as when she was male. She does not display "masculine" aggressiveness as part of "androgyny." Instead, Orlando, both as male and as female, discovers some impulse to strike, but the male Orlando must be taught to exaggerate it into murderous swordplay, while the female Orlando must be trained to stifle combativeness.

This outcome, and what it may suggest for the further education of both men and women as militants or peacemakers, appear at the end of the hilarious scene of Fly Loo. Trying to escape the unwanted attentions of the Archduke Harry, Orlando engages in a courtship reduced to a competitive game, with a woman—herself—typically the prize. As she and her adversary bet highmindedly on whether bluebottle flies will settle on sugar cubes (and as Harry perhaps is betting that he can pounce on his sweet lady), Orlando resorts to cheating, by sticking dead flies on cubes. Although Harry, "no nice judge of flies," fails to notice the ruse, he is appalled when finally compelled to acknowledge that a woman, his image of innocence itself, can stoop to treachery (183). Nevertheless, since women cannot help themselves, he thinks, he gallantly forgives her. Thus frustrated in her gentler attempts to repulse her suitor, Orlando drops a toad down his shirt. Yet in "justice to her, it must be said that she would infinitely have preferred a rapier. Toads are clammy things to conceal about one's person a whole morning. But if rapiers are forbidden, one must have recourse to toads. Moreover toads and laughter between them sometimes do what cold steel cannot" (184). Women's education, usually so faulty, surpasses men's in this one area: women learn to reconcile contenders rather than to retaliate when hurt. Similarly, Woolf in *Three Guineas* will salvage from women's unpromising nineteenth-century training in "poverty," "chastity," and "derision" a sole good aspect, peacefulness. She thus redefines the three terms, respectively, as modest independence, refusal to sell one's brains for money, and humility (78–80). Here, in *Orlando,* she praises women's instruction in "toads and laughter," to recommend such training as a community-oriented technique for peace—not a spontaneous attribute of naturally serene and witty womanhood, but learned techniques valuable for both sexes.

Despite Orlando's recognition that she could stab Harry if she let herself go, she gradually yields to the nineteenth-century assignment of hostility and warring to men and of affection and nurturing to women. Once rid of Harry's attentions, she misses him—not *him*, exactly, but an occupation to give meaning to her life. Society currently is indoctrinating her that a woman's life should consist entirely of loving, with thinking and acting either relegated to the role of a distant distraction or crowded out altogether. Moreover, nineteenth-century attitudes shape the form that that loving should take. Although at Harry's departure she at first called for "Life! A Lover," not "Life! A Husband," the ring finger of her left hand begins to tingle (244, 240).

Eventually Orlando marries an active imperialist, but first she has to find him. Made restless and irresolute by her itchy ring finger, she runs in a field, where she breaks an ankle. She decides to remain stretched on the ground forever, as "nature's bride" (248). Woolf thus mocks the romantic conception of women as somehow earthier than men; because "nature" has been redeemed by Romanticism, the old medieval ascription of earthiness to women can combine with their new assignment of spirituality. Woolf, however, twits the identification with nature—"A feather fell upon her brow"—and reveals that women's confinement to the muteness of matter is actually an infirmity (248). Discussing a scene in *The Voyage Out,* in which Rachel Vinrace is similarly pressed into the ground, in her case by the combined pressure of a matchmaker and a lover (283–84), Christine Froula detects a parody of William Wordsworth's Lucy poems (81). Orlando, giving herself to "the cold embraces of the grass," even more obviously draws on Wordsworth's Lucy (D. Perkins 265). Similarly, in Woolf's *Freshwater*, the character Tennyson can shrug off the news of Ellen Terry's death: "There is something highly pleasing about the death of a young woman in the pride of life. Rolled round in earth's diurnal course with stocks and stones and trees. That's Wordsworth. I've said it too" (40). When Orlando's new suitor, the ridiculously named

Marmaduke Bonthrop Shelmerdine, rides onto the scene as the arche-
typal chevalier ready to rescue a damsel in distress, Orlando remains
passive, replying to Shelmerdine's expressions of concern, "I'm dead,
Sir!" (250). She implies that the nineteenth-century poetic conflation
of womanhood either with nature or with art objects keeps women
mute and inactive, in a kind of death in life (cf. Gilbert and Gubar,
Madwoman 41).

Yielding to the Victorian pressure to marry, Orlando also succumbs
to a prescription for fertility, but only to the extent of bearing one
child, not fifteen. To portray Orlando's impregnation and lying-in,
Woolf may be parodying both Joyce and Eliot. A high-flown paragraph
about "the red, thick stream of life" ends abruptly in the midwife's announcement, "It's a very fine boy, M'Lady" (295), which may recall
Joyce's exuberant "Hoopsa, boyaboy, hoopsa!" in *Ulysses* (383). Whereas
Joyce does not record Mina Purefoy's opinion of the connection between
her "pure" Catholic faith ("foy") and a twelfth pregnancy, Woolf invites the reader to "take courage" after the pregnancy, for Orlando will let
"nothing of the same sort" happen again (296). The birth scene is preceded
by what might be an impregnation scene, masked, in decorous Victorian
fashion, by a paragraph replete with phallic cigars slipped in cases, bulbs
thrust in earth, and a kingfisher rising across the water (293). Howard
Harper suggests that the kingfisher may allude to Eliot's Fisher King in
The Waste Land, but he thinks that Woolf is remembering fertility rituals
only to congratulate Vita Sackville-West "for continuing the male line—
something that the eighteenth-century Sackvilles had not been able to do"
(156). Far from lamenting what Harper takes to be the older Sackvilles' failure in producing only daughters, Woolf much more likely is considering the practical consequences of Eliot's nostalgia for old paradigms.
The high birth rates under his reign of fertility gods limit women's
other activities, such as writing or themselves serving as ambassador to
Constantinople.

Indeed, Eliot's supposedly timeless myths of fertility can support
ideological needs, as a Victorian monument in *Orlando* illustrates. This
"pyramid, hecatomb, or trophy"—an emblem that actually hides deaths—
jumbles bassinets with cannon, Christian cross with military helmets,

and bridal veils with telescopes and elephants (232). Despite the apparent incongruity, the maps and the mathematical instruments do not jostle each other gratuitously. A gentleman in a frock coat can sidle up to the elephant, native to India or Africa, because the Victorians were indeed expanding their Empire. The cross can be topped with a helmet, because the church was used to justify military and political control. As Leonard Woolf argued, Christians often were "unconsciously made the stalking-horse of economic imperialism" (*Empire and Commerce* 296). The cannon can accompany the telescope because science, like religion, did pave the way for territorial expansion: "An intellectual anticipation in map-making has often been a useful weapon in the carving of empire out of other people's dominions" (*Empire and Commerce* 171).

Orlando insistently calls the Victorian marker a "garish erection," because men do predominate in the church and the military, in the science, and in the commerce of the age (233). If women are excluded from these paying jobs, they nevertheless play an imperial role, too. Military men like Lieutenant Brigge need to pretend to be protecting the chastity which the bridal veils proclaim, while bassinets nurture the soldiers who will fill the ranks. Hence, when Orlando first discovers that Victorian women have fifteen children, she blurts out a startling conclusion, "Thus the British Empire came into existence" (229). She finds that her "private life" in the bedroom does have something to do with public interventions abroad. Palmerston, the statesman whom Leonard blames for an interventionist doctrine of protecting globe-trotting British subjects, even unscrupulous adventurers, meddles in Orlando's life, too: "But Orlando was a woman—Lord Palmerston had just proved it" (*Empire and Commerce* 150; *Orlando* 268). Palmerston's Victorian definitions of womanhood require that Orlando be propertyless, defenseless, and married (255). Once joined to Shelmerdine, Orlando does enjoy a happy marriage, despite his absences in South Africa—or, rather, because of them. When together, they discover a fine companionship, but not one cast in the mold of an all-absorbing "love of her life," a yoking which does not and should not exist. A marriage construed as the only career for a woman would interfere with Orlando's other interests, such as writing and visiting friends.

Despite the fact that Orlando and Shelmerdine feel at ease with each other, they take on burdensome imperialist roles during the years they are together, from Victorian times until the present, 1928. Society tries to force these friends, who would like a little separate space now and then, to be "indissolubly linked," especially in the old roles of male warrior and female reward for victory (242). Although Shelmerdine is often lauded by readers as the perfect mate who enables Orlando to be "ecstatically united with her 'Captain Self'" (Little, *Comedy* 69), the novel clearly satirizes his job as colonizer in South Africa. While he boasts of battling gales at Cape Horn, Orlando sees him as "this boy (for he was little more) sucking peppermints" (252). Reversing the label "childlike" commonly assigned by Europeans to "primitives" or "Orientals" (Said 40), Woolf reduces the European Shelmerdine's rearrangement of the map of Africa to a childish game: "Then Shelmerdine would make a little model on the ground of the Cape with twigs and dead leaves and an empty snail shell or two" (257). For all his boyish bravado, his colonial enterprise carries overtones of deadliness and emptiness.

Shelmerdine's immaturity is a function not of personal turpitude but of dangerous social training. As William Plomer laments in a book published at the Hogarth Press the same year as *Orlando*, when a South African governess tells a white boy to ignore a black playmate, he may resist beautifully for a time: "'He's not a little Kaffir!' Golgo said tearfully, 'and I don't want to be a little white boy!'" But eventually he must conform (24). Good-natured Shelmerdine, too, may not have wanted to discriminate, but by the time he marries Orlando, he insensitively mentions a black mistress in the same list as a pet monkey (258). Plomer, in his preface to *I Speak of Africa*, calls the white population of South Africa a "blight" and "uncivilised" (preface, n.p.); both Woolfs judged Plomer's works "extraordinarily good" (Bell 2: 149). Like Plomer, Leonard Woolf, in a book written as Virginia composed *Orlando*, criticizes the white presence in South Africa: "The idea that South Africa or Kenya can be permanently converted into a white man's country is a dream of political insanity. The insanity of those who dream will be visited upon the heads of their children in the third and fourth generation" (*Imperialism* 180–81). Whereas Plomer and Leonard

Woolf warn about the blight of imperialism discursively, Woolf mocks the colonizing Shelmerdine through satire: "Oh rash, oh ridiculous man, always sailing, so uselessly, round Cape Horn in the teeth of a gale!" (327).

Not only does society turn a basically nice Shelmerdine into the maker of a useless and dangerous Empire, it also insists that Orlando inspire the imperialists. The final, hilarious scene, however, parodies both the imperial mission of bringing light and its female mascot full of sweetness. Ludicrously, Shelmerdine's militaristic, phallic airplane is guided to land by the "phosphorescent flare" of Orlando's bared breasts and rich pearls (328–29). The roles of the couple here epitomize an enduring ideology. First, the definition of "man" as warrior has survived the centuries, pushing Orlando to head-hunting during Elizabeth's reign and Shelmerdine to playing hero in South Africa just in time for the Boer War. Second, the hierarchy that ranks blacks—from the Moors in North Africa to the Kaffirs in South Africa—as inferiors seems to have become only more rigid. Moreover, on the way from the Renaissance to the nineteenth century, society may have elevated women from the gutter to the pedestal, but their function as chaste, threatened, weak, and fertile vessels allows them to be co-opted into a prop for Empire.

If angelic, luminescent women are in 1928 still supposed to smooth men's rough edges and light the way to violent conquest, the contradiction that an angel aids killing goes unremarked. When the heroes return from taking other people's lands, their women still stand on shore to reward their men's deeds with their persons. The female body continues to be valued more highly than the female mind; Orlando's breasts, rather than her brain, provide the flare. That body, as sex object, has long been taught not to feel sexual pleasure of its own. Woolf, however, directs her satire against these contradictions and paradoxes to liberate both women and men: "Hail! natural desire! . . . and pleasure of all sorts, flowers and wine . . . and half-crown tickets out of London on Sundays . . . and anything, anything that interrupts and confounds the tapping of typewriters and filing of letters and forging of links and chains, binding the Empire together" (294). Woolf praises "all fulfilment of natural desire, whether it is what the male novelist says it is; or prayer; or denial; hail! in whatever form it comes, and may there be more forms, and stranger" (294). Perhaps taking a jab at the bizarre idea held by some of D. H. Lawrence's favorite characters, that women's "orgiastic 'satisfaction'" is "repulsive" (*Plumed Serpent* 463), Woolf allows to women the pleasure of their own bodies. Women might share their sexuality with women, or with men; men with men; or each by themselves; or in groups. These experiments in "more forms, and stranger" of desire interrupt the definitions of "masculine" and "feminine" as killer and nurturer, to reconceive gender roles which have long been channeled to meet the needs of an imperial state.

Between the Acts

Just as *Orlando* opens shockingly, with Orlando slicing at the mummified head of a Moor, *Between the Acts* startlingly ends the graceful clauses of its opening line bluntly: "It was a summer's night and they were talking, in the big room with the windows open to the garden, about the cesspool" (3). In both works, the introductory jolts convey social criticism behind the grotesquerie. When Orlando's biographer-narrator pretends to settle doubts about gender by pointing to swordplay, the silliness of the young man's flailing punctures the definition of masculinity as war-making. Similarly, when the characters at the beginning of *Between the Acts* lament a broken promise to bring water to the village, they imply a wider social waste land. "Cesspool" becomes a rude metaphor for everything the characters call civilization.

In fact, images of England as a waste land, a home of the dead, and an abode of darkness govern the book. The unkind juxtaposition of "Coronation" with "public lavatory," built for the royal occasion, echoes the derogatory transfer of "cesspool" from literal plumbing to figurative cleansing, the need to expel useless attitudes from the body politic (102). Wasting their lives, the characters in *Between the Acts* are indicted as the walking dead as often as those in *Mrs. Dalloway* and *The Years.* The narrator, for example, has to reassure readers, "But the master was not dead" (17). As moribund as her father-in-law, Isa admits, "There is little blood in my arm" (90). Their equally constricted guests, whether quietly inhibited or ready to break out of frustration into violence against others, know only by external signs that they have been alive: "[Mrs. Haines's] family . . . had lived. . . . There were the graves . . . to prove it" (3). Because of the deadened and deadly quality of the villagers, the last page, as monitory as the first, locates Isa and her husband Giles in a "heart of darkness" (219). Woolf thus continues the allusions, so prominent in *The Years,* to Joseph Conrad's corrupt Europeans.

The most glaring evidence in the novel that Europeans have created a heart of darkness is their readiness to slaughter each other in another cataclysmic war. As World War I dominated *Jacob's Room* and *Mrs. Dalloway,* the impending second world war drives *The Years, Three Guineas,* and *Between the Acts.* Conceived in early 1938 and completed in February 1941, *Between the Acts* appeared posthumously later that year (Zwerdling 302). References to the war punctuate the book (53, 114, 193, 199). The villagers, too superficial and/or frightened to concentrate, wander from unpleasant topics: "'It all looks very black.' 'No one wants it—save those damned Germans.' There was a pause. 'I'd cut down those trees [. . .]' 'How they get their roses to grow!'" (151). Furtive reminders of disaster disappear in clichés: "The refugees [. . .] the Jews [. . .] People like ourselves, beginning life again [. . .] But it's always been the same [. . .] My old mother, who's over eighty, can remember [. . .] Yes, she still reads without glasses. . . . I'd make it penal, leaving litter" (121). Partly through an inability to empathize, partly as a defense against empathizing too much, the distracted guests unconsciously reduce the refugee problem to litter; as a consequence, their myopia perhaps does require the glasses they disdain.

To meet this need for a more focused vision, the local playwright La Trobe provides "spectacles" with her pageant, trying to direct her audience's attention not so much to the manifestations of war as to its causes. As unwilling to soothe as an Old Testament prophet making Israel responsible for its own destruction, La Trobe accuses the villagers, "Consider the gun slayers, bomb droppers here or there. They do openly what we do slyly" (187). Like *Three Guineas,* in which Woolf detected symptoms of fascism in England as well as Germany, *Between the Acts* diagnoses specific traits that make English society waste, dead, and dark. Through La Trobe's pageant, *Between the Acts* sweepingly examines historical events and attitudes that have led to England's present role in fascism and disaster.

Zwerdling believes that Woolf blames England's problems on individualism and the loss of a former sense of community (317, 320). Although solipsism does isolate the characters, Woolf satirizes a wider range of targets. She shows that even in bygone eras, when dangerous tendencies were already incubating, a true community never existed. Founding the whole syndrome, acquisitiveness drives a competitive spirit. Society trains people to be always "pushing, striving, earning wages" (119). Social climbers, however, do not even expect to enjoy material goods; rather they postpone gratification and spend their scant savings only "when ears are deaf and the heart is dry" (119). Meanwhile, as wage-earners wear themselves out for nothing, they deplete others, too. The English, according to this novel, acquire their hoarded, unsavory possessions at the expense of four groups in particular. First, English exploitation of colonial subjects forms a major topic of La Trobe's skits relating to the seventeenth, eighteenth, and nineteenth centuries, conveying a pervasive guilt about past colonialism, not sufficiently noted in criticism of this novel.[3] Second, *Between the Acts* regrets the exploitation of the working class in England; the skits dealing with the eighteenth and nineteenth centuries, as well as the twentieth-century activities recounted in the novel, highlight the bleak conditions of servants and workers. Third, economic development proceeds at the expense of women of all classes, a problem shown in La Trobe's Age of Reason, as women are relegated to low-paying domestic jobs or the bourgeois tea-table. Fourth, the drive to amass possessions, although seeming to favor a patriarchy, also requires sacrifices of men, taught to repress vocational interests and sexual expression in favor of business or military careers. Men and women who learn to glorify money and power suffer the cost both in a figurative death—stultification and restlessness—and finally in the literal death of war.

These traits of money-getting, disdain for people seen as inferior (colonized, working-class, female), and blindness to the waste of young men regarded as expendable, have been inculcated at various points in English history, all dramatized in the pageant. La Trobe's prologues and skits criticize the past as a source of the exploitation and world wars seen in the twentieth century. For example, the pageant swiftly tarnishes the glory of the Elizabethan age. La Trobe reduces Renaissance "ingots of silver," brought back from newly discovered lands by "Hawkins, Frobisher, Drake," to silver-colored "swabs used to scour saucepans" (83–84). Just as *Orlando* almost literally knocks over such debased idols by toppling their foolish worshipers from their benches (59), *Between the Acts* similarly refuses to glorify these adventurers. On the contrary, the crone in La Trobe's Elizabethan skit tells a rosary of her century, "Each bead . . . A crime" (89).

In addition to indicting the Renaissance for its growth through "crime," La Trobe's pageant charges the Age of Reason with several injustices. Although Bart Oliver applauds the announcement that "reason holds sway," actually unreason and inequity attend Queen Anne's 1700s. Encouraged by Bart's "Bravo," a personified Reason—merely a villager in a bedspread, after all—boasts that, at her behest, the "heathen" leaves his "steaming" altar, and the warrior lays down his shield. In the ensuing peace, she claims, bees make honey in the helmets (123). Reason's noble sentiments about converting and pacifying the "heathen," however, mask a more important motive, profit, and a more ruthless method, warfare, for eighteenth-century imperialism. La Trobe exposes these realities behind the pomp by inserting a jarring note into Reason's script: "In distant mines the savage sweats" (123). This incongruous line discloses that the inhabitants of foreign lands, far from benefiting when Reason forbids them their old "unholy sacrifice," themselves become the new sacrifice, on the altar of her "Commerce." For all Reason's lyricism, she cannot avoid revealing the stark means by which her cornucopia is filled: somebody else's suffering.

As Reason glides between conversion to Christianity and conversion to Commerce, with its attendant sacrifice, La Trobe's pageant also whisks away the veils which hide force. No matter how much Reason deprecates shields, she did not obtain her "distant mines" without a fight. Her idealized picture of honeycombs forming in unused war gear

sanitizes a grislier reality. Apparently only the African warrior was sufficiently persuaded by Reason—or by the sound of technically superior
guns—to lay down shield and spear. The European warrior, in contrast, took up his weapon and kept it. As Budge the policeman admits
in La Trobe's nineteenth-century skit, he maintains "'Er Majesty's Empire" only by means of a "truncheon" (162). Budge has learned the lesson about mines and coercion that more decorous Reason only touches
on and states it more brusquely: "Let 'em sweat at the mines; cough at
the looms; rightly endure their lot. That's the price of Empire; that's
the white man's burden" (163). He adopts Rudyard Kipling's phrase
(Welch 110) to boast of carrying a burden that actually rests on the
bodies of men in mines and women at looms: both the English working class at home and colonized workers abroad.

Reason's idyll of honey in the helmets strikes a further ironic resonance.
The upside-down war gear, abandoned only temporarily, produces a commodity that figures in the ominous nursery rhyme heard recurrently
throughout the pageant: "The King is in his counting house / Counting out
his money, / The Queen is in her parlour / Eating bread and honey" (122).
This verse, recited immediately before Reason's speech, ushers in the new
gender divisions fostered by the eighteenth century. The queen in the
rhyme—along with many contemporary middle-class women—soon will
have nothing better to do than sit in their parlors, be taken care of, and
eat or serve snacks. Indeed, as soon as Reason takes center stage, La
Trobe's stagehands carry in a table with a china tea service (125).

By this simple stage set, Woolf represents a number of changes that
historians have cited as accounting for the heightened polarization of
gender roles in Reason's era. Whereas married women in the first half
of the eighteenth century had been able to contribute significantly to
the family economy, by the end of the century, the notions of women
as "dependent" and "home" as a distinct sphere for family and leisure were
firmly entrenched, both in new middle-class families, where women ceased
to earn cash, and in working-class families, where women earned less than
they had (Connell 156). One cause of these shifts is that large land-
owners had seized four million acres, nearly one-quarter of England's

arable land, absorbing forty thousand individual farms (Perry 14). This enclosure of land previously held in common, coupled with growing industrialization, affected both men and women, of course, but, as Bridget Hill argues, women's options may have narrowed more drastically. Before enclosure and the decline of handicrafts, women had been able to form an integral part of the family economy by keeping cows and growing food on the commons, engaging in cottage industries such as hand-spinning, and working in animal husbandry and a number of trades (blacksmithing, carpentry, bricklaying, coopery) that later were reserved for men (Hill 239, 259). Not only had married women helped support the family, but single women had been able to support themselves. By the end of the century, however, "the possibility of choosing a single life was steadily eroded" (Hill 239). Shut out of the commons, crafts, and trades, women found new niches in low-paying work sewing, in domestic service, or in the new "career" of marriage. Woolf takes account of these developments by portraying "Deb, her maid," trying to escape domestic servitude in the eighteenth-century skit, and by featuring Reason herself pouring out tea in the prologue's middle-class parlor.

Meanwhile, as eighteenth-century women were either eking out a living as maids or supporting themselves as bored wives eating honey, middle-class and upper-class husbands, like the king in his counting house, were making money. La Trobe's skit for this century, "Where There's a Will There's a Way," shows reason degenerating into pragmatism and the plunder of colonies. The plot revolves around efforts by Lady Harpy Harridan and Sir Spaniel Lilyliver to obtain a colonial inheritance. When Lady Harpy's Brother Bob, "Emperor of the [West] Indies," sank with the ship carrying him back to England, his daughter Flavinda was rescued, and, more to the point, his will was saved (130). The document stipulates that Flavinda will inherit her father's fortune only if she marries someone approved by her aunt. Lady Harpy, therefore, plots to marry Flavinda off to Harpy's own heartthrob, Sir Spaniel. As an eighteenth-century husband, he would acquire legal title to all his wife's property (Hill 196). Lady Harpy assumes that Sir Spaniel would then share the bounty with her, though in fact he is only flattering her in order to secure the money for himself.

This skit is often referred to as Woolf's "Restoration playlet" (Zwerdling 307) or a "Restoration burlesque" (Fussell 270). Although one of Woolf's characters, a colonel, calculates a time lapse of two hundred years between "Will" and the Victorian skit, his math is faulty. Actually, "Will" echoes eighteenth-century plays as much as it resembles a seventeenth-century Restoration comedy. In fact, at many points "Will" recalls Richard Sheridan's *The School for Scandal* (1777). Just as Brother Bob from the West Indies inspires the other characters who eye his legacy in La Trobe's skit, Sir Oliver Surface in Sheridan's drama has to decide which of two nephews deserves the fortune that he has amassed in the East. Like Sir Spaniel in "Will," Joseph Surface in *School* pretends to be in love to further his schemes. Even Woolf's choice of the name Oliver for the family that sponsors the pageant may acknowledge Sheridan; Woolf's Bart Oliver has returned from India, where Sir Oliver Surface also makes his money.

Woolf and Sheridan part company, however, over the degree of admiration due to the colonizing uncle. While Sheridan's *School* satirizes hypocrisy and backbiting, it also valorizes lavish spending and the richly profitable getting that enables it, derived from new business rather than old landowning. Sir Oliver excuses his nephew Charles, the spendthrift, ostensibly because Charles's generosity and sincerity contrast with the stinginess and cant of the other nephew, Joseph. Actually, Oliver chooses the prodigal Charles because the latter refuses to auction his uncle's picture to satisfy creditors, parting with "all but the little honest nabob" (860). Although Oliver is horrified that Charles would incur such foolish debts—and that he would sell assets at a loss to pay them—he favors Charles because the nephew gratifies his self-love, by his sentimental attachment to the portrait and, more importantly, to the ways of a nabob.

"Nabobs" were extravagantly rich returned colonizers who took on the title of the grand, despotic provincial governors of India's Mogul Empire. Coupling this appellation with Charles's word "little" is an oxymoron; "honest" may be another. Although Sir Oliver, impersonating a moneylender to test his nephews, ostentatiously scorns the Jew

Moses for charging more than 8 or 10 percent interest, he neglects to mention the hefty income in profits, bribes, and kickbacks that real nabobs made. According to the historian Geoffrey Moorhouse:

> In 1776 the political economist Adam Smith thought that between eight and ten per cent was a good profit in England, but ten years before that the normal profit in the internal trade of Bengal had been between twenty and thirty per cent and up to seventy-five per cent in some commodities such as salt, betel nut and tobacco. For a dozen years after Plassey, profits of twenty-five per cent were regarded as a sign of the moderate man, and there were to be few of those around for some time to come. (49)

When Sheridan's Moses advises 50 and even 200 percent interest, Sir Oliver chaffs the moneylender as such a good tutor that "it must be my own fault if I am not a complete rogue before I turn the corner" (852). Oliver's choice of words to dissociate himself from Moses nevertheless betrays interesting affinities with him, as this "honest nabob" has already called Charles a "wild rogue" in very indulgent acceptance of his nephew's extravagance (850). When Sir Oliver further admits, "I hate to see prudence clinging to the green succors of youth," he may indicate that he has risked his own resources wildly in India, reaped profits extravagantly, and perhaps undertaken a little roguery while he was at it (851). After all, just to give Joseph a minor present, the 12,000 pounds for which he now expects gratitude, Sir Oliver would have had to invest 120,000 pounds, if he were to keep to the rate of return he regards as reasonable (867).

Sheridan's *The School for Scandal* joins a whole group of eighteenth-century plays, from Richard Cumberland's *The West Indian* (1771) to Fanny Burney's *A Busy Day* (1800), in which the plot turns on colonial inheritance. In none of them does anyone mention the African slaves, displaced American Indians, East Indian workers, or even Europeans if they are armed. Colonizing Europeans appear only as avuncular and urbane Sir Olivers. Woolf's skit "Where There's a Will There's a Way" parodies this genre by finally indicating the source of the funds. As the jewels in the old plays seem to lie about on the ground just for the taking, Woolf's Brother Bob inhabits a West Indies "where the very stones are emeralds and the sheep-crop rubies" (130). The shift from free stones to sheep-crop slyly hints that gathering among the stubble—and the dung—might really be a dirty business. It is dirty because the stones are not free after all, but pried loose from "the reluctant earth" at a human cost, the labor of unwilling slaves (123). The unreasonable coercion that Reason could not hush up remains the crux of Woolf's eighteenth century: "In distant mines the savage sweats" (123).

The skit "Will" further undercuts the glory of colonization with Brother Bob's excessive and incongruous list of bequests: a mere "ten bushels of diamonds," "two hundred square miles of fertile territory bounding the River Amazon," a snuff box, a flagelot, macaws, and concubines, "with other trifles needless to specify" (131). Apparently Brother Bob uses Indian or African labor, reduced to the level of decorative macaws, to satisfy his sexual tastes as well as his mining needs. His sister, Lady Harpy, who treats the slaves and their sufferings as "trifles," vies with her exploitative brother in her own oppressions at home. When Flavinda foils the marriage plans of her elders, Lady Harpy consoles herself that she still possesses "messuages [houses with outbuildings and land]; tenements; napery [linen]; cattle; my dowry; an inventory," with which to entice Sir Spaniel (145). While she fares unusually well, the secondary meaning of *tenements*—i.e., slums—suggests that her tenants fare unusually ill.

She also stints on paying her servant Deb. Lady Harpy is foiled again, however, when Deb runs off with "the raggle-taggle gipsies" (148)—the same means of escape that enabled Orlando to relax her inhibitions even as it required her to give up her aristocratic snobbery. Lady Harpy cannot fathom why Deb, "fed on apple parings and crusts from my own table," would ever want to leave her stingy mistress (148). Without commenting on the obvious reason, inequity, Reason at this point "descended from her plinth," slinking rather ignominiously from the scene (148). Together, Woolf's eighteenth-century prologue and skit reveal that, while some men are taking stock in their counting houses, others sweat in the mines; the women (maids, concubines, or wives) work either menially or not at all in the parlor. As Isa guiltily learns from the nursery rhyme, in order for the privileged classes (including herself) to count profits and eat honey, "Four and twenty blackbirds"—a whole flock of the underclass—have to "bake in my pie" (178).

If La Trobe's pageant tarnishes the "glamour" of the Elizabethan age, when every bead was a "crime," and punctures the glory of the Age of Reason, when rubies were mucked from the sheep-crop (97, 89, 130), the play especially skewers the Victorian era. While Budge the policeman, in La Trobe's Victorian prologue, praises nineteenth-century life, Woolf quietly undercuts its full-blown imperialism and restrictive gender roles:

> Go to Church on Sunday; on Monday, nine sharp, catch the City Bus. On Tuesday it may be, attend a meeting at the Mansion House for the redemption of the sinner; at dinner on Wednesday attend another—turtle soup. Some bother it may be in Ireland; Famine. Fenians. What not. On Thursday it's the natives of Peru require protection and correction; we give 'em what's due. But mark you, our rule don't end there. It's a Christian country, our Empire; under the White Queen Victoria. Over thought and religion; drink; dress; manners; marriage too, I wield my truncheon. Prosperity and respectability always go, as we know, 'and in 'and. (162)

When Budge brags about all the "protection," "purity," and "correction" which he exports to the colonies, the coercive "correction" falls out of the sentence, revealing the foundation in force on which he builds an edifice not of purity but of money. "Prosperity," after all, surfaces in his speech as his one true value. Despite his claim to be helping the colonized to prosper, it is obvious that non-English hunger, whether for food or independence, counts less than his own; some "bother" in Ireland turns out to be "Famine. Fenians. What not." His indifference cancels the noble sentiments that he uses as a shield for his own profit.

Another of Budge's excuses, "security," means only that other people must mirror him in every way, including his repressive sexual mores. These strictures only produce a hypocritical voyeurism: "The ruler of an Empire must keep his eye on the cot; spy too in the kitchen; drawing-room; library; wherever one or two, me and you, come together . . . our watchword . . . respectability. If not, why let 'em fester" (162–63). He parodies Christ's words about "two or three gathered together" because he worships prosperity as his new god, with the respectability of women as its handmaiden. Orlando discovered that society engineered her into "womanliness," defined as modesty and lack of interest in sexuality, to help justify colonization. This ideological need divides people into two camps: fragile ladies and stalwart warriors, or, as La Trobe directs, Victorian maidens singing "I'd be a Butterfly" and young men chorusing "Rule, Britannia" (170). Although one member of La Trobe's audience, a colonel, may complain that she has left out the British army, actually the army is very much present in Budge's truncheon, his means to "Rule" (157). The colonel may fail to see the violence because the display of force is blatant, not masked and idealized as he is accustomed to experiencing it.

Another justification for colonization seen in the pageant is idealized missionary activity, undercut by means of the nineteenth-century skit, "The Picnic Party." A young man, Edgar Thorold, asks Eleanor Hardcastle to marry him and spend "a lifetime in the African desert" (166). Whereas he has to talk himself into a missionary calling, he assumes that living in the desert will be easier for her, a woman, "whose whole life is spent in the service of others" (165). La Trobe's pageant, however, has already sown doubts as to whether the presence of the English in Africa really serves Africans. As both Reason and Budge have confessed, colonized people only sweat in the mines. Appropriately, at the moment when Edgar and Eleanor are rhapsodizing that they will "convert the heathen" and her father is praying "for thy great gift of Peace . . . grant us to spread the light," some commotion in La Trobe's audience interrupts: "Here the hindquarters of the donkey, represented by Albert the idiot, became active" (166, 171). Just as Woolf uses references in *Jacob's Room* to dogs urinating on church pillars or defecating by the statue of Achilles to slur Jacob's Christian-trained misogyny and militarism (33, 166–67), here the donkey's interruption "defecates" on the father's pious sentiments. Moreover, when an idiot in donkey's costume carries the royal name of the queen's husband,

Albert, the combination hints that the young couple's missionary plans to serve Empress Victoria are idiotic. Instead of bringing "light," the intruders bring to Africa cultural destruction and slave wages, as Leonard Woolf carefully documented (*Empire and Commerce* 357). Instead of bringing "Peace," the nineteenth-century colonizing Europeans prepared for World War I (*Empire and Commerce* 321). La Trobe's audience, mindlessly expecting "The Picnic Party" to end in a Grand Ensemble celebrating army and navy around the Union Jack, dutifully shuffle to their feet when the gramophone needle "found the rut" for "God . . . Save the King" (157, 179, 195). However, the new war pending in 1939 will be no picnic. The same old "rut" of greed, glorification of force, and denigration of "inferiors" ends in the war trench.

When La Trobe's pageant reaches contemporary time, "ourselves" are a product of the past. The historical figures return to hold makeshift mirrors up to the audience, because the villagers ought to be able to recognize in themselves some of the attitudes portrayed on-stage. The cast creates a remarkable poem lamenting British society as less than sane, simply by reviewing a phrase or two from their lines in the preceding pageant: "*I am not* (said one) *in my perfect mind* { . . . } Another, *Reason am I* { . . . } *And I? I'm the old top hat* { . . . . } *Home is the hunter, home from the hill* { . . . } *Home? Where the miner sweats, and the maiden faith is rudely strumpeted . . . Is that a dagger that I see before me? . . . I'd be a butterfly . . . Hark, hark, the dogs do bark and the beggars* { . . . }" (185). "Home" in the eighteenth and nineteenth centuries did become a "hunter" and destroyer of women and men, if, as Woolf says in *Three Guineas,* the "private house" fostered "immorality," "hypocrisy," and "servility" (74). "Reason" might as well be an "old top hat," for all the sense in a system that turns workers into "beggars," women into frivolous "butterfl[ies]," and men into corpses on the battlefield. From the dagger of *Macbeth* to the war planes that drown out the vicar, weaponry predominates. In a history "not . . . in [its] perfect mind," the same three dangerous divisions persist in the present as in the past, separating poor from rich, women from men, and colonized from colonizer.

The problems of class, for example, which have surfaced several times during the pageant of earlier centuries, continue to characterize

La Trobe's contemporary audience. Just as the eighteenth-century skit showed Deb the maid enduring her mistress's apple parings and her temper (148), some of the audience recall nineteenth-century servants lugging heavy cans of hot water and earning only sixteen pounds a year (159). In the present, Mrs. Swithin still reduces the butcher's apprentice to the level of a tidy object: "'That'll be all right,' said Mrs. Swithin, half meaning the boy, half meaning the sandwich, as it happened a very neat one, trimmed, triangular" (35). Laying the sandwich "complacently" on the pile, she seems to trim to her own needs not only the bread but also the laborer's possibilities in life. When her nephew Giles arrives late for dinner, no one cares if the cook's time is wasted: "but what it meant to Mrs. Sands, when people missed their trains, and she, whatever she might want to do, must wait, by the oven, keeping meat hot, no one knew" (35).

Just as the warping divisions of class continue in the present, so, too, do the rigid gender stereotypes that were evident in the eighteenth- and nineteenth-century segments of the pageant. The Oliver grandchildren, for example, are already indoctrinated in the time-honored roles. Little George is learning to stifle his emotions, because boys must not cry. When his masked grandfather and the drooling dog frighten him, the old man derides the boy's tears. However, George's resentment at having to deny spontaneity and endure scorn is likely to lead him to take out frustration elsewhere. Indeed, his passage through the flowerbeds already means that "membrane after membrane was torn" (11). His sister, Caro, by contrast, will be directed to nurture others. Although Caro now tosses her bear away, the same nurse who lets George tear membranes soon will convince Caro to guard little bears and be a good mama. Isa has been similarly taught to make motherhood her only vocation, although secretly "she loathed the domestic, the possessive; the maternal" (19).

Like his son George, drilled to hide gentleness or fear in front of his grandfather, Giles has learned to damp down natural impulses. Although he had wanted to be a farmer, society directed him to become a stockbroker, so that he might acquire the substantial capital deemed necessary for marriage (47). Because Giles has repressed so many inclinations—vocational, aesthetic, emotional, physical—it is no surprise that his frustrations, like those of his son, burst out in small acts of violence, as he kicks the ground and wants to kick William Dodge, a homosexual. A socially fostered scorn for William distracts Giles from his truer contempt for himself, for refusing to face hardships as a farmer.

Moreover, Giles probably wants to be like William in ways that he has been taught to define as "effeminate," so he resents William for enacting what he has painfully denied himself. For example, William can openly praise paintings, whereas Giles has to occupy himself with stocks and bonds, which bore him. William, not Giles, can form friendships with women. Giles regards sexuality as women's only role; like many men of his culture, he has learned to dissociate sexuality from intelligence or even affection (Herek 72–73). Thus, when Giles and Mrs. Manresa go to the greenhouse, we hear of no talk between them. No matter how much pleasure they may steal there, the green fertility shrine fails to satisfy Giles's whole self, leaving him to kick the door, with hostility toward her and himself (149, 157). Women, unfortunately, often accept this same compartmentalization of sexuality, separated from mind and heart. Although Isa can accompany William to the greenhouse for one of the few examples of honest talk in the book (114), she never says what she feels to potential sexual partners, either her husband or her distant idol, Haines.

Not only is sexuality walled off from friendship, but it is also guilt-laden. Giles resents William in part because William seeks the body's pleasure so openly, even though that expression is exactly what Giles and everyone else desires: "William . . . watched [Giles] approach. Armed and valiant, bold and blatant, firm elatant—the popular march tune rang in his head. And the fingers of William's left hand closed firmly, surreptitiously, as the hero approached" (110). Cecil Eby reports that, in the years before World War I, "At some schools boys were required to have their pockets sewn up as a deterrent against self-abuse, which in the Victorian catechism was prelude to insanity, or worse" (91). Giles has been trained to avoid masturbation, to express sexuality only through intercourse and only with women, and to consider even this expression somehow a sin, a reflection of his fallen nature. His sexuality therefore becomes furtive, with Mrs. Manresa, or hostile, with his wife. His Christian training further makes him condemn the sexuality that William directs toward men, although, contradictorily, Giles's classical schooling would have taught him, as well as William, about Socrates's "left-handed," less favored, but still sanctioned homosexual route to the beautiful (*Phaedrus* 535).

Whereas Giles fears homosexuality to the point that he cannot even bring himself to utter the word, the book as a whole respects William Dodge and pities him for having to "dodge" his society's disapproval. The book especially honors William by alluding to the last page of *A Passage to India,* by Woolf's admired friend E. M. Forster. In that novel, the Indian and English characters Aziz and Fielding cannot develop a deeper friendship, both because of the political relation of master England to servant India and because of the legal prohibition against homosexuality: "[Aziz] rode against him furiously—'and then,' he concluded, half kissing him, 'you and I shall be friends.' . . . But the horses didn't want it—they swerved apart; the earth didn't want it . . . 'No, not yet,' and the sky said, 'No, not there'" (322). Woolf's version pays homage to Forster by echoing his language: "Isabella guessed the word that Giles had not spoken. Well, was it wrong if he was that word? Why judge each other? Do we know each other? Not here, not now" (61).

Giles thus learns to define masculinity as pursuing business (not aesthetics), shunning masturbation, and indulging in shared sex guiltily and only with women, whom he is unlikely to consider either intellectual partners or friends. Giles also accepts masculinity as aggression. Nevertheless, he secretly considers violence to be as boring and silly as stocks and bonds, an opinion that surfaces in the metaphor "hedgehog," which he uses to describe Europe "bristling with guns" (53). "Masculine" soldiering becomes identified with male sexuality, an equation seen in the recurrent rhyme "Bold and blatant, / Firm, elatant." Although the rhyme might suggest an erection, the sexuality more frequently is displaced onto a "pompous march tune" for the warrior (95, 160; cf. 79, 110, 163). Women, in turn, learn to accept this skewed definition of "manliness" as force, what Catharine MacKinnon calls "the erotization of dominance and submission" (quoted in Jason 126). Thus

Isa was initially attracted to Giles as hunter: "Her line had got tangled; she had given over, and had watched him with the stream rushing between his legs, casting, casting—until, like a thick ingot of silver bent in the middle, the salmon had leapt, had been caught, and she had loved him" (48). Mrs. Manresa, in a similar dynamic, judges that when Giles stomps on the toad and the snake, he somehow flatters her (107). Whereas she admires her "sulky hero," the narration deflates her enthusiasm for "valour" by juxtaposing her shallow praise with her plan to buy "Twenty-five halfpenny stamps," implying a low evaluation of all such bloody heroism (107).

In fact, throughout the novel such juxtapositions debunk militarism. When Mrs. Manresa chatters on, "T'other day I took my nephew—such a jolly boy at Sandhurst—to *Pop Goes the Weasel*," the heroes and weaponry revered at the military academy of Sandhurst shrink to the level of sly weasels and stupid toys (142), in much the same way that *To the Lighthouse* equates war-making with Jasper's childish shooting of starlings. La Trobe's skit "The Picnic Party" also mocks the ideal of conquest, from the ancient Romans in England to the nineteenth-century British in Africa: "Only when Mr. Hardcastle gets talking with Mr. Pigott about the Romans [. . .] last year they quite came to words [. . . .] But it's nice for gentlemen to have a hobby, though they do gather the dust—those skulls and things" (168). Oblivious Mrs. Hardcastle, sending her daughter and son-in-law to Africa, inadvertently equates the spread of English civilization with a grotesque collection of skulls, revealing the absurdity as well as the horror of conquest.

Just as problems of class and gender definition continue in the present, legacies of the Empire which La Trobe devalues in the historical pageant also persist at the time of the performance. The audience gossips that Mrs. Manresa has an uncle who is a colonial bishop and a former husband who supplied her with jewels "dug out of the earth with his own hands" (40). Although the villagers express only snobbishness, judging entrepreneurial upstarts inferior to the landed gentry, and colonial religious posts inferior to bishoprics at home, the narration undercuts the two relatives for a different reason. Mrs. Manresa's family unflatteringly resembles the characters satirized in the skits:

Brother Bob who scoops rubies out of the West Indian muck, and the couple whose missionizing suggests a donkey's ass. These comparisons condemn the Manresa family for continuing the exploitative money grubbing into the present.

As the Empire has contributed to the income of the guests, it has also supported the family itself. Bart Oliver, retired from the Indian Civil Service, still dreams that he is toting a gun beside "a bullock, maggot-eaten in the sun; and in the shadow of the rock, savages," and "a cascade falling. But no water" (17). Bart's recollection of past drought recalls the discussion of a present dearth of water at the beginning of the book. The passage simultaneously echoes Eliot's lines: "Here is no water but only rock" (*Waste Land* 42). La Trobe's present audience exists in a waste land, as a legacy of the past.

One reason why the society has turned into a waste land may be seen in Bart's assumption of superiority and his habit of command. He bosses "Sohrab the Afghan hound" as a kind of surrogate for the people—Afghans on the border of India, perhaps—whom he has apparently regarded as less than human: "'Heel!' the old man bawled, as if he were commanding a regiment" (12). His ability to "make a brute like that obey him" is said to be "impressive, to the nurses"—that is, only to the most cowed observers (12). Nancy Bazin explains that the dog's name Sohrab may suggest Matthew Arnold's "Sohrab and Rustum," in which "Rustum unknowingly killed his son Sohrab" (217). Bart's values—a paradoxical promotion of self (as status) with denial of self (as body and spirit)—have stifled his son at home, as they have oppressed colonized peoples abroad. Indeed, the string that Bart slips over the dog's collar is called "the noose that old Oliver always carried with him," making him a kind of walking executioner (12). He deadens others, in the same way that the Camerons in Woolf's play *Freshwater* had only death, in the form of their coffins, to take to the colonies. Bart, with his controlling noose, may think of himself as a powerful man, but really he remains, as he appears to his small grandson, a "peaked eyeless monster moving on legs, brandishing arms" (12).

Bart's former ties to Empire are resumed in his son Giles's career. Lucy twits Giles for selling stocks and shares—or "glass beads was it?"—to "savages who wished most oddly—for were they not beautiful naked?—to dress and live like the English" (47). Isa's side of the family has also benefited from the colonies, through the Civil Service; the villagers remember that her mother died in India (159). In fact, one of Isa's main preoccupations is guilt about the ongoing effects of Empire. She laments that she stumbles along as the last "donkey in the long caravanserai crossing the desert," because she is "burdened with what they drew from the earth; memories; possessions" (155). This wealth drawn from the earth recalls the key warning in La Trobe's eighteenth-century prologue that "in distant mines the savage sweats" (123); "possessions" may include Brother Bob's "two hundred square miles of fertile territory bounding the River Amazon" in the eighteenth-century skit (131). When Isa adds that the burden laid on her "in the cradle" is "murmured by waves" (155), the line may allude to another of Woolf's novels. In *The Waves,* "the waves of the sea under me" are actually the shipping lanes over which Louis operates his international finance, backed by a "hatchet" (132, 167).

Isa, whose name Isabella perhaps makes her successor to the European queen who sent ships out to create an Empire, thus feels implicated in the getting and sweating that "blister" and "crack" the hooves of the donkey (155). These hooves may also belong to acquisitive globe-trotters and especially to indigenous workers used as beasts of burden. She sees little hope of change ahead. The name of her son, George, duplicates that of the reigning king, George the Sixth, and the royal name of her daughter, Caro (probably Caroline, recalling the American colonies named after King Charles I), announces not a rebel but a "helpmeet" for the men of her time. The family's private training, in nursery and bedroom—that a man must ruthlessly tear membranes and a woman must dutifully guard children—prepares for the public violence and the hierarchies of Empire. In fact, Isa's eagerness to get rid of this guilt and her fear that change may be impossible contribute even to thoughts of suicide (104).

As Isa imagines that drowning might free her of "what we must remember; what we would forget" (155), she also briefly trusts that the impending war may somehow cleanse her society: "'Now comes the lightning,' she muttered, 'from the stone blue sky. The thongs are burst that the dead tied. Loosed are our possessions. . . . It's a good day, some say, the day we are stripped naked. Others, it's the end of the day" (156). Lucy, too, entertains flickering hopes that the destruction caused by the war may strip away ill-gotten possessions, along with dangerous attitudes of materialism and superiority. When she sees a jagged leaf that reminds her of the map of Europe, she comforts herself that "There were other leaves . . . India, Africa, America . . . couldn't the blue thread settle, if we destroyed it here, then there?" (205). If Europe were completely destroyed, the world might not miss it, might even thrive, she suggests.

Just as Isa and Lucy fitfully wish for an apocalyptic cleansing in World War II, so, too, did survivors of World War I, as La Trobe's pageant indicates. When La Trobe represents a couple rebuilding a wall and longing for "each flat with its refrigerator" (182), a reporter notes their optimism but fails to grasp the irony that dangerous attitudes are being renewed along with the architecture: "With the very limited means at her disposal, Miss La Trobe conveyed to the audience Civilization (the wall) in ruins; rebuilt (witness man with hod) by human effort; witness also woman handing bricks. Any fool could grasp that. Now issued black man in fuzzy wig; coffee-coloured ditto in silver turban; they signify presumably the League of [. . .]" (181–82). Founding the League of Nations might look promising, but, as Leonard Woolf warned, if the European states simply affixed "new fine names" (mandate) on "ancient evils" (colonies), then the only change after World War I would be that the league could hypocritically "call exploitation trusteeship, slavery labour, and profit-making patriotism" (*Empire and Commerce* 367). Indeed, La Trobe shows the old order perpetuating itself in three ways: when the reporter patronizes colonized people by labeling them "fuzzy," when the builder keeps women in an auxiliary role handing bricks, and when refrigerators become more important than people.

The reporter's unexamined assumption that World War I has swept away false values, then, proves unfounded. So, too, does Lucy's and Isa's yearning for a new beginning after the present world war. Lucy may comfort herself that a "blue thread" of civilization, broken in Europe, will resurface in Africa and Asia; but if the former colonies remain tied to Bart's definition of civilization, then her fantasy of "Islands of security" outside Europe looks naïve (205). When Leonard Woolf analyzes the legacy abroad of people like Bart, he finds a very mixed picture. On the healthy side, Europeans managed to transmit, "involuntarily perhaps," ideas from the French Revolution: "democracy, liberty, fraternity, equality, humanitarianism." On the toxic side, however, Europe also deposited "its ideas of economic competition, energy, practical efficiency, exploitation, patriotism, power, and nationalism" (*Imperialism* 44–45). If part of Lucy's "blue thread" glints with such strands, then Africa and Asia perhaps have inherited just enough rope to hang themselves.

More aware of the total colonial legacy than Lucy, Isa consciously has to abandon her hope for renewal through war, because the same greed no doubt will reassert itself after an only temporary loosing of possessions: "None [speaks] with a voice free from the old vibrations. Always I hear corrupt murmurs; the chink of gold and metal. Mad music" (156). When the same materialism, glorification of violence, and elevation of one group as "superior" to another may persist at home as well as abroad, then such an entrenched ideology simply prepares the ground for new wars.

Between the Acts epitomizes this pervasive ideology in a simple but powerful image of planting a stick—an image that unites Woolf's concern for gender relations, imperialism, and economics. When La Trobe's missionary couple in "The Picnic Party" become engaged, the young man carries "a spiked stick" to lakeside (165). He duplicates Paul Rayley and Andrew Ramsay, who "plant Rayley's stick where they had sat" by the ocean at the time of Paul's engagement to Minta (*To the Lighthouse* 117). The young men learn to claim their wives as property, just as the missionary couple will lay claim to Africa with a British flagpole. At the same time that women cease to be individuals and become merely signs of wealth, colonies become a surrogate for sexual thrills, replacing lost or repressed pleasures. Thus the sexy Manresa seems to restore to Bart his "spice islands" (41).

Further, Woolf links this imagery of imperial flagpole and phallic marker with monetary exchange. Although the missionary couple with their spiked stick leave England in the name of religion, they actually serve British "Prosperity" (162). Isa sees the relation between finance and definitions of masculinity when she reads items in a newspaper, shockingly but appropriately juxtaposed: "The paper crackled. The second hand jerked on. M. Daladier had pegged down the franc. The girl had gone skylarking with the troopers" (216). When sexuality is skewed toward possessiveness and power, a light-hearted "skylarking" turns into gang-rape by the soldiers (20). Using the same language of staking a claim, Isa's father-in-law earlier reads about M. Daladier "pegging down the franc" after the old man frightens his grandson and then scorns him as a "crybaby" (13). Because Bart recovers from his disgust by reminiscing about his experiences in India with a gun, he seems to worry that his grandson will be considered effeminate, unable to pin India down as he has done (17). Leonard Woolf points out that this mining vocabulary, of pegging claims and countries for the sake of francs and pounds, was used by Lord Rosebery to justify colonialism ("Way of Peace" 9). It is as if boys, unsure that they can ever attract a free and tender response, learn an aggression that may eventuate in the rape of women and countries, as both become dehumanized objects of exchange.

Thus, pegging claims or francs, planting flagpole or phallus, are all conflated to express a cultivated need for dominance. Ironically, women can participate in the enterprise of colonization also, as Eleanor Hardcastle in La Trobe's skit illustrates. And the fact that Giles does not enjoy his role as pushy stockbroker makes it clear that men, too, can be limited and hurt by the social system, which defines masculinity as conquest and femininity as the weakness of a butterfly. From Orlando's Renaissance to the opening years of World War II, experienced by La Trobe's villagers, this ideology warps both women and men and exposes them equally to the bombs (*Between* 193).

Conclusion

In all her books, Virginia Woolf implicitly or explicitly exposes the dominant ideology of her time. At the end of her career, in *Three Guineas,* Woolf defines that ideology as materialism, competition, and a prideful exclusivity—values that could, she believes, increase the likelihood of wars. The primacy placed on capitalist ownership, for example, may sanction exploitation or the acquisition of foreign land. Practice in competing rather than cooperating may lead to combativeness. The habit of relegating to an inferior status anyone who does not belong to one's own school, university, church, and social class may prepare the way for regarding an "enemy" as subhuman. Long before *Three Guineas,* however, Woolf's novels show how these three traits oppress outsiders and fuel wars—both imperial skirmishes and world wars.

Woolf consistently depicts the perpetuation of this dangerous ideology through the British public schools, universities, social classes, churches, professions (Jacob's law career, Susan's landowning, Louis's international finance), marriage, and gender expectations. These institutions all reinforce each other, so that a unifying imperial outlook regulates life at home and dictates behavior overseas. John MacKenzie similarly describes the dominant British ideology that took hold about 1870 and continued through the Second World War. For him, its key features are imperialism, militarism, commercialism (as expressed in the new advertising), worship of heroes, and racial bigotry, associated with Social Darwinism (2). For Woolf, such a society molds even the most likable characters to participate in the Empire, in ways that her novels as a whole satirize.

Woolf's books recognize several motives for Empire making. Most obviously, economic drives compel both well-to-do financiers and less affluent lower-middle-class adventurers. Yet Woolf goes beyond economics to identify sexual displacement as a second motive underlying both colonization and militarism. This insight forms one of her most interesting contributions to social analysis. From her earliest story to her last novels, male characters use boasting about the colonies as a courtship device, while common metaphors put "marrying a woman" in terms of "staking a territory." This cultural imagery equating land and the female body both demeans women and promotes dangerous repercussions in imperial policy. Moreover, as men in her fiction seek compensation for private hurts in global acquisitions, women become accomplices in waging war, if they cannot understand the real causes of their restlessness in prescribed gender roles. Her books further investigate how the ideology of a "civilizing mission" determines some of those restrictive roles, by requiring cultural myths of the "chaste" European woman, the "lascivious" colonized people, and the "restrained" European male.

As the most obvious motive for public policy, the desire for money colors life at home as well as abroad. Giving in to pervasive materialism, Clarissa in *Mrs. Dalloway* has allowed her passion for Sally to decay into a "passion for gloves" (15). A voracious Susan in *The Waves* wants not just onions but *more* onions, hams, and everything else—including India (173). The Pargiter family, whose lives Woolf hoped would sum up everything—"history, politics, feminism, art, literature"—that propelled a whole society from 1880 to "here and now" (*Diary* 4: 129, 152), identifies so completely with finance that they hold their grand reunion in business offices (*Years* 397). The acquisitive ideal of Empire imbues the Pargiters to such an extent that one of them even mistakes an invitation to the reunion as a call "to Africa" (348).

These possessive characters do not so much succumb to individual greed as acquiesce in a larger economic system that assures one person's well-being at the expense of someone else's. Thus, Rachel Vinrace in *The Voyage Out* grows uneasily aware that taking up her assigned role as a middle-class wife means accepting that the servant girl be scrubbing on her knees every morning at 10:30 (36). Rachel further discovers that her ability to play the piano depends on keeping her father's South American workers "beggars," as he himself admits (196). The people at whose expense the Empire operates, at home and abroad, pay higher and higher costs: poverty, loss of indigenous tradition, loss of life. Louis in *The Waves*, for instance, is well aware of the "rumours of wars" produced by his dependence on the Suez Canal, yet he is able conveniently to block out such knowledge by focusing on picturesque women carrying red pitchers along the Nile (95). *Between the Acts* admits bluntly that, from the eighteenth century on, if "Commerce from her Cornucopia pours the mingled tribute," then, to make that tribute to England possible, in "distant mines the savage sweats" (123). The character Isa in this novel expresses a guilt that hangs over all Woolf's characters (some aware of its causes, some not): "How am I burdened with what they drew from the earth; memories; possessions. . . . That was the burden . . . laid on me in the cradle . . . what we must remember: what we would forget" (155). Isa's phrasing alludes to Kipling's "white man's burden," which has proved crushingly arrogant. Woolf's novels are a constant "remembering" of the costs of the Suez Canal and the African mines: in beggary, warfare, and scorn for people defined as inferior.

Money motivates Empire-makers not only among entrepreneurs like Willoughby Vinrace, with his competitive desire to "win the race," but also among the lower-middle and working classes who have scarcely been allowed to enter the race at all. Ralph Denham in *Night and Day* briefly entertains a plan to go to India, to gain the recognition denied him in a rigid class system and to escape stifling family life. Woolf is aware, however, that those dominated often want to join the race in order to dominate others rather than to change the economic or social system. Ralph, for instance, though he supposedly resents family life, would stifle Katharine in a new family built on the same model. Similarly, Charles Tansley in *To the Lighthouse* resents his poverty, yet as soon as he feels accepted by middle-class men, Tansley is compared in the text to a naval commander (169). To be a "top dog," he would accept the need for a fleet: fangs to lash out at new curs below him.

Boredom combines with limited economic opportunities to provide another motive for Empire and war. In *Jacob's Room,* the men of

Scarborough, a town as mummified as its museum pieces, have left home only once—gladly—to fight in the Crimean War. In a draft of *The Years,* Eleanor Pargiter explicitly discovers the dangerous effects of drab conventionality: "That's why war is possible. It's so much better for most people than the lives they are leading, the women can feed their children. The men get excitement" (quoted in Radin 70). As long as societies rely on war and Empire to bolster the economy, provide an outlet for people unintegrated into advancements at home, or distract them from boredom, then ordinary, well-meaning folk may be drawn into violence. Geoffrey Moorhouse, benefiting from hindsight, assesses the reasons why preceding generations of average Britons may have endorsed the Empire:

> . . . their fundamental decency was greatly outweighed by their ignorance and even more by a primitive need not to have the foundations of their world disturbed. My grandfather had been a young volunteer soldier in the Boer War and he still spoke of his time at Ladysmith and on Spion Kop with excitement and pride. He would have been shocked if someone had told him that he had been an imperialist aggressor, engaged in a morally indefensible act: to him it had been something between a duty to Queen and Country and a chance for adventure far from the dismal back streets of his home mill town. (12)

For Woolf, the Ralph Denhams, Charles Tansleys, and Eleanor Pargiters of England all possess such a "fundamental decency." Nevertheless, she exposes the ways in which they, like their author and readers, may participate—obliviously or guiltily—in imperial attitudes that hurt people.

Woolf thus grants that economic causes, including the lures and resentments of the class system, are strong forces fueling imperialism and militarism. Her novels, however, show many other incentives at work. She goes beyond commentators who would add "prestige" to commerce in explaining the motives behind Empire (Graham 225), by speculating that money and prestige both might displace other concerns, often sexual. Avoiding a monolithic explanation, her books delineate a complex set of reasons linking Empire, military, and gender relations, the elements of Woolf's most characteristic juxtapositions.

References to imperialism and militarism often occur together because, once a country accepts the need for colonies, it must rely on force to put down local rebellions and fend off other European nations. Leonard Woolf insistently blamed economic imperialism's "rivalry, cupidity, aggression, [and] fear of aggression" for contributing to World War I: "By sowing dragon's teeth in Africa we may reap a most bloody crop of armed men in Europe as well as a most lucrative rubber crop" (*Empire and Commerce* 45). Some later historians have agreed: "The conflict of empires was a contributory cause of both World Wars of the twentieth century" (Snyder 444). In all her novels, Woolf similarly names the greed and ignorance of Empire as causes for war: from the pre–World War I travelers in *The Voyage Out* who cannot inspect trade prospects without also noting the overseas fleet, to the villagers in *Between the Acts* who hear in a pageant about the mines in the colonies, as warplanes fly overhead, auguring World War II.

Empire and military, in turn, constellate with gender relations for a number of reasons. Men's training to expect women's inferiority unhealthily prepares them to accept other hierarchies. Women, dominated by men, may be tempted to imagine dominating someone even lower, perhaps foreigners or laborers. Jacob's lessons at the chapel and the university—that women cannot preach, teach, or take degrees—render him that much less capable of hearing other excluded groups. He remains oblivious, for example, to the poor outside his door (*Jacob's Room* 109). Drilled to rank whole groups as less human than he, he more easily becomes a tool of war. Jacob's visit to the prostitute Laurette epitomizes this relationship of gender roles to world affairs. He learns that he can command Laurette's services and leave a pittance on the mantelpiece; meanwhile, a statue of Britannia, leaning on her spear, presides on that same ledge as an appropriate sign of Jacob's initiation into unequal relations (104–5).

More than prostitution, marriage in England at various times may have taught men a habit of command that paved the way for behavior in the wider world. Sir William Blackstone, in *Commentaries on the Laws of England in Four Books* (1753), endowed the husband with an exclusive "empire," including his children (quoted in Hill 198). In life and even in death, he controlled his offspring and could assign them to guardians other than their mother. Moreover, his private imperial domain included his wife, since "a married woman had no legal existence" (Perkin 13). Woolf's Orlando in the eighteenth century discovers that the law courts have brought charges against her: "(1) that she was dead, and therefore could not hold any property whatsoever; (2) that she was a woman, which amounts to much the same thing" (168). Indeed, until the 1880s, a woman in England kept no property of her own, and after that she still could forfeit her interests to serve her husband's. Acting imperiously already during their betrothals, Terence in *The Voyage Out* wants Rachel's piano playing to be less important than his writing (292), and Ralph in *Night and Day* insists that there be no place in Katharine's mind where he does not hold sway (489). Middle-class wives were supposed to give up fulfilling work, such as Rachel's music or Katharine's mathematics. Thus middle-class Clara in *Jacob's Room* can only pour tea. Yet the ideology that keeps her in the drawing room is not confined to the home. *Jacob's Room* carefully juxtaposes the scene of tea-pouring Clara, limited by her family, with a reference to Morocco, controlled by France, because the two oppressions reveal a common habit of dominance (166).

That the public mind did indeed associate Empire and gender relations is apparent from the fears expressed about women's suffrage bills in England. Ray Strachey reports in *The Cause* that, during the debate in 1918, before the vote was partially granted to women, "their Lordships were still saying that women's place was in the home, and that Women's Suffrage would endanger the British Constitution and the safety of the Empire" (365). Woolf refers to Ray Strachey's book in *A Room of One's Own* (58). Two reasons might explain why women's taking a more public role—whether in voting or earning an income—was thought to endanger "the safety of the Empire." Publicly active women might not bear so many children, and they might not provide such an inspiring mythical image.

One of the most obvious ways women contribute to the imperial civil service and the armed forces is by supplying them with sons. Woolf is sardonically aware of the burden that this contribution places on women, through the time and effort involved in raising large families and the grief associated with losing children in wars. In her short story "A Society" (1921), "Lord Bunkum" claims that he accepted his peerage only "because my wife wished it"; he goes on to boast that he and his professional friends work fifteen hours a day, leaving them no time to read. "'But why do you work so hard?' 'My dear lady, with a growing family—' 'But *why* does your family grow?' Their wives wished that too, or perhaps it was the British Empire" (*Complete Shorter Fiction* 132). In the 1923 version of *Freshwater,* a painter similarly hints that the Empire fosters large families. He explains that in his allegorical painting, "Maternity" means "two million horse marines" (77). Already in *Melymbrosia,* an earlier draft of *The Voyage Out,* a young man calculates "that if every man in the British Isles has six male children by the year 1920 and sends them all into the navy we shall be able to keep our fleet in the Mediterranean; if less than six, the fleet disappears; if the fleet disappears, I shall no longer be able to pursue my studies in the university of Cambridge" (quoted in Ingram 127). The young man's cryptic connectives imply that merchant and military fleets carry and protect a lucrative trade, from which his family makes the money to ensure his advancement. Although this line about the six sons does not occur in the published version of *The Voyage Out,* Mrs. Dalloway there nevertheless connects childbearing and Empire in exactly the same manner. Effusing over "all we've done" in India and Africa, she gushes, "We *must* have a son, Dick" (*Voyage Out* 50). Later she "skimmed" toward some warships (69). Mrs. Dalloway's superficial, skimming mind has uncritically internalized the message that she should be not the variously talented mother of variously able children, but a factory turning out single-minded imperialists, arming for war.

Englishwomen become necessary to maintain the Empire not only as providers of sons but also as embodiments of an inspiring image: "The mothers of Pimlico gave suck to their young. Messages were passing from the Fleet to the Admiralty" (*Dalloway* 9). Although this juxtaposition might seem to contrast a giver of life with an instrument of death, the coziness implies no such opposition of aims. Instead, the mothers seem to facilitate the passing of war messages. They do so because, in fact, the Admiralty needs an icon of motherhood. The chaste mother and the helpless baby join with the virgin young woman to form a particularly effective ideology of Empire. This ideology construes a threat to chaste womanhood as an excuse to keep supposedly rapacious "natives" in the preventive detention of colonialism.

Several of Woolf's books blast the hypocrisy and destructiveness of this myth. One of her most vivid and damning juxtapositions shows an irascible colonizer calling for more troops in the colonies; his shouts "echoed strangely across the way in the ears of girls buying white underlinen threaded with pure white ribbon for their weddings" (*Dalloway* 26). This juxtaposition is not as incongruous as it might at first appear, for the brawler and his society require pure white virginity as one of the justifications for quelling rebellions. Woolf had already commented explicitly on this motive in her essay "The Royal Academy" (1919). After caricaturing a sentimental and bloodthirsty duke, she explains his function: "scenes from Rudyard Kipling must take place with astonishing frequency at these parties in order that the English maidens and gallant officers may have occasion to insist upon their chastity on the one hand and protect it on the other, without which, as far as one can see, there would be no reason for their existence" (*Collected Essays* 4: 208). Without chastity, upon which "all the property in the world depends," as Samuel Johnson claimed, the couple would lose the social basis for marriage, to pass inheritances from father to son (quoted in Hill 180). Or, as Orlando learns, the "tribe of the respectable" insist on women's chastity in part because it gives the middle-class city men "Wealth, Prosperity, Comfort, Ease" (137). Similarly, without chastity the prosperous Empire would lose one of its key ideological props, the ostensible need to protect European women from sexual contact with colonized men.

Cynthia Enloe has analyzed the importance to Empire building of "the respectable lady," like the girls in their emphatically white underlinen whom Woolf parodies: "She stood for the civilizing mission which, in turn, justified the colonization of benighted peoples" (Enloe 48). This alibi requires the construction of several ideological players, imaginary in the sense that their qualities are assumed to be shared not just by a few but by all members of the designated class.

The script calls for "the rapacious native male," for example; all native males become, by definition, sexually unrestrained. Mrinalini Sinha argues that the British of the late nineteenth-century Raj elaborated an image of lascivious Bengali men because that image announced them as unfit to govern themselves. The British also called the Bengali men "effeminate" (Sinha 218), although this new version of feminine men as passionate conflicted with the mid-Victorian ideal of genteel femininity, "passionlessness" (Showalter, *Sexual Anarchy* 21). Despite the contradiction, to be "like women" further guaranteed that Indian men would be considered unfit to govern. The construction of feminine and/or uncivilized Indian men warrants the imposition of "civilization." Thus Lady Bruton in *Mrs. Dalloway* needs to imagine "barbarian hordes," although her very name exposes her as the brute (274).

In addition to casting a lascivious colonized male, the ideology of a civilizing mission requires the figure of the "respectable" European woman. Woolf was aware of several falsifications in this prescription. When Lady Bruton stands with a bouquet against the portrait of a general whose baton parallels her flowers, the stance supposedly contrasts a chivalrous man, violent to protect her, and a demure woman, delicate as the flowers she holds. Actually, Lady Bruton, far from dainty, would prefer to ride down the "hordes" herself. The label "respectable woman" thus glosses over the aggressiveness that might reside in women as well as men.

The label further glosses over and denies women's sexuality. Woolf shrewdly shows that Orlando, for example, to meet imperial needs, must become a respectable woman and repress her sexuality. The moment of her sex transformation significantly coincides with the revolt of the Turks against the sultan, as the presence of "ladies" justifies intervention in a local conflict: "English ladies in the company [. . .] I own that my hand went to my cutlass" (127). In the telescoped time of the novel, Orlando's transformation and escape to the gypsies takes place in a matter of weeks, actually the 1600s to the 1800s. Thus the scene of a Turkish rebellion in the 1600s can also reflect the nineteenth-century British desire to take advantage of the power vacuum provided by the decline of the Ottoman Empire. The British military, however, rather than admit that they would like to incorporate Constantinople into their own Empire, resort instead to the more glowing ideology that they are protecting ladies. Orlando becomes a woman for the imperial age because the Empire needs a woman—and womanhood of a certain sort. As she wakes up in her new female state, Chastity, Purity, and Modesty throw the naked Orlando a towel—not at all to her liking (138). The soldiers need not just any woman, but a chaste woman under attack from local men, to excuse their own display of arms.

Although the icon of the respectable woman seems designed to praise women, it also controls them. As Orlando complains, womanhood "meant denying her love, fettering her limbs, pursing her lips, and restraining her tongue" (163). The contrast between the supposed power attributed to the inspiring woman and her real lack of power vividly appears in the engraving *Britannia and Her Boys,* by G. Durand, from the *Illustrated London News,* 1885.

Britannia in her horse-drawn chariot stands above dozens of men, all soldiers, including both Britons and colonized men in the service of Great Britain. Because this woman has a classical helmet, a shield, and a flagstaff, and because only a ship's mast in the background looms higher, she dominates the engraving as a strong Athena figure. Nevertheless, closer inspection reveals that two men hold the bridles at the mouths of the rearing horses. Although Britannia looks autonomous and venerated, she is really not even driving her own steeds. Moreover, for all her military regalia, she remains demure in her fluttering drapery, a contradiction that moves her subtly from the battlefield to the boudoir. Her isolation as the only woman in the crowded scene further reduces the initial impression of powerful womanhood. No real woman could stride onto the field of public activity, only this single idealized vision.

If a real woman did arrive with helmet and shield—or even with less threatening gear, such as a notebook in the hands of an investigator seeking to reform the dairy industry—the audience for the *Illustrated London News* probably would be scandalized. Mrs. Ramsay, who only dreams of such dairy reforms, is a good example of the respectable woman who both resents and endorses the ideology which keeps her at home. When she lets herself be framed as Madonna against an "authen-

Britannia and Her Boys, by G. Durand. *Illustrated London News,* 1885. Courtesy of The Mansell Collection, Limited, London.

ticated" painting by Michelangelo, and again when she stations herself under a picture of Queen Victoria, she exposes the constructed nature of her identity as Mother and as Inspirer of the British Empire (25, 48). Mrs. Ramsay accepts her society's flattering "interpellation" of her as saintly "subject" (Althusser 171), as Madonna or Angel in the House, because she hears as personal adoration the homage that men have been taught to give to the myths. Feeling as if *she* has the power to make men bow down, she can further express her unused strength by matchmaking, replicating herself in the creation of new Madonnas. The Luriana scene at the end of *To the Lighthouse* mocks this ideology in a comic parody (165–67). Mr. Carmichael, a mild, unsuited imperialist, his mustache yellowed from the opium he probably began using during his years in India, humors Mrs. Ramsay by bowing to her. Meanwhile, this ludicrous priest consecrates the newly engaged Minta as the next Angel in the House. Woolf, showing how "saintly" Motherhood and "civilizing" Empire require each other, satirizes them both.

When Mrs. Ramsay identifies with the Angel and with Victoria, empress of India, Woolf accurately reflects late Victorian ideology, which linked the two images. In *Queen Victoria Opens the Imperial Institute,* which appeared in the *Illustrated London News* in 1893, Victoria stands in a portico, while directly over her head hovers Britannia on the model of a Renaissance angel, complete with wings and trumpet.

This angelic Britannia, like the respectable Victoria, mother of many children, guarantees that the imperial enterprise answers a godly purpose. Britannia does, however, wear a robe slashed to the top of her thigh. Her difficult dual role, as both disembodied saint and risqué dancer, coincides with the impossibly contradictory requirements for women exposed by Woolf in Peter Walsh's dream of a tree-woman. While his visionary woman, in her character as inanimate and remote angel, gives him "charity" and "absolution," she must at the same time remain available for a "carouse" (*Dalloway* 86). If respectability in women is construed to mean lack of sexuality, and if people are taught to seek out only sexual partners of the opposite sex, then two options are left for shared sexuality. Either passionless women must occasionally "submit"; or the ideology must materialize some sexual women who are not

THE IMPERIAL INSTITUTE
AN ILLUSTRATED RECORD OF THE
Opening Ceremony by Her Majesty the Queen

" With soaring voice and solemn music sing !
High to Heaven's gate let pealing trumpets ring !

To-day our hands consolidate,
The Empire of a thousand years"—LEWIS·MORRIS

THE NATION'S TRIBUTE TO QUEEN VICTORIA

Queen Victoria Opens the Imperial Institute, by G. Durand. *Illustrated London News,*
1893. Courtesy of The Mansell Collection, Limited, London.

respectable: "loose" women, such as Jacob's Laurette or Florinda, or "native" women.

Although Virginia Woolf (for reasons discussed in the introduction) did not portray any colonized women, Leonard Woolf depicted some sexually active local women in a short story, "A Tale Told by Moonlight" (1921). The narrator, Jessop, recounts how a nervous, cultivated European, Reynolds, buys Celestinahami—idealized, celestial angel and earthy whore—out of a brothel in Ceylon and sets her up in a bungalow on the beach. Prostitution is said to exist not because of some supposed sexual uncontrollability in the women but because of power relations under colonization, creating "this hovel in the warren of filth and smells which we and our civilization had attracted about us" (*Diaries and Stories* 260). Jessop (and perhaps the author) does subscribe, to some extent at least, to the stereotypes of cerebral, white-skinned man and instinctual, dark-skinned woman: "He was a civilized cultivated intelligent nervous little man and she—she was an animal, dumb and stupid and beautiful . . . she had grown to love him . . . as a bitch loves her master" (263). When Celestinahami's devotion begins to get on Reynolds's nerves and he cannot talk to her about his novel, he loses interest. The story, however, undermines the narrator's stereotypes and reveals Reynolds's callousness. Rather than being "stupid," as Jessop judges, Celestinahami is merely uneducated in the areas important to Reynolds. Her attempts to get Reynolds back by dressing in European clothing give evidence not of animal contentment in a cozy lair but of human vulnerability. When Reynolds leaves for Aden, she drowns herself, "bobbing up and down in her stays and pink skirt and white stockings and shoes" (264). Although Jessop's audience had thought that it wanted to hear about "real" battles rather than insignificant "white kid gloves and omnibuses and rose leaves," the small, domestic details of the water-logged white stockings and pink skirt capture the real human devastation that results from unequal relations between much larger political entities (255).

The ideology of the civilizing mission to benighted souls generates, then, several stock players: the animalistic colonized woman, the always lascivious colonized man, and the asexual European woman. The same myth also assumes a colonizing male who is always restrained, to differentiate him from the colonized male and to account for European ascendancy. Restraint, of course, conflicts with a key lure of the East, sexual adventure. As Moorhouse summarizes, "It was a far from celibate world for those early [East India] Company employees and many unions were made with Indian women inside and out of wedlock, with the happy result that racial prejudice was almost unknown until it surfaced in the nineteenth century with the assistance of Evangelical dogma" (117). Marriages with local women may have become more difficult over time, but the Raj encouraged prostitution in the nineteenth century by frowning on the presence of English soldiers' wives, licensing local women as whores, and regarding the latter as a necessary "commodity" (Liddle and Joshi 151–52). More extended affairs also continued, with Indian mistresses at times "pensioned off" when an English wife eventually arrived (Masani 54). Nevertheless, the ideal for Englishmen, promoted through such organizations as the Boy Scouts, was sexual self-control. A scout "could never lower himself to behave like a beast, nor would he allow a woman to ruin herself with him" (quoted in Enloe 51). According to Enloe:

> The Boer War, following in the wake of the Crimean War, shook Britons' confidence that their men were masculine enough to maintain the empire. Robert Baden-Powell founded the Boy Scouts in 1908 because venereal disease, intermarriage of the races and declining birthrates were allegedly endangering the maintenance of Britain's international power. Baden-Powell and other British imperialists saw sportsmanship combined with respect for the respectable woman as the bedrock of British imperial success. (49–50)

Baden-Powell's ideal of rigid self-control, epitomized in the scout's posture at attention, may have heightened the guilt and violence associated with licentiousness in the colonies. William Plomer expressed such a view in *I Speak of Africa* (1927), whose manuscripts in 1925 were judged "extraordinarily good" by both Woolfs and published at their Hogarth Press (Bell 2: 149). Plomer's graphic and innovative stories, set in South Africa, portray characters who alternate between sexual repression and sadistic sexual expression.

To idealize the restrained man may be hypocritical, then, if he is really engaged in sexual affairs or even attacks, as Leonard Woolf and William Plomer suspect. Virginia Woolf also suggests that the ideal may be hypocritical, when she identifies a strong motive for colonization and militarism in displaced sexuality. She goes beyond the sensational cases depicted by Leonard or Plomer to discern a whole cultural dynamic. In fact, her investigation of displacement forms one of her most interesting and original contributions to an understanding of the late nineteenth and twentieth centuries. Throughout her novels, men who are unsure of themselves sexually try to enhance their prowess by positioning themselves next to the immensity of the Empire. Men who resort to talk of colonies as a conspicuous courtship device occur in many of her fictions, including her first surviving story, "Phyllis and Rosamond" (1906), in which a suitor attempts to suggest his virtues by mentioning India (*Complete Shorter Fiction* 21). In *The Waves,* Bernard similarly approaches a mistress by offering "India, Ireland or Morocco" as vicarious evidence of potency (255). Martin in *The Years* courts a "virginal girl" at a party with chatter about Ireland (250). In all these cases, an appeal to Empire compensates for doubts about sexual attractiveness.

In Woolf's novels, men's fears of inadequacy may fuel militarism as well as imperialism. When Sara Pargiter sees her father "Pirouetting up and down with his sword between his legs," she implies that he places the sword where his genitals should be because he worries that his wife really prefers his brother (*Years* 144). Many observers other than Woolf have commented on the way some cultures elide weaponry or war with sexuality. Claire Culleton notes that postcards from World War I picture women "straddling the shells and riding orgastically across the atmosphere" (109). Simone de Beauvoir complains in 1949 about a continuing vocabulary of war to describe sexual "conquest" and "surrender" (375). In an essay on Vietnam War literature, Philip Jason finds that "In the crude semantic equations of the battlefield, killing gooks is the same as fucking them—and being a man in the military environment 'means' being a killing and fucking machine" (126).

Jason tries to explain the equation of war with sex by referring to Otto Rank's classic theory that men who fear women associate sex with "chaos, irrationality and death"; women, according to Rank, "do not fear sex because they accept their basic biology and mortality" (127). Men in this theory seem to want to avoid sex. The World War I postcards, on the other hand, suggest an almost cynical conspiracy to entice men to enlist, as if offering them sexual release on the battlefield (Culleton 109, 112). Jason also considers Mark Gerzon's speculation that a soldier's "fear of being considered a woman [i.e., a person with feelings] . . . is the sexual underbelly of combat" (quoted in Jason 126). In all these cases, a fear of sexuality or emotion, plus a continued need for both, seems to generate dangerous sexual surrogates in a kind of international swagger.

One of Woolf's clearest examples of Empire making and war making as displaced sexuality occurs in her portrait "Scenes from the Life of a British Naval Officer," probably written in late 1931 (*Complete Shorter Fiction* 232–34, 306). The officer in his cabin, surrounded by instruments enabling him to dominate the Red Sea, is constantly measuring, weighing, counting, dividing, or ordering something. Named Captain Brace, he is braced not only against the blasts of the world but also against himself. To preclude any spontaneous reactions, he has allotted "three seconds precisely" or "precisely two seconds" before responding to a gong or a salute (233). His brace-like rigidity recalls Baden-Powell's ideal of masculinity; in the scout master's *Rovering to Success*, a man, white, stands at attention with chest thrust out, near a smaller black man, dressed in baggy attire, who looks up admiringly: no loose clothes, limbs, or sexuality for the scout or the officer (Enloe 50).

Yet for all Captain Brace's self-control, he clearly derives a substitute sexual pleasure from his career in the navy. The gong, for example, seems to him to stimulate the atmosphere into "sharp muscular contractions" (233). Even more tellingly, the telescope encloses "the penetration of his sight. When he moved the telescope up and down it seemed as if his own long horn covered eye were moving" (234). Brace has replaced the risks of touch with more distant, safer sight, and he has displaced himself into his machine. As an extension of himself in metal and glass, the telescope lets him engage, while still remote and protected, in erotically described horniness, penetration, and thrusting.

Although Brace enjoys a kind of symbolic intercourse with the world he sees, he does so not to interact with that world but to control it. He establishes no reciprocal relationships with whole, complex people: "Of the servants who put plates before him he had never seen more than the white hands . . . When the hands were not white, they were dismissed" (233). As Baden-Powell draws a weak black man and puts woman on a confining pedestal, Brace disdains blacks and idealizes a woman kept at home who inspires his exploits: "On the wall behind the Captain's back hung seven or eight white faced instruments. . . . In the centre of the instruments hung the photograph of a lady's head surmounted by three ostrich feathers" (232). Just as Brace has converted himself into an invincible machine, here the "white faced" instruments predominate over the human face. The dehumanized image of a woman serves as his mascot, although her ostrich feathers—of a cabaret dancer? of a matron?—may not make her quite as respectable as Baden-Powell would like.

Brace's relationships must all exalt him to absolute power: "His face had a carved look as if it had been cut by a negro from a well seasoned log . . . erected before grovelling multitudes as their idol" (232). The description ironically turns him into the African sculpture that he probably would not recognize as art, let alone as an object of legitimate worship. Whereas his government may excuse his policing the Red Sea as "converting the heathen" (*Between* 166), the story reveals Brace as the real idol worshiper, devoted to his own power. As a civilizer, moreover, he has no message, since he is the self-proclaimed god "to whom questions have been put for many centuries without eliciting an answer. . . . The suppliants might well address their prayers to back or front indifferently" (232). Nevertheless, Brace's personal hollowness resounds worldwide. As Gregory Herek argues, the continued definition of heterosexual masculinity in Western culture as "exclusively social relations with men and primarily sexual relations with women," both ties based on aggression, success, status, independence, and the repression of emotion, not only may confine a man individually but also may "increase the likelihood of interstate warfare and thereby be maladaptive" for the species (72–73). Thus Brace's desire to pin down the entire Middle East seems to develop from his need to button down and protect his own fragile ego.

As, in Woolf's novels, a man courting may inflate a faltering sense of self-worth by reminding himself of Empire, so, too, a man who has lost at the game of love may compensate for absence or failure, either by substituting control of the Red Sea for an ostrich-feathered woman, or simply by dreaming of colonization.[1] Thus, when Evan Williams in *Jacob's Room* cannot prevent his wife's affair with Jacob, he starts praising past Empire-builders. Evan would like to possess his wife, and when he cannot, he takes vicarious pleasure in the overseas possessions of "great men" (143). Jacob, too, follows Evan's method of assuaging pain by inflicting it elsewhere. When he falls into a gloomy mood after visiting the prostitute Laurette, probably because he senses how ephemeral that relationship is, he compensates by hardening his position on Ireland, deciding that it should not have Home Rule after all—as if the eternal union of Empire would ensure the eternal union of the couple, fantasized as "lovers" but actually master and slave.

One of Woolf's most frightening analyses of imperial and other totalitarian impulses as compensation for self-doubt occurs in the portrait of Louis in *The Waves*. Feeling not so much abandoned by one particular lover as forsaken by a whole community, Louis treats the telephone, by which he arranges international business deals, as a mistress: "I love the telephone with its lips stretched to my whisper" (168). When the school authorities forget to prepare a Christmas gift for the alien boy from Australia, as an afterthought they give Louis the Union Jack from the top of the tree. Although he claims to be furious, Louis, in fact, accepts the Union Jack of Empire as his life's project. Lacing the globe with his steamship lines, he wraps up the Empire as his own private present. Ironically, Louis's effort to belong to an accepting group only sets other people adrift from their roots: "Dark men and yellow men migrating east, west, north and south" (167). Because Louis's poignant fear of being unloved must be felt by everyone at some time, such longings become a particularly alarming motive for Empire.

When a society converts sexuality into militarism, or a need to be included into the desire for an all-embracing Empire, one effect may be a pervasive cultural image linking women and land. This metaphor works in both directions to debase into possessiveness the relations of men to women, and to indict as substitute sexual thrills the relations of England to its colonies. Several of Woolf's books describe courting a woman or taking a wife in terms of staking a territory. Thus Captain Barfoot, with "something military in his approach," supports himself on his way to Betty Flanders by leaning on a "flagstaff" (*Jacob* 25–26). The captain claims Betty as evidence of his attractiveness, as he believes in securing India and Ireland as proof of English power (91). Paul Rayley in *To the Lighthouse* plants his stick in the tide at the moment of his engagement to Minta Doyle (117). Learning to define virility as ownership, he stakes out Minta as he would claim a piece of property. Similarly, when a couple in the nineteenth-century skit of *Between the Acts* becomes engaged, the man carries a "spiked stick" to lakeside (165). Because his fiancée's life as a woman is already earmarked as sacrifice to others, she might as well "serve" in the colonies, too, he thinks, and "convert the heathen" (166). Woolf, however, mocks this enterprise by interrupting the blessing on the couple with the observation, "Here the hindquarters of the donkey, represented by Albert the idiot, became active" (171). By assigning the royal name Albert to the village idiot in donkey costume, Woolf designates as asinine both the institution of Victorian marriage and the couple's royally approved colonial project.

The comparison of woman and land, *mater* and matter, has, of course, a long history, carried in language. Gerda Lerner argues that Aristotle, having assigned matter to women and soul to men, went on to justify slavery by transferring his gender definitions. He insists that slaves are like women, that neither slaves nor women have rationality, and that both groups, therefore, need to be ruled (Lerner 207). With such precedents, the equation of women and land proved particularly useful in the age of imperialism. In fact, by linking women and territory, Woolf anticipates later analyses of colonialism as a compensatory delusion of sexual power. Mary Louise Pratt, for instance, detects a "fantasy of dominance" in nineteenth-century European travel writing (143). The language of information-gathering, Pratt argues, often confuses attitudes toward countryside and women: "The eye 'commands' what falls within its gaze; the mountains 'show themselves' or 'present themselves'; the country 'opens up' before the European newcomer, as does the unclothed indigenous bodyscape" (143). Such supposedly neutral, scientific language, Pratt believes, prepared the way for an appropriation of land.

This description of land as a mute, waiting woman persisted into the twentieth century, still underpinning colonialism. Simone de Beauvoir complains that traditional imagery of city, state, or nation as enclosing, feminine space can easily be misused. She quotes a "shameful" poem in which Paul Claudel calls Indochina, a French colony, "That yellow woman" (177–78). Cynthia Enloe finds that colonial postcards "were frequently eroticized and surprisingly standardized," in a way that identifies women with land (42). A card from the early 1900s, for example, captioned "The Beauty of the Kraal, Zululand," seems to announce landscape (43). Instead, it presents a bare-breasted woman, half-lying on the ground. The female subjects of the postcards lie or sit directly on the earth. They look at the viewer, either at eye level (making the viewers important) or from below (beseeching). Interestingly, Woolf's Orlando meets her future husband Shelmerdine, a South African colonizer, when she is lying on the ground, in a Wordsworthian identification as "nature's bride" (248). Woolf, however, parodies the romantic, free-spirited earth woman ("A feather fell upon her brow") by protesting that Orlando was confined to the ground involuntarily, because her ankle was broken (248). The paradigm of woman as land does not benefit either Orlando, now restricted in the work she can undertake, or South Africa, which Shelmerdine controls as nonchalantly as one of the snail shells childishly arranged to explain his exploits at the Cape (257).

A few years before writing *Orlando,* Woolf had invoked the link between women and other people's land. She begins her 1925 review of the memoirs of Harriette Wilson, a courtesan in the time of Byron, by remarking, "Across the broad continent of a woman's life falls the shadow of a sword" (*Collected Essays* 3: 227). On the sunny, respectable side of the sword, women behave chastely, "escorted by gentlemen, protected by policemen, wedded and buried by clergymen" (227). If women are protected, they are themselves also policed and restrained, already half-buried at marriage; as Orlando tells Shelmerdine when they become engaged, "I'm dead, Sir" (*Orlando* 250). Only on the "shady" side of life can a woman admit that she, too, experiences sexual desires. Whereas men "can cross from sun to shade," from propriety to condoned affairs, "with perfect safety" in terms of their careers, a woman with a lover incurs disapproval. The community and even former lovers scorn the rebellious woman, "and the Queens are left sitting on three-legged stools shivering in the cold" (227). Although Wilson ends her life in poverty, Woolf insists that "it would be a grave mistake" to imagine that the courtesan regretted having "stepped across" the shadow of social expectation into a nontraditional life (228).

Woolf's image of the "continent of a woman's life" shadowed by a phallic sword further recalls Sigmund Freud's characterization of female sexuality as the "dark continent," which he proposed to explore: "In using this phrase in English, Freud ties the image of female sexuality to the image of the colonial black and to the perceived relationship between the female's ascribed sexuality and the Other's exoticism and pathology. . . . Freud continues a discourse which relates the images of male discovery to the images of the female as object of discovery" (Gilman 257).[2] Although the Woolfs' publishing house printed translations of Freud's writings from the early 1920s (Woolmer 37), Virginia Woolf is not known to have read his work until 1939 (*Diary* 5: 248). Her image of a woman's life as a shadowed continent suggests, however, that she knew Freud's phrase and converted the continent from inherently dark to socially darkened. Moreover, she converts the courtesan Wilson from a passive object of discovery to an active explorer of her own possibilities (*Collected Essays* 3: 228, 230). By drawing attention to both the literal continent, open to colonization by the "sword" (or the Gatling gun), and the women figuratively seen as territory, Woolf evokes sympathy for both.

In thus showing Betty, Minta, Harriette, Orlando, and the woman in *Between the Acts* all pressed into mute land under the flagstaff or sword, Woolf was reflecting upon an ideology graphically illustrated in a German cartoon from 1900 mocking the difficulties encountered by a series of English generals in the Boer War.

Lord Roberts Takes a Slice of South Africa. Reprinted from *Klodderadatsch,* 1900.

The cartoon pictures the new arrival, General Roberts, trying to insert an enormous knife into a slit at the lower end of the African continent. With West Africa providing a mammalian bulge, the map resembles a feminine torso; Europe sits a little above Africa as the head governing unthinking femininity and "savagery." The whole globe is an apple. Drawing on biblical iconography depicting the female as temptress, this feminized Africa becomes a fruit ripe for the plucking— if only the English generals could handle their knives as well as the Germans could.

Woolf ridicules all such fantasies of power when Peter Walsh in *Mrs. Dalloway* follows a woman on Cockspur Street while surreptitiously opening and closing a knife. At the same time, to give himself courage to imagine an affair, Peter recalls his position as administrator in India. Betraying a lack of confidence under his bravado, Peter displaces sexuality into ruling colonies. In so doing, he identifies the life-giving phallus with deadly weapons.

When foreign lands are regarded as women available to be raped, and women are reduced to the status of inert land, both lands and women look like victims of men's faults or fears. Nevertheless, Woolf does not ignore the complicity of women themselves in Empire and war. She warns that if conditions for women do not improve, they may actually solicit the cataclysm of war. Two forces promote this endorsement of jingoism. First, hostilities may provide women a psychological release for bottled-up resentments. Betty Flanders, for example, feels exhilarated, without really articulating her feelings, when her young son plays with a knife, because she would like to cut a few possessive men herself (*Jacob* 16). When her grown-up sons still handle the weapons of war, she approves. Simone de Beauvoir agrees that frustration may push women toward chauvinism, making them no more inherently pacifist than men: "During the War of Secession no Southerners were more passionate in upholding slavery than the women. In England during the Boer War, in France during the Commune, it was the women who were most belligerently inflamed. They seek to compensate for their inactivity by the intensity of the sentiments they exhibit" (601).

The unarticulated resentments of Woolf's Betty Flanders thus exacerbate a kind of apocalyptic longing to slash away everything. As C. J. Keep has pointed out, the avidity with which late-Victorian and Edwardian audiences read of the destruction of "their street or their relatives' church," in popular fiction about impending war, attests to both fear and "a curious desire to see those very things destroyed" (8). Keep attributes this masochism to a desire to "purge deep-set anxieties" about industrialism, technology, or class antagonism (3). One could also add the dangers involved when women like Betty Flanders vent unexamined and misdirected anger. Woolf implicates Betty's need for avenging violence—expressed, for example, when she gelds an unwanted suitor's cat—as one of the factors, on some level, making her fail to protest militarism.

A second reason Woolf suggests why women might actually welcome war and colonial conquest is that these pursuits provide a way of escaping the private house. Just as boredom made the Boer War or a New Zealand sheep farm seem an exciting change to men, so does monotony push some women to endorse anything that liberates them from traditional roles within which they may not fit. As Woolf remarks sardonically in *A Room of One's Own,* the Crimean War and World War I offered the first opportunities for women to leave home independently, as nurses or factory workers (112). Woolf also blames prudery, as well as the limitation of female occupations to mothering and housekeeping, for making the domestic scene so oppressive. In an arch introduction to a 1930 exhibition of paintings by her sister Vanessa Bell, Woolf imagines a thwarted female painter driven to missionary work in China. Adopting the voice of a prudish visitor to the gallery, Woolf muses:

> That a woman should hold a show of pictures in Bond Street . . . is not usual, nor, perhaps, altogether to be commended. For it implies, I fancy, some study of the nude, and while for many ages it has been admitted that women are naked and bring nakedness to birth, it was held, until sixty years ago[,] that for a woman to look upon nakedness with the eye of an artist, and not simply with the eye of mother, wife or mistress was corruptive of her innocence and destructive of her domesticity. Hence the extreme activity of women in philanthropy, religion and all pursuits requiring clothing. ("Foreword" to *Recent Paintings,* n.p.)

Woolf pictures this overly clothed, enforcedly chaste, and artistically frustrated woman fleeing to China: "Hence again the fact that every Victorian family has in its cupboard the skeleton of an aunt who was driven to convert the native because her father would have died rather than let her look upon a naked man" (*Recent Paintings*).

The need to escape limitations at home thus contributes to women's cooperation in dangerous Empire making. As Enloe admits, "To describe colonization as a process that has been carried on solely by men over-looks the ways in which male colonizers' success depended on some women's complicity. Without the willingness of 'respectable' women to see that colonization offered them an opportunity for adventure, or a new chance of financial security or moral commitment, colonization would have been even more problematic" (16). Enloe adds an example from American imperialism: in 1901, some women teachers sailed to the Philippines "to help establish American rule" (46). Susan B. Anthony, of the American suffrage movement, "found she had few follow-ers when she protested to President McKinley in 1900 that annexation of Hawaii and colonial expansion in the Caribbean and the Pacific did little more than extend American-style subjugation of women. Indeed, some suffragists in the United States and Europe argued that their *service* to the empire was proof of their reliability as voters" (47). More like Anthony, Woolf invited women not to serve any Empire. In *Three Guineas*, she explicitly warned that, if conditions did not improve for the dependent woman, like Betty Flanders, she might be lost to the cause of peace: "So profound was her unconscious loathing for the edu-cation of the private house with its cruelty, its poverty, its hypocrisy, its immorality . . . [that] consciously she desired 'our splendid Em-pire'; unconsciously she desired our splendid war" (39).

Woolf evolved this analysis through a series of fictional women who collaborate in the work of Empire. Not admirable though understand-able, Evelyn Murgatroyd in *The Voyage Out*, anticipating domesticity as confinement, rebels only so far as to identify with Renaissance con-quistadores—a group derided elsewhere in the book. Betty Flanders leaps from her own inability to earn a living to the oppression of some-body else, coveting Cochin Chinas (a breed of chickens whose name makes them her own private empire) and asking no questions when a son goes to Singapore. Susan in *The Waves* would accept vicarious achievement through her sons in India. In the same novel, Jinny, reversing her own anti-authoritarian principles, suddenly sanctions flag waving in the colonies; after glimpsing her own mortality, she translates a wish to conquer death into a need to conquer "savages."

If Woolf satirizes women as sometimes in league with male colonizers, she also portrays women as parallel to the colonized (cf. Gilbert and Gubar, *Sexchanges* 36, 63–64). The demeaning metaphor of women as land linked them to colonies in general. The more specific connection to colonized peoples appears, for example, in "Phyllis and Rosamond." As already noted, the suitors in this story discuss "India in the Sixties," as if the government's military victories constituted an infallible sign of the men's personal qualifications to enter the women's beds (*Complete Shorter Fiction* 21). These Victorian Hibbert sisters, reduced to one of their few available "professional arena[s]," the marriage market, assess the men as a "merchant in the Stock Exchange" might scrutinize potential buyers (18). Although the women are really items of exchange, they magnify their one moment of choice and imagine themselves as merchants. The system dehumanizes both partners, whether the generally powerful male or the temporarily powerful female. Moreover, the women gain their brief control by identifying not only with merchants but with rebels among the colonized. At the very moment when a suitor recounts the assassination of Lord Mayo by Indian rebels in 1872, Rosamond "shoots down" the men's chances, so to speak, by signaling Phyllis to reject them (21). The timing implicitly equates the noncompliant sisters with the colonized in revolt.

Both the sisters and the rebels, however, remain ineffectual, subject to a new governor. After the party, "Lady Hibbert's face changed at once: if she had seemed a benevolent cat playing with a mouse from philanthropic motives before, she was the real animal now in sober earnest. 'Remember,' she snapped, 'this can't go on for ever. Try and be a little less selfish, my dear'" (21). The phrase "philanthropic motives," describing Lady Hibbert's plans for her daughters' weddings, simultaneously glosses the suitors' description of "India in the Sixties," because the Empire, too, was frequently justified as a benevolent, philanthropic undertaking. The story, however, reveals the "real animal" behind both Lady Hibbert and her colonizing government. Power plays, not love, motivate the marriages of many Victorian, middle-class women, as well as the creation of colonies.

Night and Day similarly links colonized Indians with socially limited English women. Katharine Hilbery feels angry at the reminder of an Indian servant because she resents her own reduction to servant status. Usually the characters do not realize this kinship. Rosamond and Phyllis do not consciously compare themselves to assassins in the Andaman Islands, as Katharine does not see that her silent mutiny against the expectations for middle-class women puts her in line with the more openly violent Indian mutineers of 1857. Nevertheless, when she looks at relics from this mutiny as she telephones her own subversive plans, or when Clara in *Jacob's Room* unhappily pours tea as the guests murmur about Morocco, the juxtapositions reveal to readers, if not to the characters themselves, the parallels between dominated but rebellious women and constrained but restive colonies.

One could say that Woolf herself identified with the colonized as early as the Dreadnought hoax in 1910, when she dressed as an African man in a bogus delegation to a navy battleship (*Complete Shorter Fiction* 126; Bell 2: 217). Bell speculates that the prank "reinforce[d] political sentiments which had for some time been taking shape in her mind" (1: 161). He means her dislike of war, but these political sentiments might also include an incipient sense of solidarity with oppressed groups. The duped officers on the ship included a cousin of Woolf's, a conservative young flag commander, who worried only about a risk to her "feminine" reputation. He claims that after the escapade, the officers in the mess called her "a common woman of the town—and *I* have to sit and hear this in silence" (Stephen 38; Woolf, *Letters* 3: 324). Perhaps Woolf already had begun to see the common cause uniting women in a patriarchy and colonized people in an Empire. While both are said to be beneficiaries, in reality someone else's interest takes precedence. Gradually Woolf formulates explicitly the parallels between the positions of women and colonized peoples that she has been representing all along. In *A Room of*

One's Own, she castigates the possessiveness which "murmurs if it sees a fine woman go by, or even a dog, Ce chien est à moi. And, of course, it may not be a dog, I thought, remembering Parliament Square, the Sieges Allee [*sic*] and other avenues; it may be a piece of land or a man with curly black hair" (52). Her exhortation to reform in *Three Guineas* similarly links both groups, whether excluded by race or gender; the outsider must "in no way hinder any other human being, whether man or woman, white or black" (66).

Because Woolf's society did exclude so many groups, an unobtrusive memento mori resides in the corners of many of her books: sheep's skull in *Jacob's Room,* coffin in *Freshwater,* boar's head in *To the Lighthouse,* shrunken skull on the first page of *Orlando,* "skulls . . . and other trophies" collected by Susan's sons in *The Waves* (191), the bullock carcass from India remembered by Bart in *Between the Acts.* As these signs recall irremediable mortality, they also serve as warnings—the skull and crossbones on a poison bottle—against social problems that theoretically can be remedied. Woolf laments that artists acting alone cannot affect these ills: "Keats, Shelley, Wordsworth, Coleridge and so on . . . didn't have anything like the influence they should have had upon 19th century politics. And so we drifted into imperialism and all the other horrors that led to 1914" (*Letters* 6: 421). Nevertheless, she believes, writers can affect readers' education to some extent—not by direct preaching, but by indirect means, in fiction and poetry, and in nonfiction such as *Three Guineas* (*Letters* 6: 420, 422).

Thus Woolf's books, with their memento mori, reject certain attitudes as toxic. The ideology of a European civilizing mission, to be carried out by "chaste" European women, "chivalrous" European men, and "lascivious" colonized people, limits all the players. Such a delusive scenario may displace sexuality into militarism and imperialism. Englishmen may employ Empire and battles as courtship devices or consolation prizes. Englishwomen may imagine an escape from the limitations of domesticity or revel in an apocalyptic immolation. Both men and women may compensate for unavailable affection, work, or excitement by desiring more and more possessions, prestige, dominance, and an outlet for frustration in actual or vicarious adventure.

Because of these displacements, usually unconscious, European society becomes both deadening at home, in its stultifications, and deadly abroad, in its pursuit of Empire and world wars. Woolf's juxtapositions of Empire, military, and gender relations, apparently incongruous but actually reasonable, may helpfully bring such connections to consciousness.

Notes

1. Devouring the Lamb: Sex, Money, and War

1. Maria DiBattista also suggests the influence of *Ulysses* on *Mrs. Dalloway.* DiBattista, however, thinks that the difference between Joyce and Woolf is "absolute," because Joyce shies, "as Bloom's mind recoils, from those unsayable and unfigurable realities (especially Death surprising in the midst of life) hers sought to embrace" (110). On the contrary, Woolf in *Mrs. Dalloway* is not so much mourning the biological death that occurs in all times as lamenting the deathly qualities of a very particular society. Moreover, DiBattista believes that, when Woolf says she sets out to portray "what [readers] can neither touch nor see," the novelist means "spiritual" and "transcendent" truths (97–98, 107). However, rather than searching out a metaphysical world, Woolf is exposing the intangible and unseen expectations governing a society.

2. England had three prime ministers, two Conservative and one Labour, between the time Woolf started writing *Mrs. Dalloway* and the actual date of publication; in June 1923, when the book's plot takes place, the actual prime minister was Conservative Stanley Baldwin (Taylor 643–44). By not naming any of the prime ministers, Woolf seems to dismiss them as interchangeable.

3. Woolf mentions "the injustice which Turks inflict upon Armenians" in "The Prime Minister," a short story that originally formed part of a draft for *Mrs. Dalloway* (*Complete Shorter Fiction* 318). In the story, a character named Prentice criticizes both the prime minister and the workers who blindly worship this official. Although Prentice seems better than the frivolous Clarissa, the story satirizes his middle-class crowd for congratulating themselves so smugly on just sympathizing with working-class conditions.

4. This personification of Conversion as a goddess who coerces people to share her own narrow views may have been suggested by Woolf's cousin Dorothea Stephen. Dorothea's condescension to "Brahmans" in India and her disapproval of Vanessa Bell's sexual partners made Woolf fume in 1921 about her cousin's "odious selfcomplacency; her extreme brutality—I felt as if she had a thick stick as well as a thick leg; and if I did anything unseemly she would kick and beat" (*Letters* 2: 492; cf. 2: 488).

5. The violets as a sign of erotic exchange may also encode a reference to Violet Trefusis, "with whom Vita [Sackville-West], often disguised as a man, had had a passionate and dramatic love affair between 1918–21" (*Diary* 3: 162n).

6. Just as Sara reminds North caustically of the "switch in your hand," a party-goer in Woolf's short story "The Evening Party," possibly written in 1918, faults the hypocritical chatter of some nearby "ladies, earnest and benevolent, with exalted views upon the destiny of the negro who is at this moment toiling beneath the lash to procure rubber for some of our friends engaged in agreeable conversation here" (*Complete Shorter Fiction* 98, 298). Although the speaker in this story can detect a social problem, he offers no solutions. In fact, he only wants to exclude the ladies from his vicinity, because they remind him of distasteful matters.

2. Staking a Territory: Marriage

1. Woolf modeled Katharine in part on her sister Vanessa Bell, for two reasons. First, Vanessa preferred her work (painting) to society life, as Katharine prefers mathematics (*Letters* 2: 400). Second, Vanessa managed an unconventional sexual life, living with Duncan Grant while remaining married to Clive Bell (*Letters* 2: 109). Duncan apparently was bisexual (*Letters* 3: 342). Angelica Bell, daughter of Vanessa and Duncan, was born one month after Woolf finished work on *Night and Day* (Bishop 47). Unlike Vanessa, whose parents had died by the time of her unusual living arrangements, Katharine still has to cope with parental outrage. Long after publication of the novel, Woolf was still recording encounters with people like Mrs. Hilbery, who have one judgment—"ugly"—for both unorthodox sexuality and any work for women that is not domestic. In 1926, she wrote to Vita Sackville-West (with whom Woolf had her own unorthodox, sapphic relationship), "Three old gentlemen, round about 60, have discovered that Vanessa is living in sin with Duncan Grant, and that I have written Mrs. Dalloway— which equals living in sin" (*Letters* 3: 241).

2. Woolf's own family consciously treated her mother, Julia Duckworth Stephen, as a Madonna. For example, Haller reports that Julia posed for Burne-Jones's painting of the Annunciation (93). Julia also had herself photographed by Julia Margaret Cameron as the Virgin Mary (White). Julia Stephen is, of course, in some ways a source for Mrs. Ramsay (*Diary* 3: 135). The Victorian habit of allegorical painting and photography, which allowed Julia to appear as the Madonna, corroborates the idea that Woolf is posing Mrs. Ramsay *as* the Madonna and Queen Victoria, so as to highlight and question these icons. Haller tries to argue for Mrs. Ramsay as "anti-Madonna," an Isis to oppose the "claims of patriarchy" (105). Nevertheless, Mrs. Ramsay does reinforce just such claims.

3. Gayatri Spivak treats Mrs. Ramsay's solution as "a marvelous deceptive deployment of undecidability" (206). Spivak accidentally reverses the children's reactions to the skull: "Cam, the girl-child, must be reminded of the animal skull; James, the male-child, not" (206). She misses the fact that Woolf's sarcasm does come down decisively, not undecidably, against Empire making. Marcus further criticizes Spivak's reading for applying imagery of gestation to Lily's

painting, with Mr. Ramsay needed as agent, when "the text actually exults in the *refusal* of Mr. Ramsay" (*Art and Anger* 228).

4. I am grateful to Yvonne Singer for this observation.

3. Securing the Circle:
The Education of an Empire-Builder

1. When Vanessa Bell engaged a tutor and a governess for her sons and some other children in order to avoid the public schools, Woolf agreed: "In fact I believe the only hope for the world is to put all children of all countries together on an island and let them start fresh without knowing what a hideous system we have invented here. . . . I mean honours, degrees, and governments and so on. Or would they hark back to the same ways of their own accord?" (*Letters* 2: 208). The experiment in home schooling lasted a year.

2. Sara Ruddick agrees that Louis is a "proto-fascist" (206). She hesitates to use the term because "it would be some years before Woolf made explicit [in *Three Guineas*] the connection between professional and sexual possessiveness and the growing tyrannies of Europe" (206). Actually, Woolf had already made the connection in *A Room of One's Own* (36). Patricia Joplin also recognizes that "it may feel outrageous to read Percival as a figure for the blond ideal of Hitler's Aryan dream, but his apotheosis in the minds of his friends is described in rhetoric chillingly like fascist propaganda in this era" (96).

3. This woman may have been inspired by Annie Besant, an English activist who started a Home Rule for India League in 1916 and was briefly president of the Indian National Congress. Her work for Indian independence was accompanied by a philanthropy that Woolf seems to have regarded as patronizing. Besant "adopted a young Madrassi named Krishnamurti as her son and pronounced him Messiah" (Moorhouse 226). When Woolf heard Besant speak in July 1919, she reacted ambivalently: "She pitched into us for our maltreatment of India, she, apparently, being 'them' & not 'us.' . . . It seems to me more and more clear that the only honest people are the artists, and that these social reformers and philanthropists get so out of hand, & harbour so many discreditable desires under the disguise of loving their kind, that in the end there's more to find fault with in them than in us. But if I were one of them?" (*Diary* 1: 293). In her shifting meditation on "them" and "us," Woolf casts herself as both inadvertent perpetrator of, and artistic protester against, Empire.

4. Playing Out History: Becoming a Woman

1. Schneider does recognize that Woolf is not mourning a culture that had "lost its authority" but rather is trying to dismiss a social code "proving altogether too tenacious" (105). Sears also helpfully underlines "the correspondence of previous ages" to present world events and destructive values still held by the villagers (224).

2. Like Orlando, the dog Flush learns "to resign, to control, to suppress the most violent instincts of his nature [i.e., his desire to mount "the spotted spaniel down the alley, and the brindled dog and the yellow dog—it did not matter which"]—that was the prime lesson of the bedroom school" (*Flush* 42, 127). In Woolf's mock biography of Elizabeth Barrett Browning's dog, Flush serves as a double for Elizabeth, because both are, in effect, kept as restrained, asexual pets.

3. Neuman recognizes that the pageant "sharply observes that literature often chronicles the conquest of other people's money or spirit," but she weakens her point by characterizing Woolf's parody as "affectionate, comic, elegiac" (71). The pageant, however, tartly aims to change the future, not to bring back the past. Further missing the tone, Cuddy-Keane claims that Woolf in *Between the Acts* is "inhibiting her satire" in favor of "amiable comedy" (277). Instead, throughout the book Woolf trenchantly satirizes dangerous attitudes.

Conclusion

1. In her diary for 1929, Woolf similarly assesses a former suitor, Sydney Waterlow, who became an official at Addis Ababa near the Red Sea and Bangkok, as "a desperate looking pompous sad respectable elderly man; worldly; but quivering as usual in his shell. Any pin pricks him in the unarmoured skin. I liked him" (3: 224). His vulnerability, shared with Woolf herself, unfortunately seems to her to motivate his participation in the Empire. He boasts of "his lancers and state at Bangkok—all to his liking. His importance very clear to him. At Oare [his home in England] he is nobody. And so he would like to go back to Bangkok and be important in the East for ever" (3: 224).

2. Finding other links between colonization and scientific discourse about women, Elaine Showalter records: "The American gynecologist Marion Sims, who experimented with a speculum in 1845, experienced himself as a 'colonizing and conquering hero'; 'I saw everything as no man had ever seen before,' Sims rejoiced . . . While male novelists [Haggard, Kipling, Conrad] describe their journeys into Kor, Kafiristan, or the heart of darkness as sexual expeditions into a primordial female body, doctors describe their invasions of the female body as adventurous quests for treasure and power" (*Sexual Anarchy* 129). Despite references to the female body, Showalter also sees these male romance quests set in colonies as encoding "the desire to avoid heterosexuality altogether," playing out forbidden homosexual fantasies (82).

Works Cited

Althusser, Louis. "Ideology and Ideological State Apparatuses (Notes towards an Investigation)." In *Lenin and Philosophy and Other Essays,* by Louis Althusser, 127–86. New York: Monthly Review Press, 1971.

Annan, Noel. "Bloomsbury and the Leavises." In *Virginia Woolf and Bloomsbury: A Centenary Celebration,* ed. Jane Marcus, 23–38. London: Macmillan, 1987.

"Armenia." *New Encyclopaedia Britannica.* 15th ed. 1988.

"Armenian Massacres." *New Encyclopaedia Britannica.* 15th ed. 1988.

Baring-Gould, William S., and Ceil Baring-Gould. *The Annotated Mother Goose.* Cleveland, Ohio: World, 1962.

Baudelaire, Charles. *Petits Poèmes en Prose (Le Spleen de Paris).* Paris: Éditions Garnier Frères, 1962.

Bazin, Nancy Topping. *Virginia Woolf and the Androgynous Vision.* New Brunswick, N.J.: Rutgers Univ. Press, 1973.

Beauvoir, Simone de. *The Second Sex.* 1949. Translated by H. M. Parshley. New York: Vintage-Random, 1989.

Bell, Quentin. *Virginia Woolf: A Biography.* 2 vols. New York: Harcourt, 1972.

Bishop, Edward. *A Virginia Woolf Chronology.* Boston: Hall, 1989.

Black, Naomi. "Virginia Woolf and the Women's Movement." In *Virginia Woolf: A Feminist Slant,* ed. Jane Marcus, 180–97. Lincoln: Univ. of Nebraska Press, 1983.

Blain, Virginia. "Narrative Voice and the Female Perspective in 'The Voyage Out.'" In *Modern Critical Views: Virginia Woolf,* ed. Harold Bloom, 231–41. New York: Chelsea, 1986.

Bloom, Harold, ed. *Modern Critical Views: Virginia Woolf.* New York: Chelsea, 1986.

Boyd, Elizabeth F. "Luriana, Lurilee." *Notes and Queries* 208 (1963): 380–81.

Bradbrook, Frank W. "Virginia Woolf: The Theory and Practice of Fiction." *The Pelican Guide to English Literature.* Vol. 7: *The Modern Age,* ed. Boris Ford. Baltimore, Md.: Penguin, 1961.

Brontë, Charlotte. *Jane Eyre.* Ed. Margaret Smith. New York: Oxford Univ. Press, 1975.

Carroll, Berenice A. "'To Crush Him in Our Own Country': The Political Thought of Virginia Woolf." *Feminist Studies* 4 (Fall 1978): 91–131.

Chakravarti, Uma. "Whatever Happened to the Vedic *Dasi?*: Orientalism, Nationalism, and a Script for the Past." In *Recasting Women: Essays in Colonial History,* ed. Kumkum Sangari and Sudesh Vaid, 27–87. New Delhi: Kali for Women, 1989.

Chapman, Wayne K., and Janet M. Manson. "Carte and Tierce: Leonard, Virginia Woolf, and War for Peace." In *Virginia Woolf and War: Fiction, Reality, and Myth,* ed. Mark Hussey, 58–78. Syracuse, N.Y.: Syracuse Univ. Press, 1991.

Chatterjee, Partha. "The Nationalist Resolution of the Women's Question." In *Recasting Women: Essays in Colonial History,* ed. Kumkum Sangari and Sudesh Vaid, 233–53. New Delhi: Kali for Women, 1989.

Chevigny, Bell Gale. *The Woman and the Myth: Margaret Fuller's Life and Writings.* Old Westbury, N.Y.: Feminist, 1976.

Clements, Patricia, and Isobel Grundy, eds. *Virginia Woolf: New Critical Essays.* Totowa, N.J.: Barnes, 1983.

Connell, R. W. *Gender and Power: Society, the Person and Sexual Politics.* Cambridge, England: Polity, 1987.

Conrad, Joseph. *Heart of Darkness.* Ed. Robert Kimbrough. 3d ed. New York: Norton, 1988.

"Crimean War." *New Encyclopaedia Britannica.* 15th ed. 1988.

Cuddy-Keane, Melba. "The Politics of Comic Modes in Virginia Woolf's *Between the Acts.*" *PMLA* 105 (Mar. 1990): 273–85.

Culleton, Claire A. "Gender-Charged Munitions: The Language of World War I Munitions Reports." *Women's Studies International Forum* 11 (1988): 109–16.

Dante Alighieri. *The Divine Comedy.* Translated by H. R. Huse. New York: Holt, 1954.

Daugherty, Beth Rigel. "The Whole Contention Between Mr. Bennett and Mrs. Woolf, Revisited." In *Virginia Woolf: Centennial Essays,* ed. Elaine K. Ginsberg and Laura Moss Gottlieb, 269–94. Troy, N.Y.: Whitson, 1983.

DiBattista, Maria. "Joyce, Woolf and the Modern Mind." In *Virginia Woolf: New Critical Essays,* ed. Patricia Clements and Isobel Grundy, 96–114. Totowa, N.J.: Barnes, 1983.

DuPlessis, Rachel Blau. "Feminist Narrative in Virginia Woolf." *Novel* 21 (Winter-Spring 1988): 323–30.

———. "WOOLFENSTEIN." In *Breaking the Sequence: Women's Experimental Fiction,* ed. Ellen G. Friedman and Miriam Fuchs, 99–114. Princeton, N.J.: Princeton Univ. Press, 1989.

Eagleton, Terry. *Marxism and Literary Criticism.* Berkeley: Univ. of California Press, 1976.

Eby, Cecil Degrotte. *The Road to Armageddon: The Martial Spirit in English Popular Literature, 1870–1914.* Durham, N.C.: Duke Univ. Press, 1987.

Eliot, T. S. *The Waste Land and Other Poems.* New York: Harcourt, 1958.

Embree, Ainslee T., ed. *1857 in India: Mutiny or War of Independence.* Boston: Heath, 1963.

Enloe, Cynthia. *Bananas, Beaches and Bases: Making Feminist Sense of International Politics.* London: Pandora, 1989.

Ewell, Judith. *Venezuela: A Century of Change.* Stanford, Calif.: Stanford Univ. Press, 1984.

"Fawkes." *New Encyclopaedia Britannica.* Micropedia. 15th ed., 1988.

Forster, E. M. *Abinger Harvest.* 1936. Rpt. New York: Meridian, 1955.

————. *A Passage to India.* New York: Harcourt, 1952.

Fox, Alice. "Virginia Liked Elizabeth." In *Virginia Woolf: A Feminist Slant,* ed. Jane Marcus, 37–51. Lincoln: Univ. of Nebraska Press, 1983.

Friedman, Albert B., ed. *The Viking Book of Folk Ballads of the English-Speaking World.* New York: Viking, 1956.

Froula, Christine. "Out of the Chrysalis: Female Initiation and Female Authority in Virginia Woolf's *The Voyage Out.*" *Tulsa Studies in Women's Literature* 5 (Spring 1986): 63–90.

Fussell, B. H. "Woolf's Peculiar Comic World: *Between the Acts.*" In *Virginia Woolf: Revaluation and Continuity,* ed. Ralph Freedman, 263–83. Berkeley: Univ. of California Press, 1980.

Gates, Henry Louis, Jr., ed. *"Race," Writing, and Difference.* Chicago: Univ. of Chicago Press, 1985.

Gilbert, Sandra M. "Costumes of the Mind: Transvestism as Metaphor in Modern Literature." In *Writing and Sexual Difference,* ed. Elizabeth Abel, 193–219. Chicago: Univ. of Chicago Press, 1982.

Gilbert, Sandra M., and Susan Gubar. *The Madwoman in the Attic: The Woman Writer and the Nineteenth-Century Literary Imagination.* New Haven, Conn.: Yale Univ. Press, 1979.

————. *No Man's Land: The Place of the Woman Writer in the Twentieth Century.* Vol. 2: *Sexchanges.* New Haven, Conn.: Yale Univ. Press, 1989.

Gilman, Sander L. "Black Bodies, White Bodies: Toward an Iconography of Female Sexuality in Late-Nineteenth-Century Art, Medicine, and Literature." In *"Race," Writing, and Difference,* ed. Henry Louis Gates, Jr., 223–61. Chicago: Univ. of Chicago Press, 1985.

Ginsberg, Elaine K., and Gottlieb, Laura Moss, eds. *Virginia Woolf: Centennial Essays.* Troy, N.Y.: Whitson, 1983.

Gottlieb, Laura Moss. "The War between the Woolfs." In *Virginia Woolf and Bloomsbury: A Centenary Celebration,* ed. Jane Marcus, 242–52. London: Macmillan, 1987.

Graham, Gerald Sandford. *A Concise History of the British Empire.* London: Thames, 1970.

Green, Martin. *The English Novel in the Twentieth Century: The Doom of Empire.* London: Routledge, 1984.

Gubar, Susan. "Mother, Maiden and the Marriage of Death: Women Writers and an Ancient Myth." *Women's Studies* 6 (1979): 301–15.

Haller, Evelyn. "The Anti-Madonna in the Work and Thought of Virginia Woolf." In *Virginia Woolf: Centennial Essays,* ed. Elaine K. Ginsberg and Laura Moss Gottlieb, 93–109. Troy, N.Y.: Whitson, 1983.

Handley, William R. "War and the Politics of Narration in *Jacob's Room.*" In *Virginia Woolf and War: Fiction, Reality, and Myth,* ed. Mark Hussey, 110–33. Syracuse, N.Y.: Syracuse Univ. Press, 1991.

Harper, Howard. *Between Language and Silence: The Novels of Virginia Woolf.* Baton Rouge: Louisiana State Univ. Press, 1982.

Herek, Gregory M. "On Heterosexual Masculinity: Some Psychical Consequences of the Social Construction of Gender and Sexuality." In *Changing Men,* ed. Michael S. Kimmel, 68–82. Newbury Park, Calif.: Sage, 1987.

Hill, Bridget. *Women, Work, and Sexual Politics in Eighteenth-Century England.* New York: Blackwell, 1989.

Holroyd, Michael. "Bloomsbury and the Fabians." In *Virginia Woolf and Bloomsbury: A Centenary Celebration,* ed. Jane Marcus, 39–51. London: Macmillan, 1987.

Homer. *The Odyssey.* Translated by E. V. Rieu. New York: Penguin, 1946.

Hughes, Robert. "Return of the Native." *Time* 124 (15 Oct. 1984): 96–97.

Hussey, Mark, ed. *Virginia Woolf and War: Fiction, Reality, and Myth.* Syracuse, N.Y.: Syracuse Univ. Press, 1991.

Ingram, Angela. "'The Sacred Edifice': Virginia Woolf and Some of the Sons of Culture." In *Virginia Woolf and Bloomsbury: A Centenary Celebration,* ed. Jane Marcus, 125–45. London: Macmillan, 1987.

Jack, Homer A., ed. *The Gandhi Reader: A Sourcebook of His Life and Writings.* New York: Grove, 1956.

Jakobson, Roman. "Linguistics and Poetics." In *The Structuralists: From Marx to Lévi-Strauss,* ed. Richard T. DeGeorge and Fernande M. DeGeorge, 84–122. Garden City, N.Y.: Anchor-Doubleday, 1972.

Jason, Philip K. "Sexism and Racism in Vietnam War Fiction." *Mosaic* 23 (Summer 1990): 125–37.

Jensen, Emily. "Clarissa Dalloway's Respectable Suicide." In *Virginia Woolf: A Feminist Slant,* ed. Jane Marcus, 162–79. Lincoln: Univ. of Nebraska Press, 1983.

Joplin, Patricia Klindienst. "The Authority of Illusion: Feminism and Fascism in Virginia Woolf's *Between the Acts.*" *South Central Review* 6 (Summer 1989): 88–104.

Joyce, James. *Ulysses.* 1922. Rpt. New York: Modern Library, 1934.

Kamuf, Peggy. "Penelope at Work: Interruptions in *A Room of One's Own.*" *Novel* 16 (Fall 1982): 5–18.

Keep, C. J. "Fearful Domestication: Future-War Stories and the Organization of Consent, 1871–1914." *Mosaic* 23 (Summer 1990): 1–16.

Kimmel, Michael S., ed. *Changing Men.* Newbury Park, Calif.: Sage, 1987.

Knight, Ian. *Queen Victoria's Enemies.* Vol. 3: *India.* London: Osprey, 1990.

Knopp, Sherron E. "'If I Saw You Would You Kiss Me?': Sapphism and the Subversiveness of Virginia Woolf's *Orlando.*" *PMLA* 103 (Jan. 1988): 24–34.

Lawrence, D. H. *The Plumed Serpent.* 1926. Rpt. New York: Vintage, 1959.

———. *The Woman Who Rode Away and Other Stories.* New York: Knopf, 1928.

Leonardi, Susan J. "Bare Places and Ancient Blemishes: Virginia Woolf's Search for New Language in *Night and Day.*" *Novel* 19 (Winter 1986): 150–63.

Lerner, Gerda. *The Creation of Patriarchy.* New York: Oxford Univ. Press, 1986.

Lewis, David Levering. *The Race to Fashoda: European Colonialism and African Resistance in the Scramble for Africa.* New York: Weidenfeld, 1987.

Liddle, Joanna, and Rama Joshi. "Gender and Imperialism in British India." *South Asia Research* 5 (Nov. 1985): 147–65.

Lilienfeld, Jane. "Where the Spear Plants Grew: The Ramsays' Marriage in *To the Lighthouse.*" In *New Feminist Essays on Virginia Woolf,* ed. Jane Marcus, 148–69. Lincoln: Univ. of Nebraska Press, 1981.

Little, Judy. *Comedy and the Woman Writer: Woolf, Spark, and Feminism.* Lincoln: Univ. of Nebraska Press, 1983.

———. "(En)gendering Laughter: Woolf's *Orlando* as Contraband in the Age of Joyce." *Women's Studies* 15 (1988): 179–91.

Lloyd, T. O. *The British Empire: 1558–1983.* New York: Oxford Univ. Press, 1984.

Lukács, Georg. *The Meaning of Contemporary Realism.* Translated by John Mander and Necke Mander. London: Merlin, 1963.

Lunn, Eugene. *Marxism and Modernism: An Historical Study of Lukács, Brecht, Benjamin, and Adorno.* Berkeley: Univ. of California Press, 1982.

Macaulay, Thomas Babington. "Lord Clive." In *The Victorian Age: Prose, Poetry, and Drama,* ed. John Wilson Bowyer and John Lee Brooks. 2d ed. New York: Appleton, 1954.

MacDonald, Robert H. "A Poetics of War: Militarist Discourse in the British Empire, 1880–1918." *Mosaic* 23 (Summer 1990): 17–35.

MacKenzie, John M. *Propaganda and Empire: The Manipulation of British Public Opinion, 1880–1960.* Manchester, England: Manchester Univ. Press, 1984.

Marcus, Jane, *Art and Anger: Reading Like a Woman.* Columbus: Ohio State Univ. Press, 1988.

———. "Other People's I's: Class and Colonialism in Virginia Woolf's *The Waves.*" Colloquium presented at the Univ. of Hawaii, 12 Jan. 1990.

———. "Other People's I's (Eyes): The Reader, Gender and Recursive Reading in *To the Lighthouse* and *The Waves.*" *Reader* 22 (Fall 1989): 53–67.

———. *Virginia Woolf and the Languages of Patriarchy.* Bloomington: Indiana Univ. Press, 1987.

————, ed. *New Feminist Essays on Virginia Woolf.* Lincoln: Univ. of Nebraska Press, 1981.

————, ed. *Virginia Woolf and Bloomsbury: A Centenary Celebration.* London: Macmillan, 1987.

————, ed. *Virginia Woolf: A Feminist Slant.* Lincoln: Univ. of Nebraska Press, 1983.

Masani, Zareer. *Indian Tales of the Raj.* Berkeley: Univ. of California Press, 1987.

McNeillie, Andrew, ed. *The Essays of Virginia Woolf.* Vol. 1: *1904–1912.* New York: Harcourt, 1986.

Meyerowitz, Selma S. *Leonard Woolf.* Boston: Twayne, 1982.

Miller, J. Hillis. "*Mrs. Dalloway*: Repetition as the Raising of the Dead." In *Critical Essays on Virginia Woolf,* ed. Morris Beja, 53–72. Boston: Hall, 1985.

Moi, Toril. *Sexual/Textual Politics: Feminist Literary Theory.* New York: Routledge, 1985.

Moorhouse, Geoffrey. *India Britannica.* New York: Harper, 1983.

"Moroccan Crises." *New Encyclopaedia Britannica.* Micropedia. 15th ed. 1988.

Naremore, James. *The World Without a Self: Virginia Woolf and the Novel.* New Haven, Conn.: Yale Univ. Press, 1973.

Neuman, Shirley. "*Heart of Darkness,* Virginia Woolf and the Specter of Domination." In *Virginia Woolf: New Critical Essays,* ed. Patricia Clements and Isobel Grundy, 57–76. Totowa, N.J.: Barnes, 1983.

Nicolson, Nigel. "Bloomsbury: the Myth and the Reality." In *Virginia Woolf and Bloomsbury: A Centenary Celebration,* ed. Jane Marcus, 7–22. London: Macmillan, 1987.

Ohmann, Carol. "Culture and Anarchy in *Jacob's Room.*" *Contemporary Literature* 18 (Spring 1977): 160–72.

Ovid, *The Metamorphoses.* Translated by Horace Gregory. New York: Mentor—New American, 1958.

Perkin, Joan. *Women and Marriage in Nineteenth-Century England.* Chicago: Lyceum, 1989.

Perkins, David, ed. *English Romantic Writers.* New York: Harcourt, 1967.

Perry, Ruth. "Finding Our Foremothers." *The Women's Review of Books* 8 (April 1991): 14–15.

"Pitt, William." *New Encyclopaedia Britannica.* Micropedia. 15th ed. 1988.

Plato. "Phaedrus." In Plato, *Euthyphro, Apology, Crito, Phaedo, Phaedrus,* 413–579. Translated by Harold North Fowler. Cambridge, Mass.: Loeb—Harvard Univ. Press, 1914.

————. *Republic.* Translated by Benjamin Jowett. In *Critical Theory Since Plato,* ed. Hazard Adams, 19–40. New York: Harcourt, 1971.

Plomer, William. *I Speak of Africa.* London: Hogarth, 1927.

Pratt, Mary Louise. "Scratches on the Face of the Country; or, What Mr. Barrow Saw in the Land of the Bushmen." In *"Race," Writing, and Difference,* ed. Henry Louis Gates, Jr., 138–62. Chicago: Univ. of Chicago Press, 1985.

Radin, Grace. *Virginia Woolf's* The Years: *The Evolution of a Novel.* Knoxville: Univ. of Tennessee Press, 1981.

"Rosebery." *New Encyclopaedia Britannica.* 15th ed. 1988.

Rosenbaum, S. P. "Virginia Woolf and the Intellectual Origins of Bloomsbury." In *Virginia Woolf: Centennial Essays,* ed. Elaine K. Ginsberg and Laura Moss Gottlieb, 11–26. Troy, N.Y.: Whitson, 1983.

Rosenman, Ellen. *The Invisible Presence: Virginia Woolf and the Mother-Daughter Relationship.* Baton Rouge: Louisiana Univ. Press, 1986.

———. "Sexual Identity and *A Room of One's Own*: 'Secret Economies' in Virginia Woolf's Feminist Discourse." *Signs* 14 (Spring 1989): 634–50.

Rougemont, Denis de. *Love in the Western World.* Translated by Montgomery Belgion. New York: Harper, 1956.

Ruddick, Sara. "Private Brother, Public World." In *New Feminist Essays on Virginia Woolf,* ed. Jane Marcus, 185–215. Lincoln: Univ. of Nebraska Press, 1981.

Said, Edward W. *Orientalism.* New York: Vintage-Random, 1978.

"Salisbury." *New Encyclopaedia Britannica.* Micropedia. 15th ed. 1988.

Sammons, Todd H. "'As the Vine Curls Her Tendrils': Marriage Topos and Erotic Countertopos in *Paradise Lost.*" *Milton Quarterly* 20 (Dec. 1986): 117–27.

Sangari, Kumkum, and Vaid, Sudesh, eds. *Recasting Women: Essays in Colonial History.* New Delhi: Kali for Women, 1989.

Schlack, Beverly Ann. "Fathers in General: The Patriarchy in Virginia Woolf's Fiction." In *Virginia Woolf: A Feminist Slant,* ed. Jane Marcus, 52–77. Lincoln: Univ. of Nebraska Press, 1983.

Schneider, Karen. "Of Two Minds: Woolf, the War and *Between the Acts.*" *Journal of Modern Literature* 16 (Summer 1989): 93–112.

Sears, Sallie. "Theater of War: Virginia Woolf's *Between the Acts.*" In *Virginia Woolf: A Feminist Slant,* ed. Jane Marcus, 212–35. Lincoln: Univ. of Nebraska Press, 1983.

Shakespeare, William. *The Complete Works of William Shakespeare.* London: Hamlyn, 1958.

Sheridan, Richard Brinsley. "The School for Scandal." In *British Dramatists from Dryden to Sheridan,* ed. George H. Nettleton and Arthur E. Case, 831–76. Carbondale: Southern Illinois Univ. Press, 1969.

Showalter, Elaine. *A Literature of Their Own: British Women Novelists from Brontë to Lessing.* Princeton, N.J.: Princeton Univ. Press, 1977.

———. *Sexual Anarchy: Gender and Culture at the Fin de Siècle.* New York: Viking, 1990.

Silver, Brenda R. *Virginia Woolf's Reading Notebooks.* Princeton, N.J.: Princeton Univ. Press, 1983.

Sinha, Mrinalini. "Gender and Imperialism: Colonial Policy and the Ideology of Moral Imperialism in Late Nineteenth-Century Bengal." In *Changing Men,* ed. Michael S. Kimmel, 217–31. Newbury Park, Calif.: Sage, 1987.

Snyder, Louis Leo. *The Imperialism Reader: Documents and Readings on Modern Expansionism.* Princeton, N.J.: Van Nostrand, 1962.

Southam, B. C. *A Student's Guide to the Selected Poems of T. S. Eliot.* London: Faber, 1968.

Spenser, Edmund. *The Faerie Queene.* In *Norton Anthology of English Literature,* ed. M. H. Abrams, 1: 542–766. 2 vols. 5th ed. New York: Norton, 1986.

Spivak, Gayatri C. "Unmaking and Making in *To the Lighthouse.*" In *Contemporary Literary Criticism: Modernism through Poststructuralism,* ed. Robert Con Davis, 201–15. New York: Longman, 1986.

Squier, Susan M. "Tradition and Revision in Woolf's *Orlando*: Defoe and 'The Jessamy Brides.'" *Women's Studies* 12 (1986): 167–78.

Stearns, Peter N. "Working-Class Women in Britain, 1890–1914." In *Suffer and Be Still: Women in the Victorian Age,* ed. Martha Vicinus, 100–120. Bloomington: Indiana Univ. Press, 1972.

Steiner, George. *In Bluebeard's Castle: Some Notes Toward the Redefinition of Culture.* New Haven, Conn.: Yale Univ. Press, 1971.

Stephen, Adrian. *The "Dreadnought" Hoax.* London: Hogarth, 1936.

Strachey, Lytton. *Eminent Victorians.* New York: Random, 1918.

Strachey, Ray. *The Cause: A Short History of the Women's Movement in Great Britain.* 1928. Rpt. Port Washington, N.Y.: Kennikat, 1969.

Taylor, Alan John Percivale. *English History, 1914–1945.* New York: Oxford Univ. Press, 1965.

Tennyson, Alfred. *Poems of Tennyson.* Ed. Jerome H. Buckley. Boston: Houghton, 1958.

Tennyson, Charles. *Alfred Tennyson.* New York: Macmillan, 1949.

Thompson, Edward John. *The Other Side of the Medal.* New York: Harcourt, 1926.

Thomson, David. *England in the Nineteenth Century (1815–1914).* New York: Penguin, 1950.

Torgovnick, Marianna. *Gone Primitive: Savage Intellects, Modern Lives.* Chicago: Univ. of Chicago Press, 1990.

Vicinus, Martha, ed. *A Widening Sphere: Changing Roles of Victorian Women.* London: Methuen, 1977.

Welch, Richard E., Jr., ed. *Imperialists vs. Anti-Imperialists: The Debate over Expansionism in the 1890s.* Itasca, Ill.: Peacock, 1972.

Wheare, Jane. *Virginia Woolf: Dramatic Novelist.* New York: St. Martin's, 1989.

White, Stephen. Photography Collection. Exhibit at Honolulu Academy of Art, Honolulu, Hawaii, April 1990.

Williams, Raymond. *Marxism and Literature.* New York: Oxford Univ. Press, 1977.

Wilson, Duncan. *Leonard Woolf: A Political Biography.* New York: St. Martin's, 1978.

Woolf, Leonard. *After the Deluge: A Study of Communal Psychology.* Vol. 1. London: Hogarth, 1931.

————. *Diaries in Ceylon, 1908–1911: Records of a Colonial Administrator and Stories from the East: Three Short Stories on Ceylon.* London: Hogarth, 1963.

————. *Empire and Commerce in Africa: A Study in Economic Imperialism.* New York: Macmillan, [1920?].

————. "Fear and Politics: A Debate at the Zoo." In *In Savage Times: Leonard Woolf on Peace and War,* by Leonard Woolf. New York: Garland, 1973.

————. *The Future of Constantinople.* London: Allen, 1917.

————. *Growing: An Autobiography of the Years 1904 to 1911.* New York: Harcourt, 1961.

————. *Imperialism and Civilization.* New York: Harcourt, 1928.

————. *In Savage Times: Leonard Woolf on Peace and War.* Introduction by Stephen J. Stearns. New York: Garland, 1973. Each essay is paged separately.

————. "The Way of Peace." In *In Savage Times: Leonard Woolf on Peace and War,* by Leonard Woolf. New York: Garland, 1973.

Woolf, Virginia. *Between the Acts.* New York: Harcourt, 1941.

————. *Collected Essays.* Ed. Leonard Woolf. 4 vols. London: Hogarth, 1966–67.

————. *The Complete Shorter Fiction of Virginia Woolf.* Ed. Susan Dick. 2d ed. New York: Harcourt, 1985.

————. *The Diary of Virginia Woolf.* Vols. 1–5. Ed. Anne Olivier Bell and Andrew McNeillie. New York: Harcourt, 1977–84.

————. *Flush: A Biography.* New York: Harcourt, 1933.

————. "Foreword" to *Recent Paintings by Vanessa Bell,* by The London Artists' Association. London: Favil, 1930.

————. *Freshwater: A Comedy.* Ed. Lucio P. Ruotolo. New York: Harcourt, 1976.

————. "Indiscretions." In *Virginia Woolf: Women and Writing,* ed. Michèle Barrett, 72–76. New York: Harcourt, 1979.

————. "Julia Margaret Cameron." In *Victorian Photographs of Famous Men and Fair Women,* by Julia Margaret Cameron, 13–19. 1926. Ed. Tristram Powell. Rpt. Boston: Godine, 1973.

————. *Jacob's Room.* New York: Harcourt, 1950.

————. *The Letters of Virginia Woolf.* Vol. 2: *1912–1922.* Ed. Nigel Nicolson. New York: Harcourt, 1976.

————. *The Letters of Virginia Woolf.* Vol. 3: *1923–1928.* Ed. Nigel Nicolson and Joanne Trautmann. New York: Harcourt, 1977.

————. *The Letters of Virginia Woolf.* Vol. 6: *1936–1941.* Ed. Nigel Nicolson and Joanne Trautmann. New York: Harcourt, 1980.

————. *Moments of Being.* Ed. Jeanne Schulkind. 2d ed. New York: Harcourt, 1985.

————. *Mrs. Dalloway.* New York: Harcourt, 1953.

————. *Night and Day.* New York: Harcourt, 1948.

————. *Orlando: A Biography.* New York: Harcourt, 1956.

————. *The Pargiters: The Novel-Essay Portion of* The Years. Ed. Mitchell A. Leaska. New York: New York Public Library, 1977.

————. *Roger Fry: A Biography.* New York: Harcourt, 1940.

————. *A Room of One's Own.* New York: Harcourt, 1957.

————. *Three Guineas.* 1938. New York: Harcourt, 1966.

————. *To the Lighthouse.* New York: Harcourt, 1955.

————. *The Voyage Out.* New York: Harcourt, 1948.

————. *The Waves.* New York: Harcourt, 1959.

————. *The Years.* New York: Harcourt, 1937.

Woolmer, J. Howard, and Mary E. Gaither. *A Checklist of the Hogarth Press, 1917–1938.* London: Hogarth, 1976.

Zwerdling, Alex. *Virginia Woolf and the Real World.* Berkeley: Univ. of California Press, 1986.

Index